Dialogues on Disability and Inclusion
between Isfahan and Hamburg

First results gained in a research project within the DAAD program
"Higher Education Dialogue with the Islamic world"

Dialogues on Disability and Inclusion between Isfahan and Hamburg

First results gained in a research project
within the DAAD program
"Higher Education Dialogue with the Islamic world"

Sven Degenhardt
Amrollah Ebrahimi
Hamid Nasiri Dehsorkhi
Joachim Schroeder
(Editors)

Funding Notes
Funded by the German Academic Exchange Service (DAAD) with funds
provided by German Federal Foreign Office (Auswärtiges Amt).

Bibliografische Information der Deutschen Nationalbibliothek:
Die Deutsche Nationalbibliothek verzeichnet diese Publikation in
der Deutschen Nationalbibliografie; detaillierte bibliografische
Daten sind im Internet über http://dnb.de abrufbar.

© 2018 Hrsg./Editors: Sven Degenhardt, Amrollah Ebrahimi,
　　　　　Hamid Nasiri Dehsorkhi, Joachim Schroeder

Herstellung und Verlag: BoD – Books on Demand, Norderstedt

ISBN: 978-3-7528-4562-4

E-Book-Formate:
epub: ISBN: 978-3-7528-0888-9
mobi: ISBN: 978-3-7528-0888-9

Content

I **Project Presentation** 7

  1   Fact Sheets 7

  2   Dialogues on Disability and Inclusion between Isfahan and
     Hamburg: frame work, content, structure and objectives of
     the tree-years project
     (Amrollah Ebrahimi, Joachim Schroeder) 10

II **International Discussions** 27

  3   Disability Inclusion in a Global World: Moving towards
     Disability Inclusive Development – Development Cooperation
     before and after the adoption of the UN Convention on the
     Rights of Persons with Disabilities
     (Veronika Hilber) 27

  4   Agenda 2030 and UN CRPD as the basis for a worldwide and
     diverse discussion on inclusion and disability – ideas from
     Ladakh and Isfahan
     (Nele Schell) 37

  5   A Cross-Cultural Cooperation and Research Project on
     Special Education between the Universities of Oldenburg in
     Germany and Dohuk in Northern Iraq (2013-2018)
     (Monika Ortmann, Sönke Thies) 51

III **Experiences and Research: Isfahan** 65

  6   Epidemiology of disability in Isfahan
     (Sayed Mohsen Hosseini) 65

  7   Physical Activity in People with Intellectual Disability
     (Hamzeh Baharlouei, Javid Mostamand) 84

  8   Family conflicts and disability
     (Mostafa Arab-Varnousfaderani,
     Kowsar Arab-Varnousfaderani, Maryam Ashrafi) 92

  9   Faculty development regarding disability
     (Nikoo Yamani, Habibollah Rezaei) 96

10 The Attitude of Isfahan People to Disabilities: A Pilot Study
(Hamid Nasiri Dehsorkhi, Saeid Nasiri,
Sedigheh Sadrameli, Batoul Aminalzarbian) 102

11 Feasibility of using mathematical and physical principles in
evaluation the disabled-specific orthoses: A scientific report
(Mohammad Hossein Ebrahimi, Ali Mohammadi) 116

IV Experiences and Research: Hamburg 123

12 Accessibility to Education and Therapy for Juvenile Refugees
with Disabilities in Hamburg
(Frauke Meyer) 123

13 Depression among asylum seekers in Germany
(Negin Shah Hosseini) 140

14 Trauma in Mentally Disabled People
(Farid Mosharaf Dehkordi) 149

15 Supporting educational and coping processes in hospital
schools of child and adolescent psychiatric units
(Tobias Hensel) 157

16 Inclusive School without Barriers (InkluSoB) – A service centre
at Universität Hamburg
(Marie-Luise Schütt, Manfred Steger) 173

17 Basic education for people with disabilities in Hamburg
GRUND:BILDUNG research project: 2012-2015
(Uta Wagner) 183

18 Accessibility in public space and public buildings – an
observation protocol for research and teaching at universities
(Sven Degenhardt, Marie Geldmacher,
Valentin Keller, Torben Scholz) 201

Alternative text for images 217

Authors 229

I   Project Presentation

1   Fact Sheets

Dialogues on Disability and Inclusion between Isfahan and Hamburg

Facts
Partner country: Iran
University in Germany: Faculty of Education, Universität Hamburg
Project managers:
Prof. Dr. Joachim Schroeder
Prof. Dr. Sven Degenhardt
Partner University: Isfahan University of Medical Sciences
Project managers:
Dr. Amrollah Ebrahimi
Hamid Nasiri Dehsorkhi

DAAD Deutscher Akademischer Austauschdienst
German Academic Exchange Service

Universität Hamburg
DER FORSCHUNG | DER LEHRE | DER BILDUNG

Project focus
What challenges do both cities and universities face if all aspects of the UN Convention on the Rights of Persons with Disabilities (CRPD) must be taken into account in public spaces, educational and rehabilitation facilities, and access to academic teaching at the universities?

Project
- Empirical studies on the living situations and requirements to support people with disabilities in both cities and universities
- Joint meetings in Isfahan and Hamburg
- Joint workshops on barrier-free universities (Hamburg, Isfahan)

- Networking with experts working with people with disabilities in Hamburg and Isfahan

Target groups
Students, doctoral students and teachers at both universities as well as rehabilitation and educational experts working with people with disabilities in Isfahan and Hamburg

Planned long-term effects
- Create barrier-free structures for students with disabilities in terms of access, curriculum and teaching at both universities
- Set up two networks between the universities and local experts that will be continued beyond the project period
- Establish teaching formats that support practice-oriented teaching and learning for students and doctoral students; identify architectural, visual, acoustic, media and educational barriers in the cities and universities; develop suggestions for improvements

Figure 1: examples of barriers and accessibility
(For the descriptions, go to "Alternative text for images" page 217)

Fields of dialogue

- International dialogue
  Exchange on key terms such as disability, rehabilitation, inclusion, barrier-free, Universal Design, etc.
  Methodological issues within inclusion research in the fields of education, rehabilitation and therapy
  Exchange on the ongoing research projects at both universities
- Community dialogue
  Foster cooperation between the universities and the work with people with disabilities in both cities

Networking in the fields of supply, education and psychosocial support (Isfahan) and with local schools (Hamburg) with regard to people with severe disabilities
- Institutional dialogue

Further development of curricula and teaching formats to foster inclusion
Additional training offers for teachers at both universities
Discussions on opportunities for "barrier-free universities"

Surveys

- Facts and data on people with disabilities in Isfahan and Hamburg
- Attitudes of students and teachers to people with disabilities
- Types of barriers to access and participation in studies at both universities

Support for young researchers

- Several relevant dissertations are currently being prepared in Hamburg (disability and migration, international comparison of attitudes, Universal Design)
- Two Doctoral students from Isfahan have already completed short study visits to Hamburg
- Several master's students at both universities will be prepared for doctoral studies
- Study trips will enable students to consider international aspects of working with people with disabilities

2 Dialogues on Disability and Inclusion between Isfahan and Hamburg: frame work, content, structure and objectives of the tree-years project

(Amrollah Ebrahimi, Joachim Schroeder)

Inclusion as a challenge for academic education

In line with the fundamental human rights, the United Nations General Assembly adopted in 2006 the "United Nations Convention on the Rights of Persons with Disabilities" (abbreviated as UN Convention here), which is signed by Iran and Germany. Disability is part of everyday life, and it has been estimated that 11% to 25% of the world's population have a disability (WHO 2011). Disabled people suffer more from medical, psychological and social problems and benefit less from job, educational and welfare opportunities. The UN Convention focuses on people with disabilities as individuals who are capable of making decisions for their lives based on their free consent, respecting their individual skills and talents and reaffirming that they must enjoy all human rights and freedoms. Depicting the different aspects and facets of freedom and social rights, it covers all areas of social life, starting from the right to life, to aspects such as education, schooling, work, employment, health, living, mobility, privacy, access to information and participation in political, public and cultural life as well as leisure and sports.

The scientists of the Universities in Isfahan and Hamburg involved in the project here want to continue and deepen their dialogue on the social and cultural challenges as well as on the education- and curriculum-related issues in putting the UN Convention into practice in both cities. The dialogue between the Iranian and German scientists has among its main objectives, based on scientific discourse and educational exchange, the discussion of individual action paths, the current status and the requirements for translating the UN Convention into effective practice in both the Cities and the Universities of Isfahan and Hamburg:

- Universities may be autonomous bodies, but they are also part of the respective *urban or rural culture*. The scientists from Isfahan and Hamburg involved in this project deal with aspects such as support, counseling,

Amrollah Ebrahimi & Joachim Schroeder

education, assistance and rehabilitation for people with disabilities. At both universities it has to be continuously critically examined whether empirical data on the problems and needs of people with disabilities living in Isfahan and Hamburg is precise enough. Furthermore, it is necessary to ask again and again how the universities can contribute to making the two cities barrier-free and inclusive.

• Like all *social institutions*, universities have to critically reflect upon whether they have successfully managed to put the UN Convention into practice or whether there is still room for improvement: What attitude do students and instructors have toward people with disabilities and toward different disabilities? What organizational, architectonic/structural or technical modifications at the universities are required to enhance accessibility to higher education for students with disabilities? In what way can the topic of inclusion be embedded in teaching?

Previous dialogues and existing cooperation
An international congress held at the University of Isfahan, Iran, in 2007, with participation of some German scientists, has brought about fruitful discussions of the scientific board on the project "Developing the Field of Psychosomatic Medicine in Iran" and, in the course of the project, the idea of scientific and cultural exchange was born. Dr. Dehkordi (University of Marburg) took the lead in organizing the contact with the University in Isfahan and regularly travels to Iran to foster, maintain and develop this contact. Prof. Dr. Schroeder (University of Hamburg) visited with Dr. Dehkordi the universities in Sari, Isfahan und Shahr-e Kord in the course of a lecture tour in October 2012. In various discussions and workshops, possibilities for cooperation in research, teachers' training and support and advisory services were examined.

Supported by the DAAD, Dr. Dehkordi and Prof. Dr. Schroeder visited the Faculty of Medical Sciences and Health Services and the Faculty of Psychology of the University of Isfahan for one week in December 2013. As part of the program, the Faculty of Rehabilitation and the Institute of Special Needs Education of the Faculty of Education were also visited for discussion, and so were various institutions providing psychological and educational assistance to children and adolescents with a disability in Isfahan and nearby Shahr-e Kord. Apart from presentation and lecture activities, topics for possible common research and teaching projects were determined together with Dr. Ebrahimi and Mr Arab during the stay. Also, a "Memorandum of Understanding between Isfahan University of Medical Sciences (IUMS) and the University of Hamburg (UHH)" was signed (December 2013/February 2014).

From 15th to 19th September 2014, funded by the DAAD, ten members of Isfahan University participated in a study visit held at the Institute for Special Needs Education, University of Hamburg. The focus was on the scientific discussion of methods and examples of interdisciplinary research in the field of disabilities. Dr. Dehkordi, Prof. Dr. Schroeder, Christoph Henriksen and Prof. Dr. Degenhardt participated in the workshops, giving an overview of international research in fields of disability work and of educational support programs for families of adults with mental disabilities as well as of research on attitudes toward people with disabilities in Germany, China and Egypt, and of research on inclusive school development (theoretical and methodological principles). Field visits were organized to an inclusive day care center, the "Educational Center for Blind and Partially Sighted People" and to the institutions of the association "Living with Disabilities Hamburg".

Again with the support of the DAAD, Prof. Dr. Degenhardt, Dr. Dehkordi, Christoph Henriksen and Prof. Dr. Schroeder visited Isfahan from 8th to 12th February 2016. Together with the Iranian colleagues, quite different institutions for the disabled were inspected there: a residential facility for adults with severe disabilities, a family-oriented, district-embedded institution providing early intervention services for blind and visually impaired children and a regional center for the medical and psychosocial treatment of children and adolescents with disability, in which many (IUMS) students do their internship.

Reflecting upon the two study visits in Hamburg (2014) and Isfahan (2016), many similarities as to existing problems and concepts could be found, but also significant differences. The Hamburg team, for instance, has relatively well-established contacts with local organizations working for the disabled, conducts evaluations in the different institutions, provides support or further training and participates in different local networks. Likewise, the team in Isfahan actively promotes interdisciplinary cooperation within the university, aiming at bringing together all faculties relevant to the topic of disability and inclusion. The Hamburg team was particularly impressed by the Medical Education Research Center, which supports the different faculties in the further development of teaching in terms of curriculum design.

As an interim conclusion, both teams agreed on the fact that the exchange so far has been very informative, led to fruitful results and a first overview of the different urban and academic contexts and brought about common research questions. Both groups want to intensify their exchange, with more thematically focused activities, to involve students and doctoral candidates of both universities in this exchange and to collaborate not only via conferences and workshops but also through common seminars or lecture courses. The group is convinced that the topics associated with the UN Convention – dealing with disability in different social contexts, attitudes toward people with disabilities and toward different forms of disability, disability in the context of religion and culture, gender or migration, higher education policy instruments and didactic concepts to enhance accessibility/inclusion at universities – are ideally suited for the thematic structuring of a productive intercultural higher education dialogue.

The concept of Inclusion from a philosophical perspective

Some scientists are defining Inclusion as a philosophy, in which learners, families, teachers, and members of the community work together to create schools and other social institutions based on admission, sense of belonging and collective sense (Salend 2001). Inclusive education is about creating schools, classes, training programs and activities for empowering students with different learning disabilities to make participation together (Adedoyin & Okere 2017). Theoretically, inclusion is created in schools to provide a collaborative, supportive, and educational environment for teachers. Therefore, teachers serve all students at each level of their ability and reconcile their programs according to their needs. In these respectful environments, learning opportunities are provided for different people (ibid.). Inclusion requires a broad vision and competences for all teachers in the education system.

Salend (2001) highlighted four important principles in which the framework and philosophy of inclusion are based. In order to have a better understanding of the theoretical foundations and the philosophy of inclusion, we will have a brief overview of these principles.

Principle I: Diversity-effective inclusion provides an educational system in which all students beside each other in a normal environment have an equal opportunity to learn and practice regardless of different learning abilities, racial, linguistic, economic status, gender, the style of learning, previous cultural backgrounds, religion, family structure, and gender orientation.

Principle II: Individual Needs-effective Inclusion: Inclusion involves sensitivity to needs and the acceptance of the needs of individuals due to their individual differences. In the inclusive classes, all students are considered valuable and have a capacity to learn and participate in social life.

Principle III: Reflective Practice-effective Inclusion: Inclusion requires reflective educators to regularly refine their attitudes, practices, and classroom management practices, and continually adapt to the needs of students.

Principle IV: Collaboration-effective Inclusion: Inclusion requires collective effort. This effort includes collaboration between educators, other professionals, students, families and community agencies to provide services and support that students can learn in normal classes.

According to these principles, people work in a collaborative and reflexive way and share resources, responsibilities, decisions, and support of the interests of students. Inclusion and providing equal opportunities for the living of the disabled is a vital, human and fundamental right. The *United Nations Convention on the Rights of Persons with Disabilities* has been an important political step, which the two countries, Germany and Iran, have signed and are bound to implement. Obviously, the implementation of parts of our work as faculty members in the University requires research and intercultural dialogue. Through scientific work, and intercultural and inter-academic dialogues, barriers to the inclusion and realization of the rights of persons with disabilities and the achievement of equal opportunities in life can be identified.

A review of research literature and political documents shows that some steps have been taken in this regard. Among them, the Stinso Center in the United States conducted an Iranian-American Intercultural Dialogue on Disability Rights in the context of the Convention on the Rights of Persons with Disabilities, and reported by Allen Moore & Sarah Kornblet entitled "Advancing the Rights of Persons with Disabilities: A US-Iran Dialogue on Law, Policy, and

Advocacy." The report states that one of the problems faced by disabled people in the Iranian society is stigmatization and the lack of adequate knowledge of the material, emotional and social needs of people with disabilities from the community and governments is mentioned (Moore & Kornblet 2011).

With regard to the pros and cons of inclusion, many studies have been done. For instance, a comprehensive review study by Alquraini & Gut (2012) can be mentioned. In this overview of literature, which deals with the necessary steps to be taken to inclusion around the world, the effective work required to inclusion around the world has been mentioned. Its focus, which lies on the Critical Inclusion Components, has succeeded in providing stakeholders with engagement that can effectively engage students in inclusive schools (ibid.).

Related to Iran, research has also been carried out on facilities and accessibility for disabled people in urban buildings and academic environments. For example, in the one research, Bayat Bodaghi & Zainab (2012) studied twelve buildings of urban libraries and universities in Iran in terms of how to make and access disabled people (ramps, entrance, interior design, ambient space, parking areas, etc.). In this study, the viewpoint of the disabled as well as the view of the architect engineer was taken. The viewpoints of disabled people and engineers were similar. In the case of ramps and interior design of buildings, according to architects, 53.8% of libraries lacked ramps, and 63% lacked an exterior space suitable for disabled people. The view of the disabled user showed that there were more obstacles than engineers said (ibid.).

The prevalence of disability in the world and in Iran

Disability is a global phenomenon that is accompanied by economic and social costs that are imposed on the individual, the family, the community and the system of treatment and rehabilitation. Based on new definitions of disability by the WHO and ICF criteria, disability is the result of people's interaction with injuries, environmental barriers and attitudes that prevent their active and appropriate participation in the community based on equal opportunity with others (WHO 2012).

According to the Global Burden of Diseases (GBD), about 975 million (19.4%) of people over 15 with disabilities and 190 million people in the world (3.8%) live with severe disability (WHO 2007). According to the 2011 census in Iran, the

---

prevalence of disabled people is 13 per 10,000 people with the highest incidence was related to physical handicap 80, mental disability 44, hearing 13, and vision 13 per 10,000 people (Soltani et al. 2015).

Because of different sources and methodologies for estimating disabilities in the world, various data are available from its prevalence. For example, according to the WHO report, Disability estimation based on GBD, Surveys and WHO study, in the whole world, including developed, developing and underdeveloped countries, are 15%, 7%, and 16%, respectively (WHO 2011).

Given the increasing prevalence of the number of people with disabilities worldwide, it is necessary to formulate intercultural proposals for addressing the situation of the disabled, particularly in Iran, and realizing their rights. On the other hand, the Universal Convention on the Rights of Persons with Disabilities encourages signatories to fulfill the conditions for improving the quality of life of the disabled, which requires international scientific interactions.

For these reasons and based on provided opportunities this academic project between Isfahan University of Medical Sciences and University of Hamburg were designed entitled "Dialogues on Disability and Inclusion between Isfahan and Hamburg".

Organization and academic content of the project

The project is conducted by the Faculty of Medicine/Psychosomatic Research Center at the Isfahan University of Medical Sciences (IUMS) and the Faculty of Education/Institute of Special Needs Education at the University of Hamburg (UHH). It was approved for funding by the DAAD in March 2017. The project deals with the question of how both universities can enhance their curriculum and teaching method as well as their organizational and architectural structures to better meet the special needs of students and instructors with disabilities and of how both institutions can be modified in general terms as to be fully accessible to all people. At the same time, close cooperation between the universities and their community/their respective urban environment and providers of further education and training as well as the development of networks aim at raising awareness on the topic of inclusion within their urban and rural contexts. Moreover, with one research component the project also provides empirical data on the life situations of people with disabilities in Isfahan and Hamburg. The project involves a number of postdoctoral and doctoral researchers, and master's degree students in Hamburg and Isfahan – more than half of them young women – and supports their academic development.

Content, working packages and time frame for the project

Facets of dialogue	2017	2018	2019
International dialogues			
IUMS/ UHH	Colloquium I: Disability and inclusion in a global world (May; Hamburg)	Field trip I: Disability and inclusion in rural areas (May; Hamburg)	Future workshop I: Is there a future for inclusion? (May; Hamburg)
	Colloquium II: Disability and inclusion in a global world (October; Isfahan)	Field trip II: Disability and inclusion in rural areas (October; Isfahan)	Future workshop II: Is there a future for inclusion? (October; Isfahan)
	Colloquium-related publication	Joint article	Recommendations
Municipal dialogues			
IUMS	Two network meetings (planning for 2018/2019)	Various activities (e.g. further training, support offers)	Various activities (e.g. further training, support offers)
UHH	Two network meetings (planning for 2018/2019)	Various activities (e.g. further training, support offers)	Various activities (e.g. further training, support offers)
IUMS/ UHH	Exchange during the meetings	Exchange during the meetings	Exchange during the meetings

Institutional dialogues(and Project IV)			
IUMS	Phase I: Development of an educational program (Project IV)	Phase II: Development of an educational program (Project IV)	Phase III: Development of an educational program (Project IV)
UHH	A workshop each: Barrier-free university in Hamburg (May) and Isfahan (October)	A workshop each: Barrier-free university in Hamburg (May) and Isfahan (October)	A workshop each: Barrier-free university in Hamburg (May) and Isfahan (October)
Project I			
IUMS	Conducting the sub-study 1a in Isfahan	Conducting the sub-study 1b in Isfahan	Final report Articles
Project II			
IUMS/ UHH	Joint method workshop (May; Hamburg)	First evaluation workshop (May; Hamburg)	Final evaluation workshop (May; Hamburg or Isfahan)
	Empirical study/data collection in Hamburg and Isfahan	Continuation of the empirical study in Hamburg and Isfahan	Joint article
Project III			
IUMS/ UHH	Joint method workshop (May; Hamburg)	First evaluation workshop (May; Hamburg)	Final evaluation workshop (May; Hamburg)
	Empirical study/data collection in Hamburg and Isfahan	Continuation of the empirical study in Hamburg and Isfahan	Photo documentation Checklist

Facets of dialogue and forms of dialogues

In the course of the first project application, the project teams focused very much on providing a common understanding of the term "dialogue" and on identifying different levels of the common higher education dialogue. The project intends to strengthen three facets or areas of dialogue: (1) the *International dialogue* between the two universities, (2) the *Municipal dialogue* between the individual university and its urban or rural environment as well as (3) the *Institutional dialogue* for putting the UN Convention into practice in the respective university context.

1) **The International dialogue** means mutual discussion of central concepts such as disability, rehabilitation, inclusion, accessibility, universal design etc. in different local, social and cultural contexts. This includes methodological problems of inclusion research in the areas of education, rehabilitation and therapy as well as an exchange of information on related research projects conducted at the two universities. The international dialogues are to focus on the development of a common transcultural and interdisciplinary discussion on the rehabilitation and inclusion of people with disabilities as the basis for the enhancement of academic education at both universities.

2) **The Municipal dialogue** tries to strengthen the existing cooperation of the two universities with different local organizations and institutions working for the disabled. Networking activities between university and city focus thematically on care, education and psychosocial support for people with severe disabilities. The University of Isfahan intends to intensify work with an already existing loose network of out-of-school institutions, and the University of Hamburg seeks to cooperate more closely with local schools, since in Hamburg children and adolescents with severe disabilities are hardly taken into account as yet when it comes to inclusion.

3) **The Institutional dialogue** focuses on deepening the discussion on disability and inclusion at the two universities and on the further development of the curriculum and of teaching formats. For this, the University of Isfahan requires empirical data that will be collected in the course of three minor research projects and will form the basis for the development and implementation of a university

training program on the topic of inclusion for teaching staff. The University of Hamburg, in turn, will continue to move the project of a "Barrier-free University" forward. Moreover, it also aims to promote regular dialogue – previously non-existent – within the university on the topic of inclusion, migration and transnationalism.

For the sake of clarity, the three facets of dialogue are illustrated separately here; in practice, though, they will be addressed simultaneously, with possible overlaps and interrelations. The teams from Hamburg and Isfahan have different functions within the three areas of dialogue: critical, yet constructive discussion partner in the international dialogue, critical, yet constructive source of impetus "from the outside" in the respective local networks, initiator of common training/research seminars and innovator in terms of curriculum development in the respective university context.

Research-based teaching and learning

In order to empirically support the dialogues, data is to be collected in studies following the principle of research-based learning. In general, the aim of these cross-cultural research studies is to analyze and assess the physical, psychological, social and cultural aspects of the life of people with disabilities in the two cities, based on various methods and instruments as well as on discussion and experience gained in international research. The procedure for each part is explained in the following.

1) Development of an epidemiological study of people with disabilities and of a study on the prevalence of psychosomatic symptoms in the city of Isfahan: The intention of the two studies is a data-based approximation to the number and characteristics (age, sex, civil and social status etc.) of persons with disabilities living in the city of Isfahan. For Hamburg, this data is already available. Until now the corresponding statistics for Isfahan have not been analyzed and systematized. Special attention will be paid to psychosomatic symptoms, because this phenomenon is reported as very common in the day care centers.

2) Some studies will investigate particularly relevant "barriers" to the full integration and participation of persons with disabilities in society: Studies

will examine public attitudes toward disabilities in the two cities, because research shows that attitudes have a big impact on promoting inclusion in society.

3) Other studies will describe different kinds of physical and architectonic barriers which make it difficult for persons with disabilities to get free access to the different public spheres (streets, public transport, schools, universities, playgrounds) in Isfahan and Hamburg. How barrier-free are the playgrounds in the city? What kind of understanding of disability do students have who want to become teachers or social workers? What sort of support do parents of a child with disabilities wish for? How accessible are the universities and the study courses for people with disabilities?

These studies will provide a detailed quantitative overview of the situation of persons with disabilities in Isfahan and Hamburg. Qualitatively derived data will moreover lead to valuable insights as to the life situations of persons with disabilities, the forms of exclusion and the public attitudes toward this group of people in both cities. Thus, these empirical studies form the basis for developing and testing awareness programs for the teaching staff at the two universities. As already mentioned one of the main goals of this cooperative project is the joint organization, testing and evaluation of teaching/learning settings (seminars, workshops, and teaching projects) in order to sustainably and efficiently implement the different facets of the UN Convention in the academic education of students at both universities.

A close combination of research and university teaching throughout the whole project is the guiding didactic principle here. Junior academics, in particular, are given the opportunity to engage in this. In interdisciplinary and cooperative seminars and methodological workshops, students are to be prepared by the university teachers involved here for empirical questions. Moreover, in special workshops and student projects, the students will be involved in the data collection process early on and encouraged to do their own research on the life situations and needs of people with disabilities in the city. Titles and objectives of the research projects

Project I: Disability epidemiology and prevalence of psychosomatic symptoms in Isfahan
Sub-study (1a): Investigating the disability epidemiology in Isfahan
Sub-study (1b): Investigating the prevalence of psychosomatic symptoms in people with disabilities

Project II: Disability and inclusion as social and cultural phenomena: Comparative analysis of public attitudes toward disability in Hamburg and Isfahan

Project III: Inclusion and urban culture: Determining architectonic/structural barriers for people with disabilities in the public sphere in the city of Isfahan and Hamburg

Project IV: Developing an educational program concerning the needs of the disabled for the students of rehabilitation

The whole objectives and the goals of these research projects that expected to reach are:

• To determine the difficulties and problems faced by disabled in Isfahan and Hamburg
• To assess and determine the disabled people life barriers and how to overcome those problems
• To recognize the barriers of disabled individuals to access to education and facilities and how to solve those issues.

In order to achieve these main goals divided in specific objectives as follow:

• Determining the prevalence of disability in Isfahan in terms of demographic variables and kinds of disability
• Determining the signs and complaints of psychosomatics in disabled persons in Isfahan and comparing them with Hamburg
• Determining the mental health status of disabled persons in Isfahan and comparing the findings with Hamburg

Amrollah Ebrahimi & Joachim Schroeder

- Determining the signs of stress and trauma in disabled persons in Isfahan city and comparing them with Hamburg
- Determining the people's attitude toward the disabled in terms of their job, education, age, gender, financial and social status, religious beliefs
- Determining the people's attitudes in terms of having or not having a disabled person in their house
- Determining architectonic/structural barriers for people with disabilities in the public sphere in Isfahan
- Analyzing the accessibility of the University of Isfahan and possible ways of overcoming barriers (roadmap)
- Needs assessment for the empowerment program of students in relation to disabled people
- Determining the educational needs of students by means of a questionnaire and via interviews
- Determining the ideas of instructors in rehabilitation majors and other related fields such as psychology, social sciences, social work in relation to educational needs of students
- Determining the ideas of graduates majoring in rehabilitation concerning educational needs of students
- Determining the ideas of disabled people in relation to educational needs of students and also their hidden needs and sufferings Determining the aims and syllabus using focus group
- Determining the educational methods and also assessment methods in rehabilitation periods, using workshops, seminars and student projects
- Determining the students' attitude and awareness before and after the implementation of the empowerment program

International Conferences: Disability and Inclusion in a global world

As outlined, two conferences on the topic of "Disability and Inclusion in a global world" were held in 2017. Isfahan and Hamburg are multicultural and multi-ethnic cities and as such they are also a mirror image of the Iranian or German society. For Hamburg, for instance, it is important to learn more about different cultural and social perspectives on disability and inclusion, not least in order to promote the necessary – due to immigration – intercultural opening in the field of disability work in the city. For Isfahan it may be stimulating to talk to migrants who have been living in Hamburg for a long time and to discuss their needs, hardships and their experiences with institutions working for the disabled in Hamburg.

The three-day congress in Hamburg (1-3 July 2017) was attended by 44 people in addition to the two project groups. From Iran there were two researchers from the University of Yazd, one colleague from the University of Shiraz as well as one representative of the Iranian Society of Psychosomatic Medicine and Psychotherapy. Also the Vice President of IUMS attended the conference. Through the DAAD we had learned of a similar project carried out by the University of Oldenburg (Prof. Ortmann) in cooperation with the University of Duhok in Iraq and had got in contact with that project. The two members of that project from Oldenburg as well as two visiting researchers from Iraq, who happened to be in Oldenburg, joined the conference. It was agreed to broaden the exchange. For the keynote, the Christoffel-Blindenmission Deutschland e.V. could be won. Furthermore, a number of German institutions attended the conference, among them Lebenshilfe Hamburg, Alsterdorf Stiftung Hamburg, Nikolauspflege Stuttgart, Abesa Hamburg and FLUCHTort Hamburg.

The three-day congress in Isfahan (23-26 September 2017) has been attended by about 60 participants in addition to the two project groups. Apart from several Iranian researchers, students as well as experts working for the disabled in Isfahan have registered for the conference. It should be pointed out here that the Mayor of Isfahan could be won as speaker, which is particularly remarkable as it means an important step for the municipal dialogue in the city. Following this, two courses had been jointly organized: In a methodological workshop students from Hamburg and Isfahan have been instructed on how to plan, conduct and interpret small research projects on different barriers at the universities as well as in the urban public space. In a second workshop a questionnaire developed by the University of Hamburg for determining students' attitudes toward people with disabilities has been adapted for use in the context of Isfahan, and problems in data collection and interpretation will be examined with the research group.

Since the both 2017's conferences and the related study visits and workshops have yielded interesting presentations and discussions with scientists and students

Amrollah Ebrahimi & Joachim Schroeder

as well as with representatives of religious groups, migrant and other organizations on historical, religious and philosophical perspectives on disability, on the change in attitudes due to migration, globalization etc., we decided to publish the contributions in this conference reader.

Conclusion

It can be said that the intercultural project due to the fulfillment of the components which are mentioned earlier, is aimed at achieving a minimum of different aspects of the rights of the persons with disabilities, which is within the competence and authority of the faculty members of the universities. These tasks are related to the assessment of the status of the disabled and their physical and psychological problems, as well as the physical, social, cultural obstacles and also the way to overcome them. The other task include development of educational programs related to people with disabilities, the movement towards the free-barriers city, university and educational centers, and providing counseling support to improve the quality of life of persons with disabilities.

In the end, we need to appreciate the DAAD for their always effective support.

References

Adedoyin O., Okere E. (2017): The Significance of Inclusion Concept in the Educational System as Perceived by Junior Secondary School Teachers: Implications for Teacher Training Programs in Botswana. Global Journal of Social Sciences Studies, 3(1), 13-28.

Alquraini T., Gut D. (2012): Critical components of successful inclusion of students with severe disabilities: literature review. International Journal of Special Education, 27(1), 42-59.

Bayat Bodaghi N., Zainab A.N. (2013): Accessibility and facilities for the disabled in public and university library buildings in Iran. Information Development 29(3), 241-250.

Moore A., Kornblet S. (2011) (Editors): Advancing the Rights of Persons with Disabilities: Iran and America: A Dialogue on Disability. A US-Iran Dialogue on Law, Policy, and Advocacy. The Henry L. Stimson Center. Washington, DC.

Salend, S. (2001): Creating inclusive classrooms: effective, differentiated and reflective practices. State University of New York.

Soltani S., Khosravi B., Salehiniya H. (2015): Prevalence of Disability in Iran. Iranian Journal of Public Health, 44(10), 1436-1437.

WHO (2007): International Classification of Functioning, Disability, and Health: Children & Youth Version: ICF-CY. Malta: World Health Organization.

WHO (2011): World report on disability 2011. WHO Library Cataloguing-in-Publication Data. *www.who.int*

WHO (2012): World report on disability 2012. Malta: World Health Organization.

II   International Discussions

3   Disability Inclusion in a Global World: Moving towards Disability Inclusive Development – Development Cooperation before and after the adoption of the UN Convention on the Rights of Persons with Disabilities

(Veronika Hilber)

Starting with Christoffel

In 2006, the United Nations adopted a new human rights treaty, the UN Convention on the Rights of Persons with Disabilities (UNCRPD). The adoption stands at the end of decades long intense lobbying and advocacy of the disability rights movement. The Treaty doesn't lay out any new or special rights for persons with disabilities. It merely spells out what human rights mean for persons with disabilities and what need to be the focus areas when we want persons with disabilities enjoy the same human rights as any other human beings.

This Treaty is remarkable in many ways. It is the first Human Rights Treaty to be ratified not only by national states- with now 174 States Parties around the world- and thus is one of the most successful human rights treaties of all times, but also the first to be ratified by a "regional integration organization", the European Union. Another innovation is its Art. 32 on international cooperation: it recognizes that, in fact, we are in a global world, in which so many things are closely interconnected and in which we can only reach our goals in close cooperation. States take mutual responsibility in promoting the goals set by the Convention and the realization of the rights it contains.

For CBM, Art. 32, but also Art. 11 on situations of risk and humanitarian emergencies are our "pet articles" of the Convention. We are a Christian development organization committed to improve the quality of life for persons with disability, their families and their communities living in so-called "developing countries" around the world. Our vision is an inclusive world in which all people enjoy their human rights and achieve their full potential, to which we aim to contribute by working towards a transformative change in structures, systems and attitudes.

CBM as an organization is over a hundred years old. We come a long way from a charity based organization increasingly becoming an organization with a needs based approach, involving national and local partners, persons with disabilities and their representative organizations (Disabled People's Organizations, DPOs) in our programs, and a human rights based approach to development.

We are on a journey, and although we are undeniably making progress, we have not arrived yet in an inclusive world. In the following minutes, I will lay out the developments international cooperation has made throughout the years, explain what has already changed in development cooperation since the adoption of the UNCRPD in 2006, and give an outlook on what still needs to be improved for a better implementation of the UNCRPD in international development cooperation. In this regard, I will briefly touch the importance of the 2030 Agenda for Sustainable Development in the context of disability inclusive development. Throughout my presentation, I will refer to examples drawn from CBM's work for illustration.

Let us start right with the beginnings of CBM as an organization and look at what development work with a focus on disability used to be over a hundred years back.

Ernst Jakob Christoffel, whose name the German version of CBM, Christoffel Blindenmission, bears in its name, was a young German pastor born in 1876. He felt a calling to work for persons- particularly children- with visual impairments in the Islamic world. His first mission led him to eastern Turkey where he was responsible for the administration of two orphanages. It was then that the particularly difficult situation of blind children first drew his attention. After World War I, he was not allowed to pursue his work in Turkey. In 1925, he moved on to Persia and by 1928, Isfahan had become the new major base of the Blind Mission, being located in the south of Persia, with then the highest concentration of blind persons. About Isfahan, Christoffel said, full of admiration "Isfahan is said to be the most beautiful city of Persia [...]. She is the city of gardens, palaces and mosques whose unreal beauty appears inebriant. The Meidan i Schah and its surroundings are like a tale from Thousand and One Nights come true in the very present."/1/

The disability and development approach at Christoffel's time was a charity approach. The focus was to help persons with disabilities, and to help them adapt to their environment. Christoffel felt like a father for "his" children, and even adopted two orphans under his care. The perspective might therefore seem rather paternalistic, although this judgment would be harsh on Christoffel and not reflect the very modern aspects of his approach. E.g., Christoffel would not restrict himself to "only" blind children. Soon, he became aware of children with other impairments like hearing impairments and tried to find ways to help them better adapt to their environment. He was a very acute observer and noticed what others wouldn't see. Today, he would perhaps work with children with mental health issues, who in our societies often are not accounted for, can't enjoy their rights and are considerably stigmatized.

Christoffel didn't take solely a medical or rehabilitation approach, but also tried to find ways to provide children with disabilities with access to education. Which was revolutionary in its way, as there were many misconceptions- and if we are honest, these misconceptions still exist today- about the capacity of children with disabilities to learn, to follow a vocational training and ultimately to earn their living with decent work. In order to be able to teach blind children to read, Christoffel even invented the Persian braille alphabet.

Christoffel was very much motivated by his Christian faith and the second Great Commandment "thou shalt love thy neighbor as thyself", he was not in-spired by the notion of human rights, a concept that didn't exist at his time the way we know it today and particularly as we understand it since the Universal Declaration of Human Rights in 1948.

What has changed with the UNCRPD?
The UNCRPD is the result of a long struggle of the disability rights movement. For decades, disability advocates from the UN, non- governmental organizations, from within governments, and persons with disabilities from all over the world have fought for a rights based approach to disability and for the recognition that *all* human rights, without exception, apply to *every* human being, again without exception, at *all times* and *everywhere* and to the *same degree*. This notion is the very essence of Human Rights being universal, interrelated and indivisi-ble. We need to particularly recognize the implication of persons with disabil-ities and their representative organizations in the creation of this new Human Rights Treaty. Not only have they been instrumental activists for their own cause,

claiming "Nothing about us without us", persons with disability have contributed to drafting the UNCRPD as it is today, making it really a convention of, not only for, persons with disabilities.

With the UNCRPD, we reach a paradigm shift from the charity model of Christoffel's time to the human rights model/2/ of disability. We understand that our point of view needs to be one that understands the human person as a rights bearer living in a particular social context that may be more or less conducive to the enjoyment of his or her rights. The enjoyment of rights being guaranteed by international human rights law, we need to look at the elements hindering human persons from enjoying their rights and work on dismantling these elements. We need to fix the environment, not the person.

The UNCRPD doesn't create new rights for persons with disabilities. It only spells out the rights we already find in the Universal Declaration of Human Rights and the two International Covenants of 1966, on Economic, Social and Cultural Rights (ICESCR) and on Political and Civil Rights (ICCPR). We have human rights such as the right to education (Art. 24 UNCRPD), health (Art. 25 UN-CRPD), work and employment (Art. 27 UNCPRD), life (Art. 10 UNCRPD), access to justice (Art. 13 UNCRPD) etc. that we also find in these two International Covenants. When we read Art. 32 of the Convention, we realize that all of these rights of the Convention need to be ensured by States Parties in international cooperation, as much by States Parties of so- called developing countries as by those of "developed" countries.

In order to help us understand how a development project, a sector becomes inclusive and compliant with the UNCPRD, the convention has not only given us the different rights, i.e. that we would have Art. 24 UNCRPD on Education and Art. 32 on International Cooperation as our only reference points for an inclusive education development project. The UNCRPD provides us with eight core principles that serve us as a guideline, a lens through which we need to take a look at policies, programs and projects to see whether they comply with the convention and where would be the areas that we need to improve.

When we look at the UNCRPD principles of Art. 3 of the Convention, we have an enormously challenging task before us. With the UNCRPD and its principles, we now know what inclusive development projects, what an inclusive world should look like, but we are still far from being able to comply with all of them and our world remains a place of exclusion, at best it is in parts integrative, but not inclusive.

The UNCRPD principles, as you surely know, are the following:

a) Respect for the inherent dignity, individual autonomy including the freedom to make one's own choices, and independence of persons
b) Non-discrimination
c) Full and effective participation and inclusion in society
d) Respect for difference and acceptance of persons with disabilities as part of human diversity and humanity
e) Equality of opportunity
f) Accessibility
g) Equality between men and women
h) Respect for the evolving capacities of children with disabilities and respect for the right of children with disabilities to preserve their identities

It would mean overstretching my time for this keynote to elaborate on each of these principles. However, in my experience with CBM, I have noticed three areas in which development cooperation and the international awareness levels with regard to the implementation of these principles still need to improve considerably:

Diversity, Participation and Accessibility

By diversity, I want to refer mainly to what is embodied in principle d) in Art. 3 UNCRPD. I like this principle very much. It implicitly states something that is very true, and at the same time, it is one of the principles of the UNCRPD that tend to be forgotten over and over again. It reminds us of the fact, that no human being is the same as another human being. Even brothers and sisters, even twins growing up in the same environment, under the same influences, are not the same. Diversity is a fact, and it is the beauty of humanity. The UNCRPD says, a little less dramatically, it is a part of humanity. Principle d) warns us to put everyone in the same sack. A wheelchair user is different from a blind person using a cane. One blind person is not like another blind person. This principle reminds us to find solutions with and for as many variables as possible, to help us all enjoy the beauty of the many colors of humanity. It also reminds us, together with principle a), that persons with disabilities are above all humans with inherent dignity, placed in an environment that enables or disables. By being aware of and respecting difference, we want to make sure that as many persons as possible enjoy an enabling environment.

In the above observance, I have also mentioned some aspects of the elements "participation" and "accessibility". We need to find solutions with persons with disabilities, not merely for them. They are the experts on their respective impairment(s) and the needs with regard to an accessible environment that facilitates the enjoyment of a person's human rights. Surprisingly, persons with disabilities are still very often not even consulted, let alone given the opportunity to shape policies, programs and projects that concern their communities and impact their lives in these communities. Very often, the central call of the disability movement "Nothing about us without us" remains unheard. Often times, persons without disabilities decide on what is in the best interest of those with disabilities. This is, of course, in complete contradiction with the Convention and human rights based approach.

An enabling environment has to be one that is as far as possible barrier free. The principle of Accessibility of Art. 3 f) UNCRPD should be self-explanatory, but still tends to be disregarded, and this often also due to the lack of awareness of diversity and the denial of the right of persons with disabilities to participate and be included in the community. For example, we may have a school building with a ramp. We cannot pretend that this building is absolutely barrier free only because of the ramp. A blind student may tell us that she doesn't need the ramp to access the building, that she doesn't find it very helpful that the teacher carries out his lessons asking students to copy content written on the blackboard and that she would love to have schoolbooks in braille instead of being provided with the meaningless piles of paper provided to students without visual impairments. Or take the example of an eye clinic: Patients going there have difficulties seeing and with seeing only, right? It cannot be that a wheel chair user needs eye care. That would be a little too much, right? So we build eye clinics without ramps, or with doors that aren't wide enough to pass through with a wheel chair, or with staircases instead of elevators. We do not provide information to patients in a format that allows them to understand when we don't provide sign language interpretation to patients with hearing impairments or easy-to-read formats to patients with learning disabilities. We have clinics where the reception is as high that any person with a wheel chair would feel like any of us felt when we were little children in a shop, trying to buy candy, but were overlooked and overtaken by adult customers, as the person behind the counter couldn't see us.

Another core challenge which recently has gotten more and more its required attention is the lacking statistical foundation for evidence-based inclusive policy making.

When we understand the UNCRPD principles and are serious about making them the principles of our disability inclusive development (DID) programs, we inevitably must understand who our target group is, how many persons with disabilities live in the area of our project and the prevalence of different types of impairments.

Even before the 2030 Agenda for Sustainable Development with its core principle to "Leave No One Behind"/3/, the lack of reliable data had been an issue. In fact, the importance of data on disability in relation with the realization of human rights for persons with disabilities is underlined by the UNCRPD itself in its Art. 31 by which States Parties have the obligation to collect data to "enable them to formulate and implement policies to give effect to the present Convention". Now this issue became even more pressing, as all governments of the world are required to report on a set of currently 230 global indicators to measure progress with the SDGs. As this shall be done in an internationally comparable manner and the 2030 Agenda requires to statistically capture those previously and most likely left behind to measure whether or not they still are, it is absolutely crucial to have an internationally comparable way of capturing disability within one's population.

The World Bank/ WHO World Report on Disability of 2011 has been a first step to see a little bit clearer. We now already know that we had for a long time under- estimated the prevalence of disabilities in our societies. However, the World Report cannot remain the only reference point forever. Data change over time, and disability rates, estimated by the World Report to 15% of the entire world population, cannot be the same anywhere. Data need to be updated regularly and collected in all countries. Prevalence is not likely to be the same anywhere, and even within countries, there are differences.

For example, a recent study supported by CBM and carried out by the London School of Hygiene and Tropical Medicine (LSHTM) in Guatemala, has shown that disability prevalence was higher in the Central and North- West Provinces of the country. The reasons for this distribution set aside; this is an important information for policy makers and programme officers.

This Study tried to approach the issue of data collection from a perspective compliant with the human rights model of the UNCRPD. It used the Washington Group Extended Set of Questions (WGESQ) and the UNICEF/WG Extended set on Functioning for children aged 2-17 years. Under the Washington group method, participants are self-assessing their own level of difficulties with regard to various functionalities, like seeing, hearing, walking, understanding or being understood etc. on a scale going from no difficulties over some difficulty, a lot of difficulty up to "cannot do".

Additionally, the study used medical tests, depending on the reported level of difficulty. An easy to use application developed for the study facilitated the collection of data. Medical assessments were also carried out with mobile applications like *PEEK Acuity* for testing visual acuity, *Hearing Test* for pure tone audiometry testing, Physical Performance Test (*PPT*) for testing physical functioning and the Patient Health Questionnaire (*PHQ-9*), a clinical depression test.

Beyond this, the study compared the barriers with regard to participation and differences in quality of life participants experienced with those of a control group with participants without disabilities, using a question set developed by the Norwegian foundation SINTEF (Stiftelsen for industriell og teknisk forskning) on participation and the WHO Quality of life- BREF instrument (WHO-QOL-BREF). The former includes 26 questions across four domains: physical health, psychological health, social relationships and the environment.

Thus, the Guatemala Disability Survey gives a rather comprehensive overview on the situation of persons with disabilities in Guatemala and has established an all age disability prevalence of 10.2%, identified regional differences in prevalence (as mentioned above), determined a higher disability prevalence of disability for women compared to men and stated that prevalence of significant limitations was highest in the domain of anxiety/depression for both adults (9.3%) and children (1.9%). The study is available for download on CBM International's Website/4/.

We are happy to say that Guatemala's National Statistics Institute (Instituto Nacional de Estadística) that had been involved in the study has expressed interest in using the Washington Group questions for the next Census in the country.

The WG questions provide an opportunity for data collection on disability that, if used internationally and without modifications, can contribute to the availability of internationally comparable data and help inform policies and programs on disability. It can also help us to identify the baseline from where we can measure progress and the impact of policies, programs and projects on persons with disabilities. The disability community, including IDDC/5/ (of which CBM is a member) and the International Disability Alliance (IDA)/6/, have just recently in June 2017 endorsed the Washington group set of questions at the 10th COSP in NY.

In Ethiopia, CBM is currently supporting DPOs in their advocacy to the Ethiopian Government to use the Washington Group questions in the next national Census in 2018.

To conclude, I want to stress again the importance of this new international political framework, the 2030 Agenda, for disability advocates. The 2030 Agenda with its many references to disability and the core principle to "Leave no one behind" provides a lot of opportunities for disability advocates to push for disability mainstreaming and data for informed policy making and accountability across the SDGs that are to a large extent reflecting human rights entitlements of persons. For example, Goal 3 on Health is underpinned by the right to life (Art. 10 UNCRPD), the right to health (Art. 25 UNCRPD) and is linked to articles 6 (Women with disabilities), 7 (Children with disabilities), 9 (Accessibility) etc. The 2030 Agenda understands the world as a place where we all live together, where we share one planet, where everything is interlinked and where the SDGs need to be reached as much in so-called developing as in so-called developed countries. In fact, for the 2030 Agenda, all countries are developing countries, even a highly industrialized country like Germany. We should use the Agenda to advocate further for the respect and realization of the rights of persons with disabilities, and as much as we can, contribute to it through our own projects, be it as NGOs working in development cooperation like CBM or as researchers. We can do this by letting us guide by the UNCRPD principles and particularly by facilitating the inclusion of persons with disabilities and their representative organizations in the design, implementation, monitoring and evaluation of development and research projects. To quote the UN Special Rapporteur on the Rights of Persons with Disabilities/7/[1], Catalina Devandas, "Times are changing … No more excuses. Nothing without persons with disabilities!"

I want to end by thanking you for the opportunity to share my thoughts with you. I wish you all a very successful and inspiring conference.

References

/1/ Sabine Thüne, Ernst Jakob Christoffel. Ein Leben im Dienst Jesu, 2007

/2/ Theresia Degener, Die UN-Behindertenrechtskonvention – ein neues Verständnis von Behinderung", 2015

/3/ *https://sustainabledevelopment.un.org/post2015/transformingourworld*

/4/ *http://www.cbm.org/Guatemala-National-Disability-Survey-ENDIS--524831.php*

/5/ International Disability and Development Consortium, *https://www.iddconsortium.net*

/6/ IDA is an alliance of eight global and six regional organizations of persons with disabilities.

/7/ *http://www.ohchr.org/EN/NewsEvents/Pages/DisplayNews.aspx?NewsID=20764&LangID=E*

4 Agenda 2030 and UN CRPD as the basis for a worldwide and diverse discussion on inclusion and disability – ideas from Ladakh and Isfahan

(Nele Schell)

Introduction

In my research, I discussed the concept of inclusion and its meaning for persons with disabilities in Germany as well as in India and Iran. I also read about these issues in other countries like Malawi, Cambodia, Kenya and China. I gained the impression that inclusion and disability are two important issues the world over. One reason for the global relevance of inclusion and disability is the discussion of these topics in several UN documents, which relate inclusion to human rights. These documents call for inclusion and non-discrimination for persons with disabilities. However, inclusion is not only demanded, but also discussed and implemented. In this article, I wish to look at both the global call for inclusion, and its discussion and implementation. I wish to focus on its meaning and impact for persons with disabilities.

The documents I refer to are the 2030 Agenda for Sustainable Development, also known as the 2030 Agenda (United Nations 2015) and the Convention on the Rights of Persons with Disabilities, or CRPD for short (United Nations 2006). I will show that the 2030 Agenda calls for inclusion in a variety of fields. This demand reinforces the CRPD, which demands equal human rights for persons with disabilities. I assume that the calls for inclusion in the UN documents make inclusion an international norm that must be implemented. The reason for using the term internationally is that the documents are signed by nation states, which essentially makes them an agreement between countries. They are not only implemented and discussed by national governments, though, which is why I prefer to use the term 'worldwide' (or 'global') when I refer to the implementation of inclusion. As previously mentioned, this worldwide implementation affects persons with disabilities. I will consider different implementations and discussions in the fields of inclusion and disability, and conclude by summarising what I have learned from these global discussions.

Concepts and definitions

When writing about inclusion and disability, it seems necessary to first define these terms. At the same time, however, a clear and precise definition of these concepts does not actually exist. Both terms are complex and their meaning varies depending on the context. Before considering inclusion with its special meaning for persons with disabilities called for by the UN (and therefore becoming a human right principle), I wish to clarify which aspects of inclusion and disability I believe are important.

According to Beck (2016), there are three theoretical lines for inclusion. The first, which she deems the most important, is the political normative question of peace, freedom and democracy. The first important documents here are the Universal Declaration of Human Rights (UDHR) adopted by the United Nations in 1948, followed by the Salamanca Statement of the United Nations Educational, Scientific and Cultural Organisation (UNESCO) from 1994, which was the first UN document to explicitly mention inclusion (Beck 2016, p. 46-47). In this article, I will mainly focus on the line and argument that the UN makes inclusion a human right principle. However, although the UN calls for inclusion, there is no uniform definition of inclusion within the UN – as is noted by Brüggemann referring to Kiuppis (2016, p. 6). Further literature is required to understand inclusion: Köpfer agrees, for example, that there is no clear definition of inclusion either in the UN or elsewhere, but states that the term is often understood as non-exclusion (2012, p. 1). As such, people should not be excluded, but rather be able to participate in specific fields like education. Participation, or being given the chance to participate, is often linked with inclusion (Antor et al. 2016, p. 456; Köpfer 2012, p. 1; Hummel & Werning 2016, p. 22). However, to achieve participation, access must be guaranteed. So creating access as well as participation are often named in the context of inclusion (Beck & Degenhardt 2010, p. 75-76). Inclusion is moreover linked with an attitude of accepting human diversity (Köpfer 2012, p. 3). This attitude as well as access have to develop or to be developed. It is for this reason that inclusion is also often described as a process (Beck & Degenhardt 2010; Brüggemann 2016; Grant & Smith 2016; Hummel 2016). To summarise, inclusion is a process of accepting different, individual people and creating opportunities for them to participate in different fields by enabling different access.

Wherever certain people are deprived of this opportunity to participate is described as discrimination (Antor et al. 2016, p. 457). Inclusion therefore also protects people from discrimination.

One group that often suffers from discrimination is persons with disabilities: according to the World Report on Disability published by the World Health Organization, "many people with disabilities do not have equal access to health care, education, and employment opportunities, do not receive the disability-related services that they require, and experience exclusion from everyday life activities" (2011, p.3).

The International Classification of Functioning, Disability and Health (ICF) defines disability as a complex interaction between a person and his/her environment (Deutsches Institut für Medizinische Dokumentation und Information, DIMDI WHO Kooperationszentrum für die Familie Internationaler Klassifikationen 2004, p. 24). A similar approach can be found in the CRPD: "disability results from the interaction between persons with impairments and attitudinal and environmental barriers that hinders their full and effective participation in society on an equal basis with others" (United Nations 2006, p. 2). These quotes could lead to the conclusion that disability also depends on the opportunities to participate given in or by the environment. If inclusion creates access and makes participation possible for everyone, it can not only protect persons with disabilities from discrimination, but also help to reduce or even eradicate disability.

For me, it also seems important that using the term "disability" can effectively construct disability as well because it also suggests the attitude that some people are less able to do something. At the same time, it is necessary to name existing problems. It is important to at least keep this in mind and to not see disability as a closed category.

Agenda 2030 and the UN CRPD: inclusion and disability as important issues worldwide

In this chapter, I wish to show how the United Nations call for inclusion in the 2030 Agenda and the CRPD, referring to human rights in both. I assume that this call makes inclusion and its implementation an international norm. A norm can be understood as a rule for behaviour (Fuchs-Heinritz et al. 2011, p. 474).

Inclusion can have a (positive) impact on every single person, so not only affects persons with disabilities. I will focus on the part of inclusion that affects persons with disabilities as a group that often suffers from non-accessibility and non-participation.

I will also take a closer look at the CRPD and its connection with 2030 Agenda.

The 2030 Agenda demands inclusion in many different fields and ways, and links in this respect to the CRPD. I will show how both coincide with one another.

The 2030 Agenda, which is also referred to as the Sustainable Development Goals, includes seventeen goals for "sustainable development" (United Nations 2015, p. 1). It describes itself as a "plan of action for people, planet and prosperity. It also seeks to strengthen universal peace in larger freedom" (ibid). This plan builds on the Millennium Development Goals of 2000 and refers to the tradition of human rights as well as to these goals (ibid). The vision of the Agenda 2030 is

"a world of universal respect for human rights and human dignity, the rule of law, justice, equality and non-discrimination; of respect for race, ethnicity and cultural diversity; and of equal opportunity permitting the full realization of human potential and contributing to shared prosperity, [...] a[n] equitable, tolerant, open and socially inclusive world in which the needs of the most vulnerable are met" (United Nations 2015, p. 2).

So the United Nations imagines an inclusive world to be a better world. By writing this on the second page, the word "inclusive" gains great significance. It is also referred to in five of the seventeen goals:

- Goal 4 on ensuring "inclusive and equitable quality education" (p. 16)
- Goal 8 on promoting "sustained, inclusive and sustainable economic growth" (p. 18)
- Goal 9 on building "resilient infrastructure, promot[ing] inclusive and sustainable industrialization and foster[ing] innovation" (p. 19)
- Goal 11 on making "cities and human settlements inclusive, safe, resilient and sustainable" (p. 21)
- Goal 16 on promoting "peaceful and inclusive societies for sustainable development, provid[ing] access to justice for all and build[ing] effective, accountable and inclusive institutions at all levels" (p. 25)
- Persons with disabilities are also mentioned within goals 4, 8 and 11:
- Goal 4.5 on ensuring "equal access to all levels of education and vocational

training for the vulnerable, including persons with disabilities, indigenous peoples and children in vulnerable situations" by 2030 (p. 16)

- Goal 8.5 on achieving "full and productive employment and decent work for all women and men, including for young people and persons with disabilities, and equal pay for work of equal value" by 2030 (p. 18).
- Goal 11.2 on providing "access to safe, affordable, accessible and sustainable transport systems for all, improve[ing] road safety, notably by expanding public transport, with special attention to the needs of those in vulnerable situations, women, children, persons with disabilities and older persons" by 2030 (p. 21)

Persons with disabilities do not only benefit from goals where they are directly named though. Goal 16 calling for better public access to information can also aid inclusion (United Nations 2015, p. 25). Both this and the whole concept of inclusion should be realized or implemented through the "global partnership for sustainable development" called for in goal 17 (United Nations 2015, p. 25).

Summarising the message of the 2030 Agenda about inclusion and its meaning for persons with disability, it can be said that inclusion should be implemented worldwide through global partnerships in a variety of fields, namely education, employment, public spaces in cities and infrastructure. The implementation of inclusion in these fields could help to protect persons with disabilities as well as all other people from discrimination. In addition, it can be said that Agenda 2030 considers the needs of persons with disabilities for different kinds of access.

This is also proven by Grant and Smith, who searched for references to persons with disabilities in the 2030 Agenda (Grant & Smith 2016). They found that persons with disabilities are explicitly referred to in the 2030 Agenda eleven times (Grant & Smith 2016, p. 4). They did not begin their search with the word "inclusive", though, but rather with references to persons with disabilities. I agree that the Agenda demands "access to education, employment, inclusive cities [and] reducing inequalities" and that persons with disabilities are explicitly mentioned in goals 4 and 11, which focus specifically on "access to education and the promotion of inclusive, resilient and safe cities" (ibid). The authors also see many connections between the 2030 Agenda and the CRPD.

The CRPD is an international convention that was adopted by the United Nations in 2006. It intends to reaffirm the universality of all human rights for persons with disabilities and the need for these right to be guaranteed to everyone without discrimination (United Nations 2006, p. 2). In one manual on disability, it states that the CRPD demands equal human rights for persons with disabilities. This is also seen as protection from discrimination. As previously mentioned, the central principles of the convention in this manual are participation and inclusion (Antor et al. 2016, p. 456-457).

In both the 2030 Agenda and the CRPD, the rights of persons with disabilities and their equality and participation are linked with inclusion. Grant and Smith demonstrate even more connections between Agenda 2030 and the CRPD: not only do they state that the 2030 Agenda supports the implementation and importance of the CRPD. They also show that they consider many similar issues, namely education, employment, access to justice and accessible living conditions as well as participation and gender equality (2016, p. 5).

From my point of view, the difference is that the Agenda 2030 takes inclusion as the starting point and names persons with disabilities as one group that benefits from inclusion. In contrast, the CRPD starts with persons with disabilities and their equal rights that should be achieved through inclusion.

Either way, it can be interpreted from both documents that inclusion is a norm, a rule for behaviour and action. In literature, inclusion is also called a human right principle (Brüggemann 2016, p.4) that is valid for different human rights, such as the right to education or the right to access public spaces (Antor et al. 2016, p. 457).

If these rights are not inclusive, then there are people like persons with disabilities who cannot enjoy their full rights. So these persons are essentially discriminated against. In the CRPD, it is also said that the discrimination of persons with disabilities means that their human rights are not guaranteed (United Nations 2006, p.4). Therefore, implementing inclusion again means protecting persons with disabilities as well as everyone else from discrimination.

As previously mentioned, inclusion can be interpreted as an international norm. But it cannot exist on its own; it must be implemented in different fields and – as Brüggemann demands, for example – this implementation must be discussed (2016, p. 5). There are in fact countless publications on how to implement inclusion that refer directly either to the 2030 Agenda or the CRPD: Hummel (2016)writes about the problems and success factors of developing inclusive education in Malawi, Kalyanpur (2016) considers the policies and practices used in Cambodia, Lee (2014) writes about mental disability in the global south, and Beck and Degenhardt (2010) share their ideas on the meaning of inclusion in Germany and China. This provides an indication of the significance of the documents themselves as well as the meaning of inclusion worldwide.

Furthermore, there are articles that do not explicitly name the 2030 Agenda or the CRPD, but also discuss inclusion and the situation of persons with disabilities in different global circumstances. Schmidt (2017) emphasises the importance of the sociocultural context of implementing inclusion and refers to Ibrahim (2014) who writes about the treatment of persons with disabilities in Kenya. A postcolonial perspective of inclusion and disability seems especially important in countries of the global south (Ibrahim 2014; Kalyanpur 2016).

It may be going too far to say that the 2030 Agenda and CRPD are the reason for a global discussion on inclusion and disability. However, it is by all means a fact that discussions are taking place the world over, and that the documents are often referred to and used as a basis. It is also important that these discussions lead to action – and that these actions are discussed, too.

Experiences and discussion in the worldwide context of inclusion and disability
I had the honour of being part of different discussions and implementations in the context of inclusion and disability.

I am studying special needs education at Universität Hamburg. Inclusion and disability are often discussed as part of the degree programme.

However, I also had the chance to witness inclusion and disability in other contexts. In India, I was able to complete an internship in a special needs class for children with disabilities at Munshi Habibullah Mission School in Kargil, which is the second largest city in Ladakh, a region in the Indian Himalayas.

I moreover had the chance to participate in the exchange programme between the University of Isfahan and Universität Hamburg on inclusion and disability. In this chapter, I now wish to describe my experiences.

I will start with my experiences in the class in Kargil: this class was established in cooperation between a German NGO called Ladakh Hilfe, a local

NGO called REWA and the Munshi Habibullah Mission School. Ladakh Hilfe was founded by the German physiotherapist Karola Wood (2013)with the aim of supporting children with disabilities in Ladakh. In cooperation with REWA, she opened a physiotherapy centre in Leh, the capital of Ladakh. This centre cooperates with different schools in Leh so that physiotherapy and school attendance can both be ensured and organized in parallel. After a while, the owner of the Munshi Habibullah Mission School in Kargil asked Ladakh Hilfe and REWA for help to offer physiotherapy and also education for children with disabilities at his school as well. So the second centre for therapy and the special class were opened. The class is open to all children with disabilities, as the school fees are paid by the NGOs. The class not only welcomes everyone, though, but also allows everyone to leave. Hence some children attend class every day, while others attend a special class for four days and another class for one day. There are also children going to the special class as well as to physiotherapy, meaning that they miss certain lessons to receive treatment. Other children receive physiotherapy and go to a normal class, sometimes even in another school. Every effort is made to find the best individual solution for each child by offering a combination of school and physiotherapy. Attempts are therefore made to ensure participation in school as well as access to healthcare in a public space. In the Ladakh area, which includes many villages that are hard to reach, it is important to make school and therapy accessible to children living in rural areas. The most successful initiative was therefore to organise a bus especially for children with disabilities that passes through all of the villages and brings them to Kargil. So-called field trips that can last from two or three days up to two whole weeks are also organised to reach even more remote areas. Many patients are visited during these trips and the NGO staff try to show them and their families how they can support physical and cognitive development. Stakeholders from different countries are involved in the project: there are physiotherapists and special needs teachers (mainly from Germany, but also from Ladakh) as well as a bus driver and the children's families. Some families even accompany their children to their physiotherapy and, in some cases, even assist the physiotherapists (*www.ladakh-hilfe.de*).

For me, this project is an attempt to implement inclusive education especially for children with disabilities as is called for in Goal 4 of the 2030 Agenda (United

Nations 2015, p. 16) and Article 24 of the CRPD (United Nations 2006, p. 17): it tries to give children with disabilities the opportunity to participate in school or to gain an education in other ways by visiting them at home. Access is also provided to a kind of a health system in the form of physiotherapy. The Munshi Habibullah Mission School even refers to an UN document about education in its brochure, stating that it aims to offer inclusive education, and quotes the UNESCO that "inclusive education means that schools should accommodate all children regardless of their physical, intellectual, social, emotional, linguistic or other conditions" (Munshi Habibullah Mission School, p. 12).

I also heard UNESCO documents quoted in a completely different context: at the University of Isfahan, when Dr. Yamani talked about the role of faculty members in training the teachers, who will ultimately teach children with and without disabilities. She refers directly to Goal 4 of the 2030 Agenda about inclusive education (United Nations 2015, p. 16) and emphasises how important faculty members are as role models in teaching to ensure high quality in inclusive education. She makes very clear that teachers at schools and universities must always question and reflect on their actions and attitudes. She demands an ongoing discussion and reflection on attitudes and teaching as the basis for the continuous development of universities and schools to implement inclusion in these institutions as well as encourage it beyond this through their influence. Her lecture formed part of the DAAD programme for "Dialogues on Disability and Inclusion between Isfahan and Hamburg". This programme involved lectures, workshops and also visits to facilities for persons with disabilities. I participated in a workshop about psychotherapy not only for persons with disabilities, but also for their families. This workshop drew my attention to the importance of the family for persons with disabilities.

This was confirmed by the lecture of Dr. Naghavi. She talked about her "development-oriented family empowerment programme" and has founded a NGO that aims to empower children. Thus she offers workshops for mothers where they can learn how to empower their own children. The project has a scientific basis consisting of psychology, sociology, philosophy, education, medicine and rehabilitation. Two aspects of this programme seemed important to me: firstly, there are many different attitudes to development, inclusion and disability. Secondly, beside the family, NGOs can also influence the lifestyle of children and also of persons with disabilities. This became clear when we visited the Iranian NGO "Heaven-children". This NGO offers further education for persons with disabilities to help them find a job. It was really impressive to visit this NGO where persons with disabilities are given the opportunity to learn how to produce art as well as to develop their computer skills. Incidentally, the NGO was founded by the mother of a boy with disabilities, which once again shows the importance of family members.

Another important NGO we learned about thanks to Dr. Pestei. He is himself a wheelchair user and has founded an NGO for persons with physical disabilities. This NGO gives people with and without disabilities the opportunity to come together to talk about their problems. It also calls for the rights of persons with disabilities in public – through demonstrations, for example. Dr. Pestei also said that they cooperate with NGOs for persons with visual and hearing impairments. However, Dr. Pestei not only talked about NGOs. He also showed pictures and shared personal experiences that highlight the difficulties a wheelchair user can encounter in Isfahan. This drew my attention to another actor – and probably the most important: persons, who are themselves affected by a disability.

What did I learn about disability and inclusion?
In this chapter, I wish to outline what I have learned about inclusion and disability from the experiences described.

Firstly, it has become clear that several different stakeholders are involved in the discussion and in the implementation of inclusion and treatment of persons with disabilities. These stakeholders are the family members, members of NGOs, teachers, faculty members and – most importantly – the persons affected by disabilities.

They belong to different institutions – to families, universities, schools or NGOs.

The stakeholders have different attitudes to inclusion and disability, and are active in different fields. Being a physiotherapist herself, Karola Wood tries to ensure this treatment for children with disabilities. The leader of the Munshi Habibullah Mission School wishes to focus on education. Dr. Yamani working at the university focuses on the attitudes to disability at universities and schools.

Other psychologists want to support families in which there are family members with disabilities by offering psychotherapy. Dr. Naghavi also wishes to support families, but through workshops about children and empowerment. Having a disability himself, Dr. Pestei prioritizes the work directly with people with disabilities by setting up their own NGO.

The different fields the stakeholders work in and the different institutions they are a part of may lead to different perspectives and to different understandings of inclusion and disability. Therefore, the second thing I learned is that there are different attitudes to inclusion and disability.

I have already shown that there is no clear definition of inclusion within the UN (Brüggemann 2016, p. 6) and that although it is always linked with participation, accessibility, non-discrimination and equal rights in literature (Antor et al. 2016, p. 456; Köpfer 2012, p. 1; Hummel & Werning 2016, p. 22; Beck & Degenhardt 2010), authors focus on different aspects, such as the field of education (Brüggemann 2016; Hummel 2016), and refer to different contexts and countries.

This is in line with the 2030 Agenda that calls for inclusion in different fields, education, employment, infrastructure, cities and society (United Nations 2015, p. 8) and at the same time wishes to be valid worldwide (United Nations 2015, p.1). Furthermore the 2030 Agenda states that a global partnership is needed to achieve its goals (United Nations 2015, p. 25).

For me, it has become clear that these partnerships must involve different stakeholders, who focus on different fields, have different understandings and contribute different perspectives. From my point of view, all these stakeholders and their perspectives are needed for the implementation of inclusion. However this perspective also needs to be discussed with the aim of reflecting on inclusion and disability.

Hummel states that to avoid setting expectations too high, inclusion should be seen as an ongoing process consisting of reflection and development. The task or perception of this process should be the minimisation of discrimination and the maximisation of access, acceptance and participation (2016, p. 2).

Thus there should be global discussions on inclusion and disability. For me, it seems important for these discussions themselves to be inclusive. This means involving different stakeholders from different fields with different perspectives.

It is particularly important to include people such as Dr. Pestei, who are directly affected by a disability, in the discussion on inclusion and disability. This is because, for me, they are the best experts on disability. Different sociocultural perspectives are also important, though, as inclusion and disability always depend on the environment and on the context – as many authors show (Lee 2014; Hummel & Werning 2016; Kalyanpur 2016). Schmidt et al (2017) and Lee (2014) both call for consideration of the sociocultural context, especially from a postcolonial view.

However, Hummel also states that there should be development. Talks and discussions are important, but at the same time, attempts should be made to achieve greater accessibility and participation. This could mean that a boy living in a village in the Himalayas receives physiotherapy and can go to school. It could mean that there is a workshop during which mothers learn to empower their children. And it could mean that persons with disabilities are given the opportunity to develop their computer skills. NGOs acting like Ladakh Hilfe e. V., REWA, Heaven-children and the NGOs founded by Dr. Pestei and Dr. Naghavi are important.

In discussing inclusion and disability, universities always play a decisive role. For the ongoing discussion, I believe it is essential to also discuss the different understandings and perspectives of inclusion and disability and their influence on implementation with members of NGOs, families and the persons with disabilities themselves. For me, this also seems to be in line with the 2030 Agenda supplemented by the UN CRPD, which can both be taken as the basis for the discussion.

References

Antor, Georg; Beck, Iris; Bleidick, Ulrich; Dederich, Markus (2016): Handlexikon der Behindertenpädagogik. Schlüsselbegriffe aus Theorie und Praxis. Stuttgart.

Beck, Iris (2016): Inklusion im Gemeinwesen. Stuttgart.

Beck, Iris; Degenhardt, Sven (2010): Inklusion. Hinweise zur Verortung des Begriffs im Rahmen der internationalen politischen und sozialwissenschaftliche Debatte um Menschenrecht, Bildungschancen und soziale Ungleichheit. In: *Schwohl, Joachim/Sturm, Tanja: Inklusion als Herausforderung schulischer Entwicklung. 2010. Bielefeld.*, p.55-83.

Biermann, Julia (2016): Different Meanings? The Translation Inclusive Education in Nigeria. In: *Zeitschrift für internationale Bildungsforschung und Entwicklungspolitik.* (3), p. 10-15.

Brüggemann, Christian (2016): Inklusive Bildung als globale Norm. Einleitende Bemerkungen zu einem entstehenden Forschungsfeld und den Beiträgen in diesem Heft. In: *Zeitschrift für internationale Bildungsforschung und Gerechtigkeit* (3), p. 5-9.

Deutsches Institut für Medizinische Dokumentation und Information, DIMDI WHO Kooperationszentrum für die Familie Internationaler Klassifikationen (2004): Internationale Klassifikation der Funktionsfähigkeit, Behinderung und Gesundheit. Cologne.

Fuchs-Heinritz, Werner; Klimke, Daniela; Lautmann, Rüdiger; Rammstedt, Ottheim; Stähli, Urs; Weischer, Christoph; Wienorld, Hanns (2011): Lexikon zur Soziologie. 5., revised edition. Wiesbaden.

Grant, Jaimie; Smith, Megan (2016): The Inclusion and Participation of Persons with Disabilities in the 2030 Agenda. In: *In: Behinderung und internationale Entwicklung. 2030 – Agenda und Inklusion* (2), p.4-9.

Hummel, Myriam (2016): Die Entwicklung inklusiver Bildung in Malawi: zwischen makro-politischer Deklaration und lokaler Umsetzung. In: *Zeitschrift für Inklusion-online.net* 2016.

Hummel, Myriam; Werning, Rolf (2016): Inclusive Education: "Same Same but Different". Examples from Guatemala and Malawi. In: *Zeitschrift für internationale Bildungsforschung und Entwicklungspolitik.* (3), p. 22-27.

Ibrahim, Mohamed (2014): Mental Health in Kenya: Not Yet Uhuru. In: *Disability and the Global South* 2014 (Vol.1, No. 2), p. 393-400.

Kalyanpur, Maya (2016): Inclusive Education Policies and Practices in the Context of International Development: Lessons from Cambodia. In: *Zeitschrift für internationale Bildungsforschung und Entwicklungspolitik.* 2016, p.16-21.

Köpfer, Andreas (2012): Inclusion. In: *http://www.inklusion-lexikon.de/Inclusion_Koepfer.php* (Last accessed: 05.03.2016).

Lee, Linda (2014): Global Mental Health, Human Rights and Development. In: *Disability and the Global South* 2014 (Vol.1, No 2), p.387-392.

Mattioli, Natalia (2016): Implementing the Agenda 2030 – The United Nations Partnership on the Rights of Persons with Disabilities as a Multi Stakeholder Platform to Advance the Rights of Persons with Disabilities. In: *Behinderung und internationale Entwicklung. 2030 – Agenda und Inklusion* 2016 (2/2016), p. 14-20.

Munshi Habibullah Mission School: Munshi Habibullah Mission School. Retaining Local Values, Creating Global Minds.

Schmidt, Kathrin; Wechuli, Yvonne; Wanjala, Stanley (2017): Relevance of Socio-Cultural Aspects in the Context of Impairment and Disability: A First Critical Look into Literature about Kenya. In: *Behinderung und internationale Entwicklung* 2017 (1/2017), p. 8-11.

United Nations (2006): Convention on the Rights of Persons with Disabilities.

United Nations (2015): Transforming our World: The 2030 Agenda for sustainable Development.

Wood, Karola (2013): Wer wir sind und wie es anfing. (Zugriff: 15.04.2016). Available online: *www.ladakh-hilfe.de/deutsch/ueber-uns/wer-wir-sind.*

World Health Organization (2011): World Report on Disability. Geneva: WHO.

5 A Cross-Cultural Cooperation and Research Project on Special Education between the Universities of Oldenburg in Germany and Dohuk in Northern Iraq (2013-2018)

(Monika Ortmann, Sönke Thies)

The Initiation of the Project

During visits to Bagdad in 2011 and to the Region of Kurdistan in Northern Iraq in 2013 Professor Monika Ortmann from the Institute for Special Needs Education of the Carl von Ossietzky University in Oldenburg started to build up networks with the aim to agree on terms for cooperation between a university in Iraq and her own university.

During her visits together with her assistant Dorin Strenge to Dohuk in November 2013 and April 2014 a deeper connection between the two universities was created. The result was a visit to the University of Oldenburg by the President of the University of Dohuk Professor Mosleh Duhoky, the Director of the Center for European Studies Dr. Mamou Othman and the Dean of the Faculty for Educational Sciences Professor Odeat Assi. Visits to different schools and institutions which are working in the area of special needs education convinced the visitors to take measures to develop structures in support of persons with disabilities in their home region. The new idea of inclusion and participation of people with disabilities were taken home by the leaders of the University of Dohuk. During their stay in Oldenburg a Memorandum of Understanding and Agreement of Cooperation were signed by the presidents of the two universities and the deans of the Faculties for Educational Sciences of both universities.

In the following months the leaders and the staff of the University of Dohuk showed strong determination and made a big effort to establish a new course of study for special needs education and showed great initiative to do so as soon as possible. This was a substantial contribution to fulfill the commitment of the Convention on the Rights of Persons with Disabilities that was signed in 2013 by the Government of Iraq. In a short amount of time impossible compared to German conditions the University of Dohuk created and implemented a new Department for Special Education in the autumn of 2014. Additionally, the new study course "Disability Studies and Rehabilitation" was created that shall prepare young people to be future teachers for special needs education. Everything was prepared for the start of this new study course in the autumn of 2014.

Already in the summer of 2014 the terrorist group of the so called Islamic State brought violence and aggression to the region. They occupied the city of Mosul which is about 50 kms from Dohuk and their hostile and intrusive attacks in Syria and Northern Iraq provoked the uprooting and migration of more than one million refugees and internally displaced people (IDP) to the governorate of Dohuk. Schools and university buildings were needed to give a home to this huge number of persons from Syria and other parts of the Iraq. Regardless of the difficult and dangerous situation in Northern Iraq the new academic year and the new study course started with a delay of several months at the beginning of 2015.

That year 54 students started with high interest and motivation. The lecturers of this new study course are former specialists in psychology, sociology or other fields. Just a small number of them have had previously attained qualifications in special needs education. The role of the University of Oldenburg in this process was to consult in counselling in the process of the development of the curriculum for the new study course and in the qualification of the staff.

With the support of the German Academic Exchange Service (Deutscher Akademischer Austauschdienst, DAAD) the German scientists around Monika Ortmann were able to intensify between 2015 and 2017 the academic partnership with the University of Dohuk. The main tasks for the scientific team from Germany in this partnership during this period were to assist and to advise the Iraqi colleagues in the process of developing the curriculum for the new study course and to offer them possibilities to improve their knowledge and their skills in the field of special needs education. As a concomitant research the German specialists from Oldenburg are realizing a formative evaluation of the new study course and the different measures in the cooperation.

Research Approach

Through the collaboration between the Iraqi and German scientists and the transparency and cooperation in the development of the formative evaluation the team around Monika Ortmann adopted the scientific approach of action research.

Action research is described by Kurt Lewin (1968, p. 280) as a comparative research of the terms and effects of social action and it produces activities as an

Monika Ortmann & Sönke Thies

outcome. "The priority reason for engaging in action research is to assist the 'actor' in improving and/ or refining his or her actions." (Sagor, 2000) The focus is on joint combined means and aims assuming that action research method lead to an improvement of the action, of the researcher's skills and of the outcome (Nielsen, 2014, p. 419).

In that way the most important goal is to improve the measures in this joint project, to enhance the professional's expertise and awareness of the staff members from the Department for Special Education in the University of Dohuk and to improve the education and the social participation of children and adolescents in Iraqi Kurdistan.

Regarding these goals, the action research is a suitable tool, because it allows the researchers to actively evaluate the process alongside the ongoing project and to correct or re-direct the process, if necessary. Via triangulation different forms of data collection methods can be used in the research process which can be of quantitative or qualitative nature. The research project has to be evaluated constantly during the process. In addition to that, there also has to be a final assessment. A constant back coupling concerning dialogic feedback with the staff of the Department for Special Education in Dohuk occurs frequently.

Statement of the Problem

The Republic of Iraq ratified the Convention on the Rights of Persons with Disabilities on 20th March 2013. Thereby the state promises "to view persons with disabilities as humans with rights, who are capable of claiming those rights and making decisions for their lives based on their free and informed consent as well as being active members of society". This means that all areas of life have to be adapted in such a manner that the social participation of Iraqi citizens with disabilities is ensured and their needs are met.

In addition to an independent life, the participation of citizens in the work place and employment and their integration into cultural life, during recreational activities and in sports should be realized. Especially the education system of a society contributes to the development of life and social skills and implements a sense of dignity and self-worth in a person. In the articles 3 and 24 of the convention the UN states that persons with disabilities should have equal access to an inclusive, quality controlled and free primary, secondary and academic education.

And that the full and equal participation in education should be ensured by the facilitation of appropriate measures to support persons with disabilities to reach their full potential (The United Nations, 2006).

Three wars in the recent past of the country, ongoing disputes and terroristic attacks lead to vast number of injured or dead soldiers and civilians. In consequence of the seizure of Mosul, the second largest city of Iraq and its surroundings in 2014 by the IS countless more people were killed and injured. The violence experienced resulted in physical and psychological damage and disabilities. In particular sexual abuse caused thousands of girls and women to suffer traumata.

Another consequence of these circumstances is that a great amount of people in Iraq have to live with a disability. Because of the wars large areas of the country are contaminated. As a result, many newborns have profound and multiple disabilities. In addition to the contamination, many hospitals and maternity wards were destroyed and therefore adequate care for mothers and their children cannot be provided. Frequently disabilities are caused by irreversible damage before, during and after birth that could have been prevented with the respective equipment.

The demographic structure in Iraq is marked by a population of over 40% under the age of 15 (WKO, 2017, p. 3) which means that there are a high number of children and teenagers who were injured in the war, disabled since their birth and are affected by the terror in their country. As no statistical data were collected, it is difficult to give an exact number of how many injured, traumatized people and people with disabilities live in the country (oral statement given by the Ministry of Health in Bagdad, Dr. Nasser, 2012).

The Situation of Children and Adolescents with Disabilities in Iraqi Kurdistan
There are just a very small numbers of studies which provide data about the situation of children and adolescents with disabilities in Iraq and in Kurdistan.

The situation is characterized by the fact that the special needs of pupils with disabilities are not considered adequate to their needs in the Iraqi school system. Until now teachers are not prepared and the institutional conditions are not suitable for children with severe or complex disabilities and children with need for care.

Disabilities can be seen as a high risk factor of being excluded from school. In Iraq in 2013 nearly 485.000 primary school aged children (8%) and over

651.000 lower secondary aged children (26%) did not go to school (UNICEF MENA Regional Office, 2015, p. 3). Just a very small number of institutes exist which are specialized in giving support to children and adolescents with disabilities. In Kurdistan Region just 810 boys and girls with disabilities benefited of these institutes in 2015. In comparison Kurdistan Region has got 4.75 million inhabitants and 46% of them are under the age of 18. (UNICEF MENA Regional Office, 2015, p. 51) Another 9.013 boys and girls with disabilities went to 445 regular schools which offer special education classes. Those are offered in an estimated 7.2% of all schools (UNICEF MENA Regional Office, 2015, p. 52). Bringing this numbers in relation to the rate of registered disabilities among children aged two to 14 years in Kurdistan Region of 19% in 2006 (UNICEF, 2007, p.63) it is not difficult to identify that a large proportion of the out-of-school pupils are children and adolescents with disabilities. (UNICEF MENA Regional Office 2015, p. 55).

As a consequence, we can identify several major barriers that hinder the school attendance of children and adolescents with disabilities:

- Lack of awareness of the importance of education of children with disabilities
- Poverty and living conditions
- Lack of school places, facilities and well trained teachers

To face this situation the Minister of Education of the Kurdistan Regional Government (KRG) introduced the Kurdistan Inclusive Education Programme (KIEP) with components for early childhood development and a special needs teacher training in 2006 (cara, 2010, p. 11). Between 2006 and 2010 a total amount of seven different trainings were offered in this programme. In each of them between ten and 227 teachers participated. In 2010 the Iraqi research team leader Dr. Al-Hashemy found out that the training offered seemed to be unfit for the purpose and that it revealed "the current dearth of qualified and experienced special-needs teachers" (cara, 2010, p. 28). The lack of formal provision for continuing professional development training amongst special needs teaching staff is a contradiction to the ratification of the Convention on the Rights of Persons with Disabilities by the Iraqi government in 2013. Hence, there is a great need to remedy the discrepancy.

The Situation of Refugees and Internally Displaced Persons

An estimated amount of more than 1.5 million internally displaced persons (IDPs) and Syrian refugees live in Kurdistan Region (KRG, 2017). Fifty percent of those people are children and teenagers. The now adolescent generation has to overcome indefinitely more developmental risks. In the future, the already high number of non-readers and functional illiterates in the population will increase.

Many of the IDPs and the refugees have been staying in the 22 camps in the governorate of Dohuk since the summer of 2014 without prospects of a good life. In the beginning, these camps were makeshift built out of various materials. Later on in early 2015, NGOs built camps out of tents and containers with international help.

During the first months, only the Kurdish population and the Kurdish Regional Government provided help for the many people living in the camps. International help progressed very slowly.

There is a multitude of people of different ages living in the camps, as well as in the rest of the population of Kurdistan Region, who have to live with congenital or acquired disabilities under hard living conditions. The region lacks prenatal care for mothers as well as health care supported by the state that would ensure regular health checks for babies, toddlers, children and adolescents. For most of the population, there is no access to affordable ways of treatment and therapy of any kind. In addition, only members of the family are responsible for taking care of persons with disabilities. People with disabilities did not have a right to education and social participation in the Kurdish society until 20.03.2013.

The care for the refugees in the camps remains scarce; especially medical care and educational offers are insufficient. Between 2014 and the beginning of 2015 no educational opportunities were available for children in the camps, no preschool, no school and no after-school. During the year 2015 International Organizations like UNICEF started to set up schools in tents or containers. Even three years later there is still a lack of basic equipment, material resources and well-trained teachers in these schools. UNICEF presumed that about 850.000 internally displaced school-aged children lived in the whole of Iraq in 2015 and about 650.000 of them have lost at least a year's worth of schooling (UNICEF MENA OOSCI, 2014). In these camps children with disabilities have got the highest risk of being out-of-school children. In this environment without enough educational resources for all children, especially children with disabilities are excluded from school as well as their sisters because they have to act as carers. People with disabilities have nearly no support and educational opportunities outside of their families.

In this situation educational paths are interrupted and stopped and a lot of young boys and girls do not get the educational, pedagogical and psychological support they need for their personal development. In addition to that a lot of them are suffering from traumata and psychological stress by experienced war, violence, escape and loss of family members.

On top of that after-school-educational paths were interrupted in this context. Many young people who went to university in their towns could not be incorporated in other universities after their escape.

University of Dohuk, College for Basic Education

The University of Dohuk is a state university founded in 1992. It offers bachelor as well as master degrees in 18 different colleges and has about 15.000 students. The gender distribution is even (UoD, 2016).

The university collaborates with a multitude of foreign universities in different European and Asian countries as well as in the USA.

The University of Dohuk has been in a process of development and expansion since its foundation. An example of this is the implementation of the for Iraq unique and new bachelor degree study course of "Disability Studies and Rehabilitation" in 2014. The graduates of this study course supported by the University of Oldenburg will work in inclusive fields, e.g. inclusive schools, in the Iraqi/Kurdish society. The Department for Special Education is the newest one of ten departments in the College for Basic Education.

The bachelor course "Disability Studies and Rehabilitation" is preparing the students in a curriculum of four academic years to be a teacher for Special Education or to study a subsequent master course.

The Progress of the Joint Cooperation Project and the Measures between 2014 and 2018

With the support of the DAAD it was possible to realize many different measures with the aim to improve the qualification of the academic staff of the new study course "Disability Studies and Rehabilitation" and to give a scientific monitoring in the process of development of the curriculum, the study contents and the practical contents in particular.

1) Conferences and Symposia

The conferences and symposia which are held in Oldenburg, Ankara and Istanbul helped to qualify the scientific teaching staff of the new course of study "Disability Studies and Rehabilitation" in Dohuk. Because the newly implemented course of study is unique in Iraq, there is no suitable, specialized and university-trained staff at the University of Dohuk or other universities in Kurdistan Region. The tense political and economic situation in this region prevents the university from acquiring qualified specialist staff from other countries.

Because of this tense situation which the German foreign ministry Berlin classified as dangerous, the project team of the Carl von Ossietzky University Oldenburg is not allowed to travel to Dohuk to hold or participate in conferences and symposia. In accordance with the regulations of the German Academic Exchange Service, the conferences and symposiums take place at the University of Oldenburg or in other designated third countries.

The contents and didactic working methods are in accordance with the needs and study-related interests of the participants of the conferences and are cooperatively planed and prepared in advance.

2) Guest Scientists in Oldenburg

Another suitable offer for the development and expansion of the university teaching and practical trainings in the course of study "Disability Studies and Rehabilitation" at the University of Dohuk is the possibility for Iraqi scientists to do an academic exchange in Oldenburg. This is a cooperation between the Iraqi project team and the Institute for Special Needs Education and Rehabilitation in Oldenburg. There is a special focus on the support of female scientists.

During this two to three months research stay, the lecturers from Dohuk get the chance to participate in disability studies and rehabilitation lectures and seminars as well as visit other institutions for the care, education and employment of persons with disabilities in the region and the city of Oldenburg to gain specialist knowledge and competences.

This research stay also provides the chance to share experiences between the scientists from both nations and universities. Knowledge about the culture specific traditions of life and manner is also shared and experienced. Participation in social and cultural life of the host country is supported.

3) Cooperations in Dohuk

Before the escalation of the political and economic situation in Kurdistan Region, there were regular study and research related visits by the project leader and project collaborators of the Carl von Ossietzky University Oldenburg to the University of Dohuk.

The implementation of the course of study "Disability Studies and Rehabilitation" was planned and executed in 2014 in cooperation with those responsible in Dohuk. The development of the curriculum for this innovative course of study was a cooperative working process of researchers from both universities. There were regular presentations and workshops in Dohuk delivered by the project team from Oldenburg as well as meetings for the scientific management when needed.

In addition, the stays of the researchers from Oldenburg in Dohuk helped them to explore and get to know the living conditions and the offers for people with disabilities in the sector of care and education in northern Iraq. In this context, the few already existing institutions for the diagnosis, support and education for this group were visited.

The Influence of the Insecure Political Situation on the Project

The insecure political situation in Iraq provokes several of the aforenamed problems. In the project and the establishment of the new study course "Disability Studies and Rehabilitation" the staff members and also the German cooperation partners were faced with different challenges. There is a great lack of studies, literature, didactical materials and financial resources. Caused by the three wars in the last four decades and the permanent conflicts between different parts of the Iraqi population the educational system was thrown back for decades. In the past years no studies were realized and current scientific literature about pedagogics, didactics or special needs education in the Kurdish or Arabic language is virtually non-existent. That makes the previously mentioned measures essential steps in the qualification of the Kurdish scientists. The continual search for current professional literature in English is for them a big support but the lack of financial resources makes it nearly impossible for them to buy expensive books from other countries.

A financial crisis that started in autumn of 2014 effects the University of Dohuk severely. The university is not able to comply with the agreement to invest 40.000 Euro per year in the Department for Special Education with the goal to use this money for equipment, material and added personal resources. The lack of money to pay their salaries effects the living conditions of all university employees and their families. Since the beginning of 2015 the government is merely able to pay a quarter of the annual salaries to the employees. This situation forces many people to look for another job, to emigrate or to accept a second job outside of university.

The Influence of Cultural Aspects on the Project

In order to achieve a constructive, rewarding and productive collaboration it was helpful to incorporate elements taken from the concept of intercultural pedagogy. As described by Schmidtke (2012, p. 70) it is essential to renounce the ethnicization of the unfamiliar and to get to know a person's social environment, their life situation and their attitudes. Furthermore, there should be an overlaying goal to promote interpersonal communication which overcomes all constructed differences. In this way, in intercultural communication a higher emphasis is placed on the process of learning of one's counterpart rather than on one's own prior knowledge (Schmidtke, 2012, p. 71). Thereby, it is possible to perceive affected people as experts of their own situation and to support and strengthen those people through the use of the principles of action research on their path of professional development in order to help them to realize their own goals as well as common goals.

The intercultural exchange between the Iraqi and the German scientists was a fundamental and important factor in the cooperation during all the time. To achieve common goals, it was always very important to listen to each other with empathy and to try to understand the subjective opinions of each cooperation partner regarding the sociocultural context of each one, the history, development and values of this environment and society. Starting from this base on it was possible to analyze the initial situation and to develop common goals that are based on a realistic and culturally sensitive view on the current situation.

An important step for the project and for the personal development of each scientist in the project was to understand the situation of persons with disabilities and the attitudes of the society behind without judging.

Different polls realized by the German scientists from Oldenburg and several conversations with the scientists from Dohuk have shown that the attitudes of the Iraqi Kurdish society constitutes great challenges. Family members with a severe visible or mental disability are often hidden by the family. People do not expect the ability to learn and to develop themselves in persons with disabilities.

Disabilities can be seen as a divine punishment or "rather as a trial from Allah, which the religiously hence spiritually strong will be able to withstand. The disabled are looked upon as people in a stage of testing." (Rispler-Chaim, 2007, p. 93) In society we can find tolerant and less tolerant attitudes towards disabled persons what should be considered in the context of the political and social atmosphere that prevailed at a particular time or place (Rispler-Chaim, 2007, p. 94).

Subsequently to the collaborative examination of the aforementioned aspects, it was possible to define common goals and measures for the project.

Furthermore, all the persons included in the cooperation have had the possibility to develop their attitudes. Respect, comprehension and appreciation for each other were growing on both sides of the cooperation partners and a reduction of prejudices was cognizably. Skepticism among the Iraqi lecturers towards the concept and the realization of inclusion was relativized and reduced through the visits to inclusive schools and institutions in Germany and the conversations with German teachers and experts from the field and from the world of science.

Future Outlook

In the autumn of 2017 students began to study the bachelor course "Disability Studies and Rehabilitation" for the fourth time. A total amount of 450 students are studying in this department. It is expected that the first 44 of them will get their bachelor's degree in the summer of 2018. The majority of this soon to be graduating young people will become teachers in schools and a small part of them will complete their studies with the new master course "Disability Studies and Rehabilitation", where they will be prepared to be future lecturers in the Department for Special Education.

Furthermore, the academic staff of the Department for Special Education at the University of Dohuk will increasingly be put in the situation to organize, to plan and to qualify themselves. The implementation of this new study course will help to improve the situation of children with disabilities in Dohuk governorate. Therefore, it will be necessary that other universities in Northern Iraq as well as in Central and South Iraq will follow the example of the University of Dohuk. The scientists from Oldenburg are pleased that they were already contacted by other universities that show a high interest in establishing a study course for disability studies themselves.

References

Council for At-Risks Academics (cara) (Ed.) (2010). *A Study of Education Opportunities for Disabled Children and Youth and Early Childhood Development (ECD) in Iraq. Phase 1 Report.* Retrieved from *https://www.escholar.manchester.ac.uk/api/datastream?publicationPid=uk-ac-man-scw:131680&datastreamId=SUPPLEMENTARY-2.PDF.*

Kurdistan Regional Government (KRG) (2017). *Mosul IDPs in Kurdistan rise to 164,000.* Retrieved from *http://cabinet.gov.krd/a/d.aspx?s=040000&l=12&a=55530.*

Lewin, K. (1968). *Die Lösung Sozialer Konflikte* (3rd ed.). Bad Nauheim: Christian.

Nielsen, R.P. (2014). Action Research As an Ethics Praxis Method. *Journal of Business Ethics,* 135:419-428.

Rispler-Chaim, V. (2007). *Disability in Islamic Law.* AA Dordrecht (NL): Springer.

Sagor, R. (2000). Guiding School Improvement with Action Research. Retrieved from *http://www.ascd.org/Publications/Books/Overview/Guiding-School-Improvement-with-Action-Research.aspx.*

Schmidtke, H.-P. (2012). Leben mit dem Anderssein im internationalen Kontext – der Beitrag der Interkulturellen Pädagogik zur Vergleichenden Heil- und Sonderpädagogik. In A. Erdélyi, H.-P. Schmidtke & P. Sehrbrock (Eds.), *International vergleichende Heil- und Sonderpädagogik weltweit* (57-72). Bad Heilbrunn: Klinkhardt.

The United Nations (Ed.) (2006). Convention on the Rights of Persons with Disabilities. *Treaty Series, 2515,* 3.

UNICEF MENA OOSCI (Ed.) (2015). *Iraq Country Report on out-of-school-children.* Retrieved from *http://www.oosci-mena.org/uploads/1/wysiwyg/150608_MENA_OOSCI_Iraq_report.pdf.*

Monika Ortmann & Sönke Thies

UNICEF (Ed.) (2007). Multiple Indicator Cluster Survey 2006 (MICS). Retrieved from *https://www.unicef.org/iraq/Iraq_2006_MICS_English.pdf*.

UNICEF MENA OOSCI (Ed.) (2014). *Displaced Iraqi children languish in deprived schools*. Retrieved from *http://www.oosci-mena.org/displaced-iraqi-children-languish-in-deprived-schools*.

University of Dohuk (UoD) (2016). *Academics*. Retrieved from *http://web.uod.ac/*.

Wirtschaftskammer Österreich (WKO) (2017). *Länderprofil Irak*. Retrieved from *http://wko.at/statistik/laenderprofile/lp-irak.pdf*.

III Experiences and Research: Isfahan

6 Epidemiology of disability in Isfahan

(Sayed Mohsen Hosseini)

Introduction

Disability is an impairment that may be cognitive, developmental, intellectual, mental, physical, sensory, or some combination of these. It substantially affects a person's life activities and may be present from birth or occur during a person's lifetime. Disability is thus not just a health problem. It is a complex phenomenon, reflecting the interaction between features of a person's body and features of the society in which he or she lives.

Disability is universal. Everybody is likely to experience disability directly or to have a family member who experiences difficulties in functioning at some point in his or her life, particularly when they grow older. Following the International Classification of Functioning, Disability and Health and its derivative version for children and youth, this action plan uses "disability" as an umbrella term for impairments, activity limitations and participation restrictions, denoting the negative aspects of the interaction between an individual (with a health condition) and that individual's contextual (environmental and personal) factors. Disability is neither simply a biological nor a social phenomenon.

Overview of the global situation

There are more than 1000 million people with disability globally, that is about 15% of the world's population or one in seven people. Of this number, between 110 million and 190 million adults experience significant difficulties in functioning. It is estimated that some 93 million children – or one in 20 of those fewer than 15 years of age – live with a moderate or severe disability. The number of people who experience disability will continue to increase as population's age, with the global increase in chronic health conditions. National patterns of disability are influenced by trends in health conditions and environmental and other factors, such as road traffic crashes, falls, violence, humanitarian emergencies including natural disasters and conflict, unhealthy diet and substance abuse.

Disability disproportionately affects women, older people, and poor people. Children from poorer households, indigenous populations and those in ethnic minority groups are also at significantly higher risk of experiencing disability. Women and girls with disability are likely to experience "double discrimination", which includes gender-based violence, abuse and marginalization. As a result, women with disability often face additional disadvantages when compared with men with disability and women without disability. Indigenous persons internally displaced or stateless persons, refugees, migrants and prisoners with disability also face particular challenges in accessing services. The prevalence of disability is greater in lower-income countries than higher-income countries

People with disability face widespread barriers in accessing services, such as those for health care (including medical care, therapy and assistive technologies), education, employment, and social services, including housing and transport. The origin of these barriers lies in, for example, inadequate legislation, policies and strategies; the lack of service provision; problems with the delivery of services; a lack of awareness and understanding about disability; negative attitudes and discrimination; lack of accessibility; inadequate funding; and lack of participation in decisions that directly affect their lives. Specific barriers also exist in relation to persons with disabilities being able to express their opinions and seek, receive and impart information and ideas on an equal basis with others and through their chosen means of communication.

These barriers contribute to the disadvantages experienced by people with disability. Particularly in developing countries, people with disability experience poorer health than people without disability, as well as higher rates of poverty, lower rates of educational achievement and employment, reduced independence and restricted participation. Many of the barriers they face are avoidable and the disadvantage associated with disability can be overcome. The World report on disability synthesizes the best available evidence on how to overcome the barriers that persons with disability face in accessing health, rehabilitation, support and assistance services, their environments (such as buildings and transport), education and employment. (WHO global disability action plan 2014-2021: better health for all people with disability)

It has been reported that more than 10% of population in the world suffer from physical, mental, and social disabilities. Of these people, 80% live in the developing countries, and one third are children Therefore, it is expected that nearly 7 million people live with various disabilities in Iran. Disability is complex, dynamic and multidimensional phenomenon that is more based on social rather than medical aspects (Over recent decades, several researchers from the social and health sciences have identified the role of social and physical factors in disability. Although disability and its consequences such as inability, depression and isolation are considered as stressful and aggravating conditions, they are not the unavoidable consequences for disabled people. The psychosocial benefit of social support among disabled people may be due to its effects on their mental evaluation of pressure factors, choosing effective coping methods, improving self-esteem, personal skills, better social life, and empowering them for help in the process of social development. Despite the increasing body of literature on the concept of social support and its association with health and psychological well-being in different populations. There is little information on the disabled people in Iran.

The country's total population	79,926,270 people
Male population	40,498,442 people
Female population	39,427,828 people
Total households	24,196,035 people
The total number of immigrants	4,709,149 people
The number of housing units	22,825,046
The number of vacant housing units	2,587,607
Sex ratio	103
Household size	3/3
Average age	31/1
Median age	30
Population density	49/1
Urbanization	74
Rural	26
Literacy rate	87/6
Number of cities	1245
The average annual population growth rate	1/24

Table 6.1: General Census of Population and Housing in 2016

According to Table 6.1, in the census, population is slightly less than the 80 million people. The number of men was slightly more than women. Population average age is also 31.1.

According to information calculated population density (proportion of population to area of the country) is 49 and the literacy rate of the population of 10 to 49 years old in 2016 is estimated 94.7% which had a good growth than the years of 2011 (92.4%) and 85 (91.7%).

The literacy rate in the country was 87.6% among them the provinces of Tehran, Alborz and Semnan with 92.9, 92.2 and 91.5%, respectively have the highest proportion of literate and Province of Kurdestan with 81.5 percent, have the lowest proportion of literates.

The highest and lowest population density is in Tehran and South Khorasan, respectively.

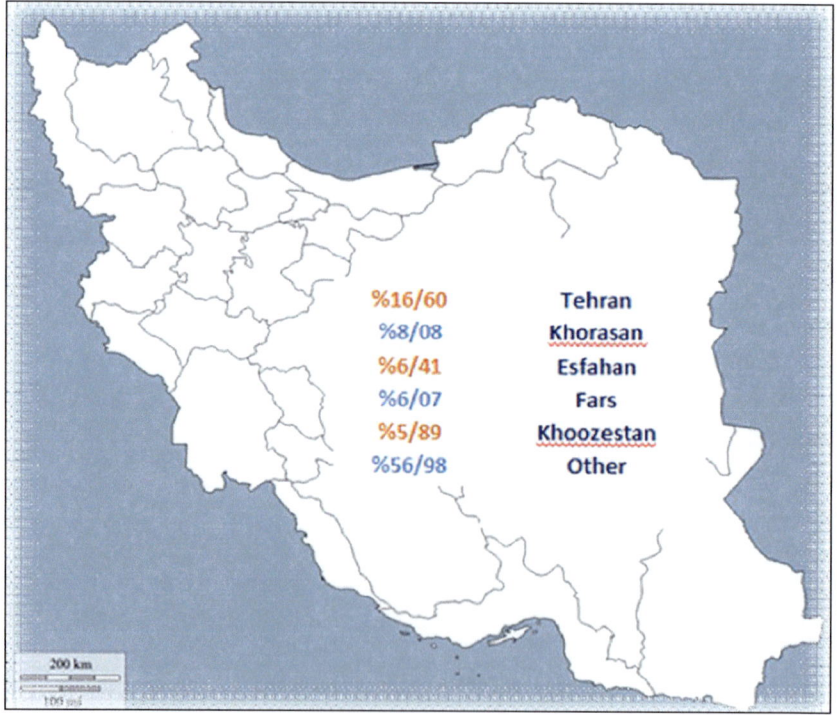

Figure 6.1: Province's population percentage of the country in 2016

The majority of population is in Tehran, Khorasan and Isfahan, respectively.

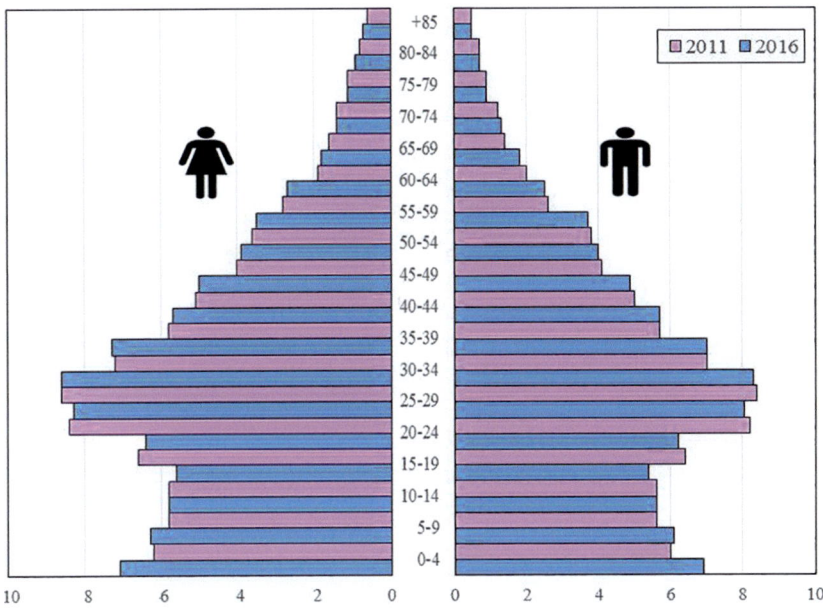

Figure. 6.2: Age pyramid of the population in 2016

The age groups of 25 to 35 years are the most population. Under 20 years old woman are more than men.

Year	Population	Male		Female		Sex ratio	Household	Household size
		Frequency	Percent	Frequency	Percent			
2007	70,495,782	35,866,362	0.509	35,866,362	0.491	104	17,501,771	4
2011	75,149,669	37,905,669	0.504	37,905,669	0.496	102	21,185,647	3,5
2016	79,926,270	40,498,442	0.507	39,427,828	0.493	103	24,185,647	3,3

Table 6.2: Population and household trends 2007-2016

Table 6.2 shows population and household trends between 2007 to 2016. Accordingly, since 2007 to 2016, household size was dropped from 4 to 3.3. Iran's population was about 80 million people in 2016 and the total number of households was 24 million households. Frequency of males was more than females in all of years.

Date	Value	Change, %
2004	1.2	0
2005	1.1	-1.11 %
2006	1.1	1.03 %
2007	1.1	-1.53 %
2008	1.1	0.39 %
2009	1.2	2.59 %
2010	1.2	3.79 %
2011	1.2	4.22 %
2012	1.3	3.17 %
2013	1.3	-1.03 %
2014	1.3	-1.70 %
2015	1.2	-3.79 %

Table 6.3: Population growth rate of country

Iran population growth rate was at level of 1.23% in 2015, down from 1.28% previous year.

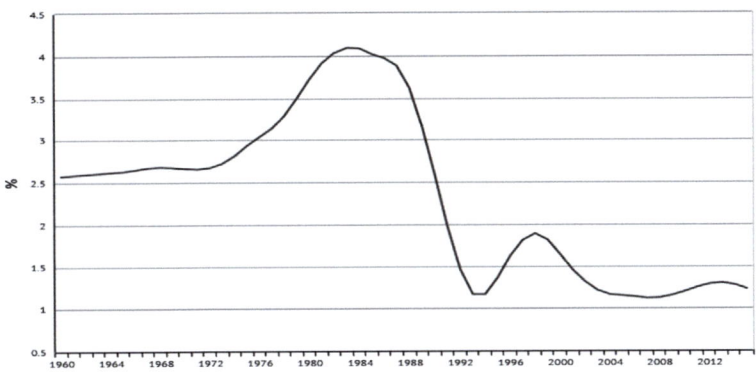

Figure 6.3: Population growth rate of country

Date	Value	Change, %
2005	67.6	0
2006	68.2	1.01 %
2007	68.9	0.92 %
2008	69.5	0.86 %
2009	70.0	0.85 %
2010	70.6	0.83 %
2011	71.2	0.81 %
2012	71.8	0.80 %
2013	72.3	0.77 %
2014	72.9	0.74 %
2015	73.4	0.71 %
2016	73.9	0.69 %

Table 6.4: Urban population of Iran

Epidemiology of disability

Urban population of Iran increased from 38.56% in 1967 to 73.88% in 2016 growing at an average annual rate of 1.34%.

Date	Value	Change %
2005	4.9	0
2006	4.9	0.39 %
2007	5.0	0.09 %
2008	4.9	-0.13 %
2009	4.9	-0.19 %
2010	4.9	-0.12 %
2011	4.9	-0.12 %
2012	4.9	-0.14 %
2013	4.9	0.21 %
2014	5.0	0.92 %
2015	5.1	1.84 %
2016	5.2	-0.14 %

Table 6.5: Population aged 65 years and above of Iran population

Population aged 65 years and above of Iran, Islamic Rep. increased from 3.45% in 1967 to 5.24% in growing at an average annual rate of 0.87%. Population ages 65 and above as a percentage of the total population. Population is based on the de facto definition of population.

Province	Growth rate (percent)
Whole country	1,24
Isfahan	0,97

Table 6.6: Annual growth rate of country and Isfahan; Province: 2011-2016

During 2011-2016, 4,776,601 people have been added to the population of the country. Annual population growth of 1.24% has been added 955,320 people to the population.

Population growth in the Isfahan province during this period was 0.97%.

Total population of the province	Male		Female		Sex ratio
	Frequency	Percent	Frequency	Percent	
5,120,850	2,599,477	51%	2,521,373	49%	103

Table 6.7: Population by sex in Isfahan in 2016

The total population of Isfahan province, is 5 million and 120 thousand and 850 people (population density per km 8/47) that of the province's population by gender is as follows: 51% male (2,599,477), 49% of women (2,521,373).

(City population: 2,094,867), 4 million and 507 thousand and 850 people (about 88%) living in urban areas and 613 thousand and 73 people (about 12%) are living in rural areas.

Type year	Physical & mobility	Mental	Chronic psychological	Elderly	Deaf	Total
	Frequency (percent)					
2008	0(0)	850(35)	680(28)	871(35)	50(2)	2451
2011	28(1)	1574(48)	1130(35)	470(15)	39(1)	3241
2012	21(1)	1151(48)	610(26)	537(23)	37(2)	2356
2013	150(2)	2600(48)	1100(15)	3000(39)	800(1)	7650
2014	30(1)	1200(34)	700(20)	1600(44)	40(1)	3570
2015	60(2)	1230(35)	851(24)	1370(38)	51(1)	3562

Table 6.8: Unit's frequency (percent) of Social Welfare Department

---

Epidemiology of disability   73

The highest units number of Social Welfare Department with 169 units is (352%) in 2012.

Year	The number of units(percent)	Growth rate
2008	40	0
2009	43	7%
2010	45	4%
2011	48	6%
2012	169	352%
2013	85	-50%
2014	92	8%
2015	150	63%

Table 6.9: Frequency (percent) of clients using the services provided by the Welfare Organization in Isfahan

Frequency of clients using rehabilitation services in all areas had been higher in 2013 than other years. Mental clients were using rehabilitation services more than other clients in 2011 and 2012. Elderly had a greater share in 2013-2015.

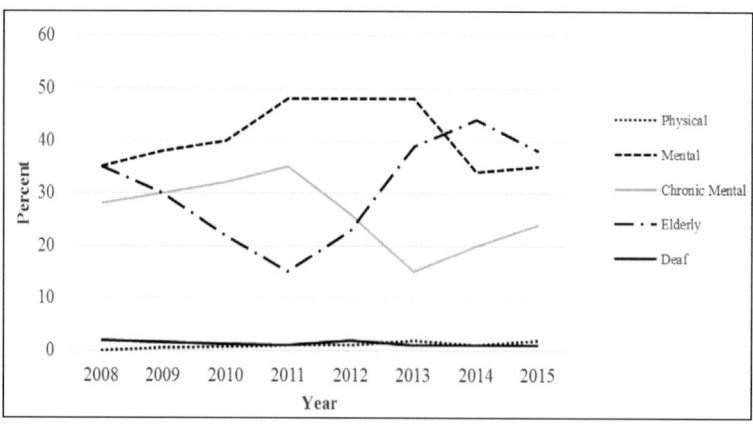

Figure 6.4: The process of clients usage of rehabilitation services between 2009 to 2015 in Isfahan

Regional	Regional population	Population of households	Disabled population Frequency(percent)	Disabled man	Disabled woman	households with disabled Frequency(percent)
1	78037	25790	1330(1.7)	791	539	1173(4.5)
2	64750	19787	1077(1.7)	733	344	922(4.7)
3	109968	36049	1497(1.4)	896	601	1347(3.7)
4	125978	39868	1917(1.5)	1196	711	1742(4.4)
5	163241	48374	1620(1.0)	1015	605	1496(3.1)
6	111625	35803	1291(1.2)	795	496	1180(3.3)
7	148680	45383	1796(1.2)	1177	619	1628(3.6)
8	237407	71060	3293(1.4)	2103	1190	2877(4)
9	73291	22573	1182(1.6)	796	386	952(4.2)
10	212369	63901	3029(1.4)	1974	1054	2660(4.2)
11	59160	17005	932(1.6)	633	299	797(4.7)
12	125681	37395	1864(1.5)	1203	661	1605(4.3)
13	118259	35696	1435(1.2)	928	507	1285(3.6)
14	167724	46722	2445(1.5)	1631	814	2132(4.6)
15	112771	33896	1999(1.8)	1355	644	1683(5)
SUM	1908941	579302	26707(1.4)	17226	9470	23479(4.1)

Table 6.10: Disabled Population and households with disabled persons by regions of Isfahan in 2015

According to Table 6.10, 1.4 percent of the Isfahan residents are disabled. About 4% of families in Isfahan are engaged.

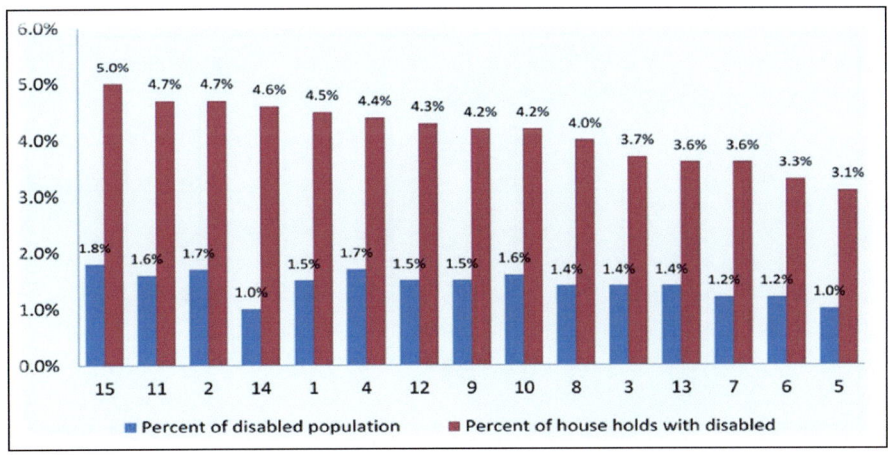

Figure 6.5: Percent of Disabled Population and households with disabled persons by regions of Isfahan in 2015

Regions with the lowest percentage of disability have a better economic level. Regions with poor and moderate economic levels have higher percentage of disability.

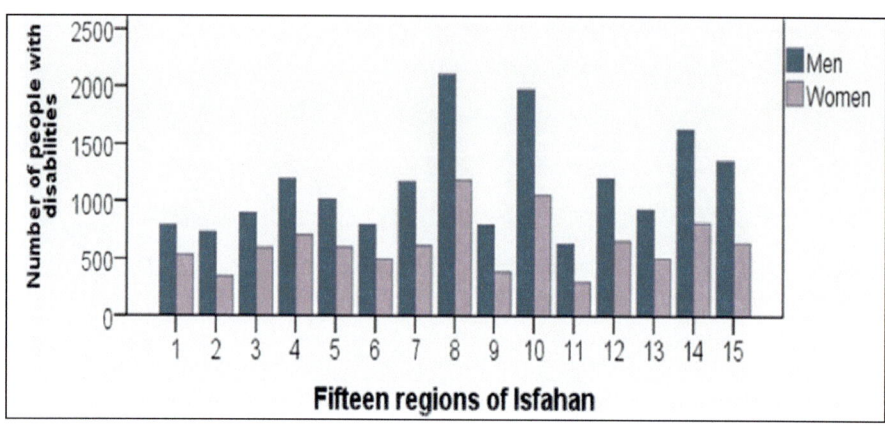

Figure 6.6: Number of people with disabilities in Isfahan in different regions of the city by gender in 2015

Disability in men is almost double than women.

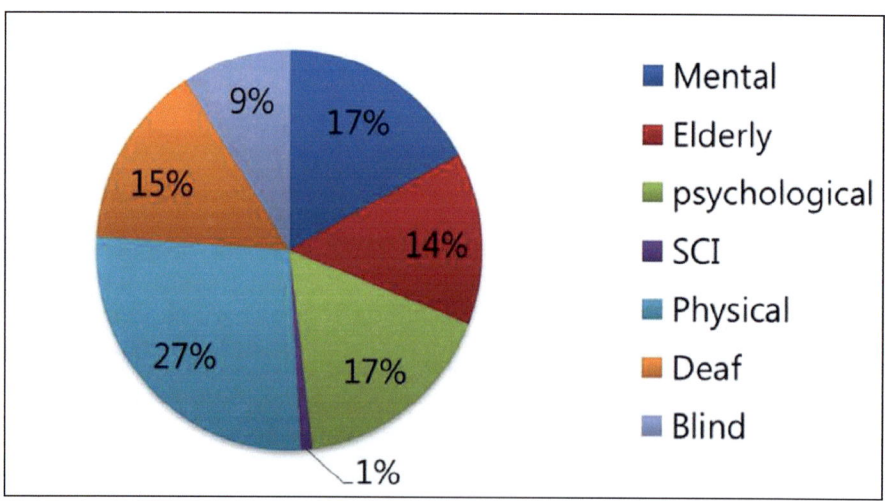

Figure 6.7: Percent of people with disabilities by type of disability in Isfahan in 2015

The highest percentage of disability was physical disability and the lowest was Spinal cord injury

Year	Age	Blind	Deaf	Physical and mobility	Spinal cord injury	Mental	Elderly	Mind	Total
					Frequency (Percent)				
	Total	3219(9)	5040(15)	9325(27)	473(1)	6081(17)	4947(14)	5747(17)	34832
	0-4	78(14)	152(28)	144(26)	13(2)	48(9)	0(0)	112(21)	547
	5-9	140(12)	342(29)	320(27)	15(1)	115(10)	0(0)	245(21)	1177
	10-14	140(11)	321(24)	404(30)	22(2)	113(9)	0(0)	312(24)	1312
	15-19	125(7)	291(15)	831(43)	20(1)	100(5)	0(0)	562(29)	1929
	20-24	155(7)	397(20)	490(24)	25(1)	219(10)	0(0)	804(28)	2090
	25-29	263(10)	541(20)	680(26)	18(1)	301(11)	0(0)	852(32)	2655
	30-34	323(9)	600(16)	1090(29)	59(2)	682(18)	0(0)	1008(26)	3762
2015	35-39	231(9)	503(20)	110(4)	51(2)	810(32)	0(0)	806(33)	3501
	40-44	282(10)	421(15)	931(33)	41(1)	725(26)	0(0)	405(15)	2805
	45-49	312(12)	298(12)	1165(45)	39(1)	648(25)	0(0)	141%)	2605
	50-54	397(20)	260(13)	695(35)	45(2)	453(24)	0(0)	125(6)	1975
	55-59	195(12)	270(17)	572(35)	32(2)	430(26)	0(0)	133(8)	1632
	60-64	178(10)	215(12)	437(25)	34(2)	502(29)	288	102(6)	2056
	65-69	147(8)	170(9)	214(11)	34(20	448(23)	846	76(4)	1935
	70-74	128(6)	130(6)	157(8)	18(10	345(16)	1329	26(1)	2133
	75 and more	125(6)	129(5)	95(3)	7(1)	142(5)	2184(80)	38(1)	2720

Table 6.11: Isfahan disabled population by type of disability and age in Isfahan in 2015

Physical and mental disabilities have highest number of disability in Isfahan province in 2011-2013.

Physical and psychological disabilities have the highest rate of disability in the province in years 2014 and 2015, respectively.

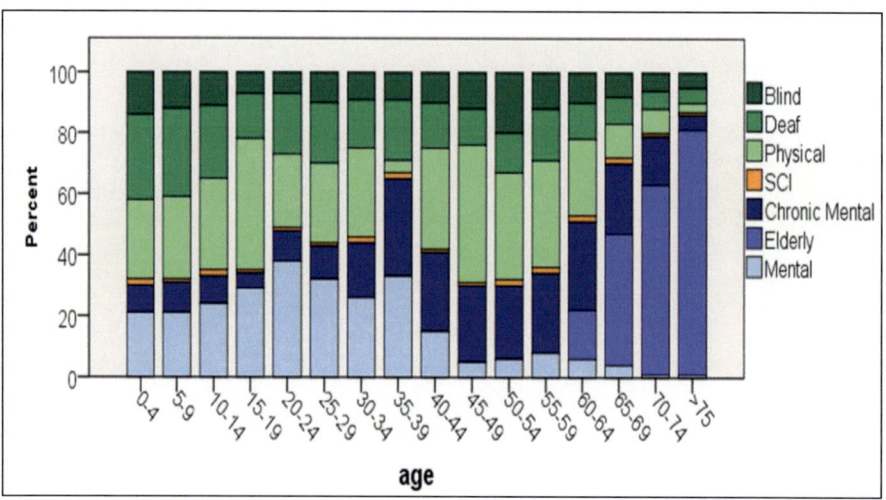

Figure 6.8: Isfahan disabled population by type of disability and age in Isfahan in 2015

Physical disabilities have the highest rate of disability in 15-19 and 45-49 years. Persons who are deaf were the highest rate of disability in children 0-9 years. Chronic mental disease have highest rate in adults over 35 years. Mental disability highest in teenagers and young adults.

Sex	Age	Mental disorder	Physical and mobility	Deaf and Speech and Impaired	Blind
		Frequency (Percent)			
Men	0-4	99(31.03)	105(32.92)	92(28.84)	23(7.21)
	5-9	302(42.72)	180(25.46)	196(27.72)	29(4.10)
	10-14	381(43.84)	281(32.34)	165(18.99)	42(4.83)
	15-19	517(43.96)	399(33.93)	216(18.37)	44(3.74)
	20-24	777(41.89)	660(35.58)	317(17.09)	101(5.44)
	25-29	819(37.57)	905(41.51)	353(16.19)	103(4.72)
	30-34	590(34.20)	809(46.90)	144(14.14)	82(4.75)
	35-39	410(26.61)	813(52.76)	226(14.67)	92(5.97)
	40-44	430(22.58)	1164(61.13)	199(10.45)	111(5.83)
	45-49	315(15.72)	1340(66.24)	254(12.56)	111(5.49)
	50-54	778(18.71)	877(59.02)	215(14.47)	116(7.81)
	55-59	169(17.39)	560(57.61)	147(15.12)	96(9.88)
	60-64	100(13.04)	489(63.75)	94(12.26)	84(10.95)
	65-69	79(11.99)	414(62.82)	91(13.81)	75(11.38)
	70-74	60(10.34)	359(61.90)	99(17.07)	62(10.69)
	75 and more	152(9.91)	935(60.95)	290(18.90)	157(10.23)
Women	0-4	56(22.95)	100(40.98)	61(25)	27(11.07)
	5-9	175(36.23)	147(30.43)	134(27.74)	27(5.59)
	10-14	274(46.28)	152(25.68)	128(21.62)	38(6.42)
	15-19	308(44.38)	186(26.80)	161(23.20)	39(5.62)
	20-24	458(43.62)	298(28.38)	234(22.29)	60(5.71)
	25-29	500(45.05)	314(28.29)	243(21.89)	53(4.77)
	30-34	413(40.06)	370(35.89)	189(18.33)	59(5.72)
	35-39	256(34.59)	284(38.38)	145(19.59)	55(7.43)
	40-44	214(28.19)	337(44.40)	160(21.08)	48(6.32)
	45-49	169(24.42)	316(45.66)	150(21.68)	57(8.24)
	50-54	131(22.39)	274(47.52)	116(19.83)	60(10.26)
	55-59	69(14.11)	286(58.49)	87(17.79)	47(9.61)
	60-64	63(13.64)	276(59.74)	80(17.32)	43(9.31)
	65-69	31(8.22)	267(70.82)	50(13.26)	29(7.69)
	70-74	148(25.92)	317(55.52)	61(10.68)	45(7.88)
	75 and more	149(9.41)	1075(67.87)	223(14.08)	137(8.65)

Table 6.12: Isfahan disabled population by sex and age in 2015

Figure 6.9 indicates disability in four areas: mental, mobility, deafness and blindness in Isfahan population by sex and age. Disability in men was higher than women.

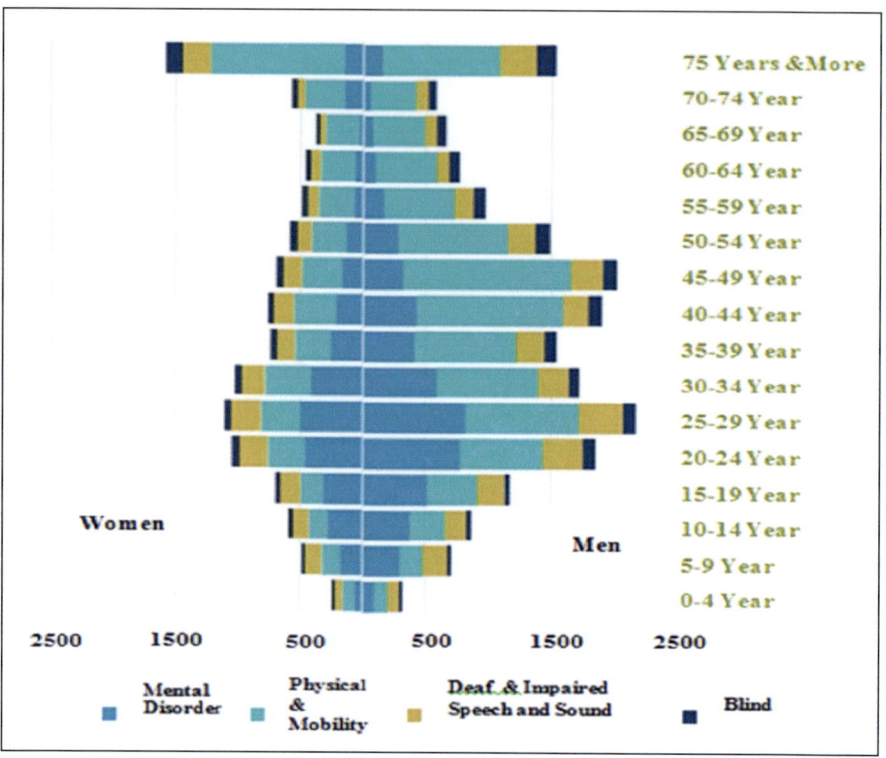

Figure 6.9: Isfahan disabled population by gender in 2015

Most problems related to physical disability in men is in the age of 45 to 50 years. Physical problems in women over 75 years are the most reported disabilities.

Conclusion

Rights and needs of persons with disabilities are: Employment opportunities, Sportive and transportation facilities, Disability insurance. Unemployment is one of the main problems among disabled people, especially disabled women in Iran.

According to a 2012 survey, 1.36% of the population was disabled and 21% of these people were unemployed. Around 1.2 million disabled people are served by welfare organizations, which mean that millions of disabled people are left to their own destinies as they receive no support and it is left to their families and others to support them.

According to a 2008 survey, of 3 million disabled people who were eligible to work, only 600,000 have been able to secure employment. This means that the majority of disabled people are unemployed and suffering from hardship.

Currently, in the cities of Iran, incomplete or improper repair of roads and streets, inaccessible and unreachable transportation, public places and parks have a significant detrimental impact on people with disabilities. Access to public transport, whether taxi, bus or metro, is so limited that attempting to use them is exhausting, and even cultural places and cinemas have few special seats for disabled people. Parking places for the disabled are easily occupied by other cars and there is no law to prevent this from happening. Persons with disabilities and elderly population are not supported by insurance including Medicare and long term care insurance (LTCI).

The Ministry of Cooperatives, Labour and Social Welfare is responsible for the area and the activities of the State Welfare Organization (SWO). "The Foundation of Martyr and Veterans Affairs" (FMVA). (Bonyad Shahid Va Omor isargran) is also an important organisation, in relating to the war disabilities, this organisation receives public funds, but is called independent and non-governmental body.

It emphasizes the accessibility of public buildings and venues; improving rehabilitative and vocational services; financial waivers for the disabled users of recreational, sportive and transportation facilities; disability insurance; employment opportunities; free education for disabled students and candidates; housing loans and facilities; and allocating two hours per week to disability programs on national television.

Healthcare and preventive services are: Medicine, Nursing, Rehabilitation, Screening and prevention services (education of caregivers).

In order to providing services to people with disabilities in Iran, There have been a number of related Ministry bodies, non-governmental public bodies working in the area elating to persons with disabilities. Iranian disability acts concluded in the ratification of the Comprehensive Act of Supporting the Disabled (or Disability Protect Act 7) by the Islamic parliament in 2004, which is considered as the first major Iranian legislation for persons with disabilities. In this regard, Welfare Organization (SWO) and Ministry of Health and Medical Education are responsible for providing this service. Welfare Organization (SWO) facilitates establishment of centres through licensing and subsidies and it also monitors the performance of these centres.

Suggestion for improvement support and services: Establishing a formal consistent organization to plan and conduct activities associated with persons with disabilities population can be a strategic measure in Iran. Planning in the form of a Network (Home Health) for providing primary health care services to solve problems of persons with disabilities and should have be done in the primary stages. All organizations should offer provincial and national plans to train enhanced support.

References

1. World Health Organization. World report on disability 2016.
2. Andrea W.M Evers, Floris W Kraaimaat, Rinie Geenen, Johannes W.G Jacobs, Johannes W.J Bijlsma, Pain coping and social support as predictors of long-term functional disability and pain in early rheumatoid arthritis. Behav ResTher. 2003; 41(11):1295-310. doi: 10.1016/S0005-7967(03)00036-6.
3. McConachie H, Colver AF, Forsyth RJ, Jarvis SN, Parkinson KN. Participation of disabled children: how should it be characterised and measured? Disabil Rehabil. 2006; 28(18):1157-64. doi: 10.1080/09638280500534507.
4. Akbarian MS. Disabillity with approach of social welfare. J Student Mohaghegh. 2007; 1(2):47-55.
5. Heidarzadeh MGA, Hagigat A, Yoosefi E. Relationship between Quality of Life and Social Support in Stroke Patients. IJN. 2009; 22(59):23-32.

6. Motl RW, McAuley E, Snook EM, Gliottoni RC. Physical activity and quality of life in multiple sclerosis: intermediary roles of disability, fatigue, mood, pain, self-efficacy and social support. Psychol Health Med. 2009; 14(1):111-24. doi: 10.1080/13548500802241902.

7. Motl RobertW, McAuley Edward, Snook ErinM. Physical activity and quality of life in multiple sclerosis: Possible roles of social support, self-efficacy, and functional limitations. Rehab Psychol. 2007; 52(2):143-51.

8. Zaki M. Validity and Reliability of social support scale at the student of Isfahan universities. J Psychiat Clin Psychol. 2008; 14(4):439-46.

9. Gol Aghaei FSB, Rafiei M. . Prevalence of depression and related factors among physical disable people in Arak city. Arak Med Uni J. 2001; 4(2):36-41.

10. Bastani S. Middle class community in Tehran [microform]: social networks, social support and marital relationships. University of Toronto; 2001.

11. Obst Patricia, Stafurik Jana. Online we are all able bodied: Online psychological sense of community and social support found through membership of disability-specific websites promotes well-being for people living with a physical disability. J Community Appl Soc. 2010; 20(6):525-31. doi: 10.1002/casp.1067.

12. Drageset J, Eide GE, Nygaard HA, Bondevik M, Nortvedt MW, Natvig GK. The impact of social support and sense of coherence on health-related quality of life among nursing home residents--a questionnaire survey in Bergen, Norway. Int J Nurs Stud. 2009; 46(1):65-75. doi: 10.1016/j.ijnurstu.2008.07.005.

13. Solar O, Irwin A. A Conceptual Framework for Action on the Social Determinants of Health. 2007.

14. Strating MM, Suurmeijer TP, van Schuur WH. Disability, social support, and distress in rheumatoid arthritis: results from a thirteen-year prospective study. Arthritis Rheum. 2006; 55(5):736-44. doi: 10.1002/art.22231.

15. Kalichman SC, DiMarco M, Austin J, Luke W, DiFonzo K. Stress, social support, and HIV-status disclosure to family and friends among HIV-positive men and women. J Behav Med. 2003; 26(4):315-32.

16. Suttajit S, Punpuing S, Jirapramukpitak T, Tangchonlatip K, Darawuttimaprakorn N, Stewart R, et al. Impairment, disability, social support and depression among older parents in rural Thailand. Psychol Med. 2010; 40(10):1711-21. doi: 10.1017/S003329170999208X.

17. Sarason BR, Sarason IG, Pierce GR. Social support: an interactional view. J. Wiley & Sons; 1990.

18. O'Brien MT. Multiple sclerosis: the role of social support and disability. Clin Nurs Res. 1993; 2(1):67-85.

19. Clingerman E. Physical activity, social support, and health-related quality of life among persons with HIV disease. J Community Health Nurs. 2004; 21(3):179-97. doi: 10.1207/s15327655jchn2103_5.

20. Eng ET, Jalilian AR, Spasov KA, Unger VM. Characterization of a novel prokaryotic GDP dissociation inhibitor domain from the G protein coupled membrane protein FeoB. J Mol Biol. 2008; 375(4):1086-97. doi: 10.1016/j.jmb.2007.11.027.

21. Jewell NP. Statistics for Epidemiology. Taylor & Francis; 2003.

22. Reisine Susan. Marital status and social support in rheumatoid arthritis. Arthritis Rheumatism. 1993; 36(5):589-92. doi: 10.1002/art.1780360503.

23. Mehrotra N. Women, Disability and Social Support in Rural Haryana. Econ Politic Week. 2004; 39(52):5640-4.

24. Fyrand L, Moum T, Finset A, Wichstrøm L, Glennås A. Social support in female patients with rheumatoid arthritis compared to healthy controls. Psychol Health Med. 2001; 6(4):429-39. doi: 10.1080/13548500126538.

25. Allen SM, Ciambrone D, Welch LC. Stage of life course and social support as a mediator of mood state among persons with disability. J Aging Health. 2000; 12(3):318-41.

26. Doeglas Dirk, Suurmeijer Theo, Krol Boudien, Sanderman Robbert, van Rijswijk Martin, van Leeuwen Miek. Social support, social disability, and psychological well-being in rheumatoid arthritis. Arthritis Rheumatism. 1994; 7(1):10-5. doi: 10.1002/art.1790070104.

27. Fyrand L, Moum T, Finset A, Glennas A. The impact of disability and disease duration on social support of women with rheumatoid arthritis. J Behav Med. 2002; 25(3):251-68.

28. Shavers VL. Measurement of socioeconomic status in health disparities research. J Natl Med Assoc. 2007; 99(9):1013-23.

Hamzeh Baharlouei & Javid Mostamand

7 Physical Activity in People with Intellectual Disability

(Hamzeh Baharlouei, Javid Mostamand)

Abstract

Introduction: Physical activity and exercise are two important factors in improving the health of people with intellectual disability. Several studies have looked at the level of physical activity, the benefits, precautions and principles of exercise in these people. The purpose of this study was to review these articles in order to achieve a general framework for improving physical activity.

Method: Various databases including PubMed, PEDro, Science Direct, were considered with some keywords such as physical activity, exercise, intellectual disability and Down syndrome. Then their information was extracted based on various categories such as physical activity levels, benefits, and principles of exercise prescription.

Results: In spite of numerous benefits, the level of physical activity in people with mental disability was lower than other groups of people. In pre-exercise examinations, attention should be paid to cardiovascular, physical, mental, and medical conditions, especially in people who are suffering from Down syndrome. Aerobic exercise, strengthening exercise, and balancing exercise are three most useful exercises for these subjects.

Conclusions: Exercise plays an important role in the health of people with intellectual disability and should be considered in pre-exercise examinations and guidelines for encouraging people to perform exercise.

Introduction

Intellectual disability is one of the most common causes of childhood disability [1]. Fernhall [2] defined intellectual disability 1977 as follows: (1) low level of intelligence (two standard deviations below the mean or level of intelligence of less than 70 for slight disability and below 35 for severe disability.) (2) Restriction of at least 2 adaptive skills including communication, self-care, housekeeping, social

---

skills, navigation, health and security, performance, work and leisure, care levels of needs3) Diagnosis of the disease before the age of 18.

These people suffer from some diseases, such as cardiovascular and respiratory diseases and cancer more than others [3]. Furthermore, problems such as infection, leukemia and early Alzheimer's have been also reported in people with Down syndrome [4]. The most important physical problems reported in this group are Ligamentous laxity, decreased muscle tone, muscle weakness, overweight, functional limitations, low aerobic capacity, and accelerated aging process [5].

Several systematic review [6] and Meta-analysis [7] have expressed that exercise is an effective way to improve people's health suffering from intellectual disability. Exercise can also increase the physical fitness associated with skill [8], public health [9], life quality [10], reducing the incidence of Alzheimer's disease [11], the incidence of diseases [12], and the isolation [13].

Physical fitness associated with skill is a type of physical fitness that is related to the ability to perform professional or occupational work and is different from health-related physical fitness. The components of this fitness include agility, balance, coordination, power, speed, and reaction [8].

Despite the above-mentioned benefits, various studies have indicated a low level of physical activity in people with intellectual disability. In this type of disorder, the individual's performance decreases in standard fitness tests such as strength, endurance, flexibility, motor coordination and cardiovascular tolerance [14]. The study by Golubović et al. [15] also showed that the physical fitness of this group was significantly lower than that of the group with the same gender and age. Considering the conflict between exercise efficiency and low physical activity in people with intellectual disability, the aim of this study was to review the articles in this field to evaluate different aspects of physical activity in people with intellectual disability.

Method
English language articles from PubMed, Science Direct, and PEDro databases were searched with the keywords such as physical activity, exercise, intellectual disability and Down syndrome, then articles were investigated to answer the following questions:

Hamzeh Baharlouei & Javid Mostamand

1. What are the causes of low physical activity in people with intellectual disability?
2. What are the dangers a. barriers in sports of people with intellectual disability?
3. What kind of sports is suitable for people with intellectual disability?
4. What kind of considerations can encourage people with intellectual disability to exercise?

Discussion and Results

Different reasons have been reported for lower physical activity in intellectual disability. The most important ones are limitation of mental abilities and low level of attention [16], motor impairment [17], lack of active lifestyle [18], and lack of motivation to show their abilities [19].

Although exercising is very useful for the general health, but all people, especially people with special needs should be examined before exercise. In people with intellectual disability, these examinations include cardiovascular, muscular strength and muscle strength and body composition examinations [20]. Examinations in Down syndrome patients are more important because half of them have congestive heart failure and Atlanto-Axial instability (Excessive movements between cervical intervertebral joints) [21].

Bartlo et al. [6] have suggested three types of exercise including aerobic exercise, resistive and balance in people with intellectual disability. Balance exercises play a significant role in the life of people with intellectual disability. Research has shown that 30% of these people fall down at least once a year, which may even lead to serious injury. Increase in risk of falling starts at a younger age in people with intellectual disability than that reported in older adults without disability [22]. Hsieh et al. [23] have studied 1515 people with intellectual disability and stated that the most important risk factors for falling are female gender, arthritis, epilepsy, using more than four drugs, use of assistive device and inability in lifting weights heavier than 4.5 kilograms.

Resistive exercises are another useful activity in people with intellectual disability. Lower limb strengthening is associated with improved agility, balance, power, strength, and response time [8]. Of course, it should be noted that exercises with moderate to severe resistance in mental abilities are not necessary because they may have no effect on functional abilities [24].

Aerobic exercises are an important part of physical activity. Walking is strongly recommended because of low level of cognitive function, acceptable cost-benefit ratio, low side effects, and the excellent compliance [20].

Day rehabilitation centers are a good place to do physical activity. At such centers, physiotherapists and staff are familiar with personality and level of mental ability, on the other hand the patient is familiar with the environment [25]. A new environment or new and unfamiliar coach can reduce the concentration or even exacerbates inappropriate behaviors [22]. The space and equipment should be provided for performing a variety of sports. On the other hand, the lower cost sports, the longer time efficacy [25]. Safety of the exercise environment should be fully ensured in order to prevent falling or fear of falling [20].

There are many ways in various articles to encourage people with mental disabilities. In the beginning, people should determine their level of activity and participation [26]. A study conducted by Podgorski et al. also shown that people who are not primarily interested in engaging in sports activities are interested in physical activity after seeing the presence of others in sports [26]. Verbal training instructions are better to be simple and concluded in a single sentence rather than repetitive sentences and then repeated regularly and verbally [20].

For many people with intellectual disability, group-based exercise is hard and they need personal attention [22]. Sometimes, it is difficult for a person with intellectual disability to concentrate. Therefore, sessions need to be arranged short and attractive [20]. The use of instruments such as balls and music balloons help encouraging the people with intellectual disability [20]. So it is recommended to encourage them to participate in competitions like the Paralympics [20].

Never ask this question to know about fatigue. Are you tired? Because in this case, most people, will respond "yes" regardless of the intensity of exercise. Instead, the following question is suggested: "Do you still want to keep up with full of energy?" [20].

However, some people with intellectual disability can reach a level to do exercise without any supervision, but for most of them, there is a need for ongoing supervision [20]. In children with Down syndrome, the probability of instability in the Atlanto-Axial joint is high. Therefore, some activities that require bending their neck or back are prohibited. In these children, there is instability and reduced muscle tone. Therefore, strengthening muscles, especially important

Hamzeh Baharlouei & Javid Mostamand

muscles around the joints is priority. Participating in sports such as martial arts and soccer should also be performed with caution [20].

Conclusion

The low level of physical activity in people with intellectual disability is due to various mental and physical reasons that can be enhanced by appropriate sports, the use of motivational methods, and exercising in an appropriate space. Aerobic, strengthening and balancing exercises are useful kind of activities for these subjects. Of course, their health status should be considered before any exercise recommendations.

References

1. Yu C, Li J, Liu Y, Qin W, Li Y, Shu N, et al. White matter tract integrity and intelligence in patients with intellectual disability and healthy adults. Neuroimage. 2008;40(4):1533-41.
2. Fernhall B. Intellectual disability. American College of Sports Medicine, editor ACSM's Exercise Management for Persons with Chronic Diseases and Disabilities. Champaign: Human Kinetics; 1977. p. 221-6.
3. Prasher V, Janicki M. Physical Health of Adults with Intellectual Disabilities. 2002.
4. Baynard T, Pitetti KH, Guerra M, Unnithan VB, Fernhall B. Age-related changes in aerobic capacity in individuals with intellectual disability: a 20-yr review. Medicine & Science in Sports & Exercise. 2008;40(11):1984-9.
5. Boer P, Moss S. Effect of continuous aerobic vs. interval training onselected anthropometrical, physiological and functional parameters of adults with Down syndrome. Journal of intellectual disability research. 2016;60(4):322-34.
6. Bartlo P, Klein PJ. Physical activity benefits and needs in adults with intellectual disabilities: Systematic review of the literature. American Journal on Intellectual and Developmental Disabilities. 2011;116(3):220-32.
7. Shin I-S, Park E-Y. Meta-analysis of the effect of exercise programs for individuals with intellectual disabilities. Research in Developmental Disabilities. 2012;33(6):1937-47.
8. Jeng S-C, Chang C-W, Liu W-Y, Hou Y-J, Lin Y-H. Exercise training on skill-related physical fitness in adolescents with intellectual disability: A systematic review and meta-analysis. Disability and Health Journal. 2016.

9.   Robertson J, Emerson E, Gregory N, Hatton C, Turner S, Kessissoglou S, et al. Lifestyle related risk factors for poor health in residential settings for people with intellectual disabilities. Research in Developmental Disabilities. 2000;21(6):469-86.

10. Walsh PN. Ageing and health issues in intellectual disabilities. Current opinion in psychiatry. 2005;18(5):502-6.

11. Lifshitz H, Merrick J, Morad M. Health status and ADL functioning of older persons with intellectual disability: Community residence versus residential care centers. Research in Developmental Disabilities. 2008;29(4):301-15.

12. Hannon F, Fitzsimon N, Kelleher C. Physical activity, Health and Quality of Life among People with Disabilities: An Analysis of the SLÁNdata: National Disability Authority; 2006.

13. Mutrie N, Campbell AM, Whyte F, McConnachie A, Emslie C, Lee L, et al. Benefits of supervised group exercise programme for women being treated for early stage breast cancer: pragmatic randomised controlled trial. Bmj. 2007;334(7592):517.

14. Franciosi E, Baldari C, Gallotta MC, Emerenziani GP, Guidetti L. Selected factors correlated to athletic performance in adults with intellectual disability. The Journal of Strength & Conditioning Research. 2010;24(4):1059-64.

15. Golubović Š, Maksimović J, Golubović B, Glumbić N. Effects of exercise on physical fitness in children with intellectual disability. Research in Developmental Disabilities. 2012;33(2):608-14.

16. Vuijk PJ, Hartman E, Scherder E, Visscher C. Motor performance of children with mild intellectual disability and borderline intellectual functioning. Journal of intellectual disability research. 2010;54(11):955-65.

17. Westendorp M, Houwen S, Hartman E, Visscher C. Are gross motor skills and sports participation related in children with intellectual disabilities? Research in Developmental Disabilities. 2011;32(3):1147-53.

18. Lotan M, Isakov E, Kessel S, Merrick J. Physical fitness and functional ability of children with intellectual disability: effects of ashort-term daily treadmill intervention. The scientific world journal. 2004;4:449-57.

19. Halle JW, Gabler-Halle D, Chung YB. Effects of a peer-mediated aerobic conditioning program on fitness levels of youth with intellectual disability: two systematic replications. Intellectual disability. 1999;37(6):435-48.

20. Medicine ACoS. ACSM's guidelines for exercise testing and prescription: Lippincott Williams & Wilkins; 2013.

21.   Dedlow ER, Siddiqi S, Fillipps DJ, Kelly MN, Nackashi JA, Tuli SY. Symptomatic atlanto-axial instability in an adolescent with trisomy 21 (Down's syndrome). Clinical pediatrics. 2013;52(7):633-8.

22.   Hale LA, Mirfin-Veitch BF, Treharne GJ. Prevention of falls for adults with intellectual disability (PROFAID): a feasibility study. Disability andrehabilitation. 2016;38(1):36-44.

22.   Hsieh K, Rimmer J, Heller T. Prevalence of falls and risk factors in adults with intellectual disability. American Journal on Intellectual and Developmental Disabilities. 2012;117(6):442-54.

24.   Carmeli E, Reznick AZ, Coleman R, Carmeli V. Muscle strength and mass of lower extremities in relation to functional abilities in elderly adults. Gerontology. 2000;46(5):249-57.

25.   Shields N, Taylor NF, Dodd KJ. Effects of a community-based progressive resistance training program on muscle performance and physical function in adults with Down syndrome: a randomized controlled trial. Archives of physical medicine and rehabilitation. 2008;89(7):1215-20.

26.   Podgorski CA, Kessler K, Cacia B, Peterson DR, Henderson CM, Taylor SJ. Physical activity intervention for older adults with intellectual disability: report on a pilot project. Intellectual disability. 2004;42(4):272-83.

8   Family conflicts and disability
(Mostafa Arab-Varnousfaderani, Kowsar Arab-Varnousfaderani, Maryam Ashrafi)

Disability is a set of physical, mental and social factors or a combination of them which in a way have an adverse effect on an individual life and deviate it from its normal path (Lucas-Carrasco et al. 2011). The disability of a child creates serious crises in the family system and prevents family members from a normal life. It also results in the family breakdown or the abandonment of the disabled child.

A disabled child also may affect social, economic and psychological aspects of family's life (Carson, 2011). The child could also be considered as a threat for family's happiness, interpersonal relationships and generally its well-being (Haring et al. 2011). The disability is reflected not only in the body of the disabled person but also much in the mindset and attitudes of the family members. This in turn creates negative feelings in parents (both toward themselves and their children). In addition, the quality of life, the level of happiness and self-confidence of parents with negative attitudes are lower comparing to other people of the society (Olsson and Hwang, 2007).

The pleasant thoughts and feelings experienced by child, resulted from mother's initial relationships will turn in to efficient internal patterns and cognitive-emotional attitudes. Therefore, the child considers himself as an important and lovely person and take other people important and trustworthy as well (Morris and Misters, 2014). The children who are provided with less attachment relationship and affection, show more aggressive and hostile behaviors than other children (Fills and yaprak, 2012).

The presence of a child with physical-motor disabilities is problematic in terms of care issues and is accompanied with stressful experiences for parents. This situation is considered as an obstacle for family to perform its normal functions such as interpersonal relationships in a desirable way. Other families also lower their relationship with the child family (Olsson and Hwang, 2007).

Today we are facing with the third wave of cognitive-behavioral therapies, of which acceptance and commitment-based therapy (ACT) is one to mention. Acceptance and commitment-based therapy benefits from an organized philosophical and theoretical framework. It is an experience-based psychological intervention that applies awareness and acceptance based strategies with commitment and behavior changing ones to increase one's psychological flexibility. The clients learn through metaphor, paradox and other practices how to encounter their physical, horrible and avoiding thoughts, feelings, memories and senses in healthy way.

With the skills learned, they are able to accept these personal events, change their context, specify their personal values and commit themselves to the required behavioral changes (Hayse, Strosahl, & Wilson, 1999).

For treating the family of the disabled person, first the consultant tried to increase individual's psychiatric acceptance about mental experiences (thoughts, feelings ...) and at the same time decrease ineffective control actions. The family is taught that any action for avoiding or controlling these unwanted mental experiences is either ineffective or has a reverse effect and will intensify them.

In other words, the experiences should be accepted completely without any internal or external reaction to exclude them. Second, the psychiatric awareness of the individual will be increased at the present time, that is, the individual becomes aware of his entire psychiatric conditions. In the third step, the individual is taught to isolate himself from these mental experiences (cognitive isolation) in a way that he is be able to act independently from them. Fourth, attempts are made to decrease one's excessive focus on self-imagination or personal story that the individual has conceived (like when the individual considers himself as a victim). Fifth, the family is helped to acknowledge its major values, specify them and turn them to specific behavioral purposes (illuminating values). Finally, the family is motivated to be committed to their action that is the focuses of activities are the purposes and values specified, besides accepting mental experiences. These mental experiences could be depressive and compulsive thoughts, thoughts related to events, social panic or anxieties (Pourfaraj, O, 2011). ACT therapy therefore is defined considering flexibility. Cognitive flexibility in turn includes six categories namely acceptance, detachment, relating to the present time, self as observer, values and committed actions.

In ACT therapy process, metaphors techniques are used to turn psychological trauma of experiential avoidance in to acceptance, isolation, past and conceptualized future to connection with the present time and conceptualized self to self as observer, inexplicitness of values to values and inactivity to committed actions. In ACT, acceptance and isolation are two major tools used for confronting thoughts and feelings, also memories and physical senses.

Acceptance is a way for reducing and solving problems related to experiential avoidance that is a situation is provided for expressing feelings, physical senses, passion and other internal experiences without struggling against them. In other words, we allow them come and go. In isolation, we watch thoughts, conceptions, memories and other cognition as they are, that is the individual is not allowed to see more than words and images. In other words, we should learn them, terrible events, binding rules and objective facts should not be considered as they are, but to consider them only as the process of an active mind and separate them from the real world. (McKay, Lev, Skeen, & Hayes, 2012).

References

Carson, J. (2011). Components social support and Quality of life in severely ill, low income individuals and general population group. Community Mental Health Journal, 34(5):459- 75.

Filiz, Z., Yaprak, B. (2012). A study on classifying parenting styles through discriminant analysis. J Theo Pract Educ. 2012; 5(2): 195-209.

Hayse, S. C., Strosahl, K., & Wilson, G. K. (1999). Acceptance and Commitment Therapy: An experiential approach to behavior change. New York: Guilford Press.

Herring, S., Gray, J., Taffe, K., Sweeny, D., Eifeld, S. (2011). Behavior and emotional problems in toddlers with pervasive developmental disordersand developmental delay: associationwith parental mental health and family functioning. Journal of Intellectual disability Research,12, 874-882.

Lucas-Carrasco, R., Eser, E., Hao, Y., McPherson, K. M., Green, A., Kullmann, L., & Group, T. W.-D. (2011). The Quality of Care and Support (QOCS) for people with disability scale: development and psychometric properties. Research in Developmental Disabilities, 32(3), 1225-12 . 34

McKay, M., Lev, A., Skeen, M., & Hayes, S. C. (2012). Acceptance and Commitment Therapy for Interpersonal Problems. New Harbinger Publications, Inc.

Muris, P., Meesters, BA. (2014). Assessment of anxious rearing behaviors with a modified version of "Egna Minnen Beträffande Uppfostran" questionnaire for children. J Psychopathol Behav Assess. 2014;25(4):229-37.

Olsson, M.B, Hwang, C.P. (2007). Depretion in mother and father of children with intellectual disability. Journal of Intellectual disability Research, 45, 535-545.

Pourfaraj, O. (2011). The effectiveness of acceptance and commitment group therapy in social phobia of students. Journal of Knowledge and Health, 6(2), 1-5.

9 Faculty development regarding disability

(Nikoo Yamani, Habibollah Rezaei)

Education for All (EFA) is an international commitment to ensure that every child and adult receives the basic education of good quality (1). It is based both on a human rights perspective and on the generally held belief that "education is central to individual well-being and national development" (2). As well as UNESCO defines inclusive education as "a process of addressing and responding to the diversity of needs of all learners through increasing participation in learning, cultures, and communities, and reducing exclusion within and from education" (3).

In universities, there are many students that live with a disability. Disability is "any restriction or lack (resulting from an impairment) of ability to perform an activity in the manner or within the range considered normal for a human being" (4). We should attend to a disabled student based on both education for all and inclusive education. There are many approaches to realizing the right of students with disabilities to inclusive education. Approaches to realizing the right of students with disabilities to inclusive education are government-wide measures, education policies and strategies to promote the right to access education, the right to quality education and respect for rights within the learning environment (2).

Education has to be of the highest possible quality to help every disable reach her or his potential, although there is no single definition of 'quality education' it is broadly understood to incorporate the opportunity for both effective cognitive learning, together with opportunities for creative and emotional development (3). The right to quality education includes securing the appropriate individualized support for students with disabilities (Provision, where needed, of holistic packages of involving support, not only in education, but also in the provision of health or social care services, technical assistance, and psychological support), developing inclusive curricula, teaching and learning methods (Adopting a curriculum to enable all students to acquire the core academic curriculum and basic cognitive skills, together with essential life skills, including respect for human rights. Creative use of assistive technology to make it easier for students with disabilities to learn, including physical resources, computers and use of ICTs, introduction of rights-based and inclusive student assessment (Measuring student progress in the general education curriculum, with clear standards and benchmarks and use multiple forms of student assessments to inform and facilitate teaching and learning), investment in teacher training (On-going, high quality professional development opportunities for teachers that address inclusive methodologies), establishing resources to provide specialist support (Development of collaborative practice and provision through networks of learning communities) (2).

Education has to be provided in a situation which supports the cultural issues, and respects the participation rights of learners (2). Respect for rights within the learning environment include right to respect for identity, culture and language (Recognition of learners' right to respect for their language and culture within their education), respect for students' participation rights (Introduction of mechanisms for ensuring that learners are able to express a view on placements, and have their views taken seriously in accordance with their situation), right to respect for personal and physical integrity(Emphasis on tolerance, respect, equity, non-discrimination, and non-violent conflict resolution within the curriculum, textbooks and teaching methods) (3).

It was mentioned in "the right to a quality education" that we should invest in teacher training. For investment in teacher training, we should respond to four questions: Why Faculty Development regarding disability? What is the role of Faculty Members? Which models in Faculty Development are appropriate? and: What do teachers need to know about students with disabilities?

Regarding the necessity of Faculty Development, Faculty Members will be in touch with disabilities in universities at least in three modes:

1. Some Faculty Members teach disabled students
2. Some Faculty Members provide health services to disables
3. Some Faculty Members train students who will provide services to disables after graduation

According to these facts that Faculty Members and students may not have the knowledge and positive attitude about disabilities (5), therefore we should design Faculty Development Programs regarding disabilities.

But, what are the roles of Faculty Members at universities?

Harden cited twelve educational roles for Faculty Members that shown in figure 9.1(6).

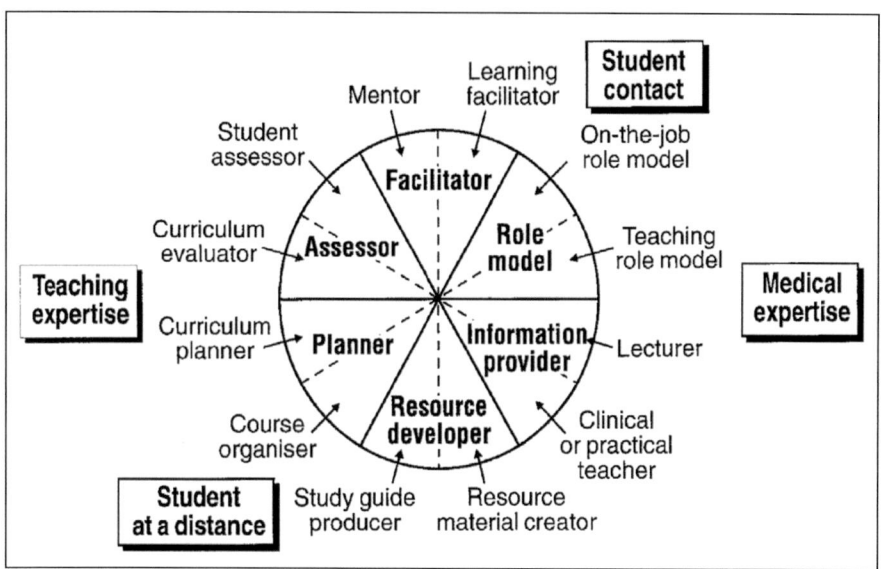

Figure 9.1: The 12 roles of the teacher

According to these roles, we should determine that in any role how we can create Faculty Development and which Faculty Development programs are suitable. Some forms of Faculty Development programs are workshops, panels, presentations, individual faculty consultations, classroom observations, teaching-related grants programs, faculty fellows programs, faculty learning communities or reading groups, Scholarship of Teaching and Learning Support (7).

In regard to Faculty Development Programs, there are many models. Such as, Armstrong and Barsion Model, Sprietzer model, Mallak and Kurstedt model, Robbins, Crino and Fredendal model, Mc Lagan and Nel model, Vogt and Murrel model, Noller model, Thomas, and Velthouse model and Laverack model (8-16). For Faculty Development regarding disability, we should select the best model from them.

But, what do teachers need to know about students with disabilities?

In interviews with some of the faculty member, they mentioned that teachers need to know issues of disabilities for family and community, the right of people with disabilities, the needs of students with disabilities, how to interact with the disabled student, how to teach the disabled student, and how to evaluate the disabled student (2, 17, 18, 19, 20).

According to literature review, issues of disabilities for family and community are anger and aggression, depression, disruption of the marital relationship, shame and embarrassment, and economic costs for the family and community. The rights of people with disabilities are education, employment, housing, marriage, provide rehabilitation aid, allowance for treatment, community participation, and equal rights with other members of the community and facilitate commuting in the city and university. Needs of disabled students are life Skills, respectful attention, independence, educational facilities, community participation, economic and facilitated commuting in the city and university. How to interact with the disabled students? In interacting with the disabled students, faculty members should attend to ability, be comfortable in the conversation, focus on sayings, give enough time and use verbal and nonverbal skills depending on the type of impairment. How to teach the disabled students? Student-centered method, individualized educational program, face to face education, flipped classroom, team learning, peer learning, extra assistance, audio-visual materials are some strategies for teaching to the disabled students. How to evaluate the disabled students? For evaluating the disabled students it is better to use global rating and give project and extra time. Using different assessment methods depends on the type of impairment and provide an environment for assessment depending on the type of impairment (2, 17, 18, 19, 20).

In summary for a proper Faculty Development Programs with the purpose of paying special attention to the needs of disabled students, first we should select an appropriate model for Faculty Development. Then we need to pay attention to developing knowledge, attitude and skills of Faculty Members regarding disability. Second, as long as faculty member have different roles, we should integrate attention to disability in every role of Faculty Members.

References

1. United Nations Educational, Scientific and Cultural Organization. A Human Rights-Based Approach to education for all. United Nations Educational, Scientific and Cultural Organization; 2007. [Cited 2017 November 18] Available from: *https://www.unicef.org/publications/files/A_Human_Rights_Based_Approach_to_Education_for_All.pdf*

2. UNICEF. The Right of Children with Disabilities to Education: A Rights-Based Approach to Inclusive Education in the CEECIS Region. UNICEF. [Cited 2017 November 18] Available from: *https://www.unicef.org/eca/Background_NoteFINAL(1).pdf*

3. United Nations Educational, Scientific and Cultural Organization. Guidelines for Inclusion: Ensuring Access to Education for All. United Nations Educational, Scientific and Cultural Organization, 2005. [Cited 2017 November 18] Available from: *http://unesdoc.unesco.org/images/0014/001402/140224e.pdf*

4. United Nations. The United Nations and Disabled Persons -The First Fifty Years. What is a disability?. Department of Economic and Social Affairs. Division for Social Policy and Development. [Cited 2017 November 18] Available from: *http://www.un.org/esa/socdev/enable/dis50y10.htm*

5. Sniatecki JL, Perry HB, Snell LH. Faculty Attitudes and Knowledge Regarding College Students with Disabilities. Journal of Postsecondary Education and Disability. 28(3): 259-275.

6. Harden RM, Crosby JR. AMEE Education Guide No 20: The good teacher is more than a lecturer – the twelve roles of the teacher. Medical Teacher. 2000; 22(4): 334-347.

7. Gravett EO. What exactly is faculty development? [Cited 2017 November 18] Available from: *http://cte.virginia.edu/wp-content/uploads/2014/01/Faculty-Development-Handout.pdf*

8. Armstrong EG, Barsion SJ. Using an outcomes-logic-model approach to evaluate a faculty development program for medical educators. Acad Med. 2006 May; 81(5): 483-8.

9. Sprietzer GM. Psychological empowerment in the workplace: dimension, measurement and validation. Academy of management journal. 1995; 38(5): 1442-1465.

10. Mallak LA, Kurstedt HA. Understanding and Using Empowerment to Change Organizational Culture. Industrial Management. 1996; 38(6).

11. Robbins TL, Crino MD, Fredendal LD. An integrative model of the empowerment process. Human Resource Management Review. 2002; 12: 419-443.

12. McLagan P, Nel C. The age of participation: New governance for the workplace and the world. New York: Berrett-Koehler; 1997.

Nikoo Yamani & Habibollah Rezaei

13. Vogt JF, Murrell KL. Empowerment in Organizations: How to Spark Exceptional Performance. San Diego, CA: University Associates; 1990.

14. Noller D. Beyond a buzzword: An empowered perspective in Andrews. Journal of Applied Psychology. 1991; 74(1): 152-156.

15. Thomas KW, Velthouse BA. Cognitive Elements of Empowerment: An "Interpretive" Model of Intrinsic Task Motivation. Acad Mange Rev. 1990; 15(4): 666-681.

16. Laverack G. Improving Health Outcomes through Community Empowerment: A Review of the Literature. J Health Popul Nutr. 2006; 24(1): 11-120.

17. Shield B. Evaluation of the social and economic costs of hearing impairment. 2006. [Cited 2017 November 18] Available from: *https://www.hear-it.org/sites/default/files/multimedia/documents/Hear_It_Report_October_2006.pdf*

18. Mass mutual. Understanding the long-term challenges of disability. [Cited 2017 November 18] Available from: *https://www.massmutual.com/mmfg/pdf/Living_with_Disabilities_Study.pdf*

19. Nikkhah H, Fadayi S. The study of economic, socio cultural and psychological needs of disabilities people. Journal of Hormozgan cultural research review. 2016; 5(10): 29-45.

20. Yektamaram A. [How to interact with people with disabilities]. Tehran: Welfare Organization; 2009. [Persian] [Cited 2017 November 18] Available from: *http://www.isaarsci.ir/conference%20sci/scibookfair/titlebook/Taamol-malool.pdf*

10   The Attitude of Isfahan People to Disabilities: A Pilot Study

(Hamid Nasiri Dehsorkhi, Saeid Nasiri, Sedigheh Sadrameli, Batoul Aminalzarbian)

Description of the project

Disability and inclusion as social and cultural phenomena: Comparative analysis of public attitudes toward disability in Hamburg and Isfahan. Various factors affect the exclusion of people with disabilities. The most fundamental of these factors is the attitude of the society (planners, professionals, employers, etc.) (Nosek et al., 2004). Likewise, any modification in lifestyle and the return of persons with disabilities to the society, the distribution of employment and social opportunities, the optimal use of the capabilities of people with disabilities and the integration of the disabled in society depend on the changes in the underlying thinking, feeling and orientation in terms of changing attitudes toward people with disabilities that will be conceptualized in attitude change (Aiden and McCarthy, 2014).

Introduction

Despite the fact that disability advocates are working to change attitudes toward persons with disabilities, public perception of such individuals is still largely negative (1). Research indicates that negative attitudes interfere with the employment, self-esteem, and health care of persons with disabilities (2). Deal (2006), a professional with a disability, found that people with disabilities who voluntarily met up with other people with disabilities collectively held the most positive attitudes towards disability (3). Thus, the role of people with disabilities in changing attitudes to disability may be very significant (1).

Attitudes are comprised of three components: affective, cognitive, and behavioral (4). The affective component represents the emotional portion of an attitude, whereas the cognitive component refers to ideas, beliefs, and opinions (5). The behavioral component describes a person's willingness to interact with the subject at hand and the manner in which they do so (6). It is important to understand the components of attitudes since understanding attitudes should help predict behavior toward persons with disabilities. Furthermore, the relationship between attitudes and behavior is complex, and attitudes only account for a small part of behavior (7). This study investigated attitudes toward different types of disabilities: congenital physical, acquired physical, and psychiatric.

Purpose of study

The purpose of the survey was to provide evidence on attitudes to disability among a representative population of males and females aged 18 and above living in the Isfahan, with specific analysis across a range of variables including gender, age, and disability status. This evidence will be used to guide future interventions and to assess, where possible, changes and their cause, in public attitudes to disability as measured in a joint Hamburg-Isfahan project.

Method

Type of present study is survey and descriptive. Because the present study is a pilot study, 400 adults, 18 years old and above, were randomly inquired. The 14-item questionnaire that was used in this study covered many topics related to attitudes to disability including: knowledge of what was a disability and general attitudes to disability, disability and education, disability and relations, disability and access, level of comfort living with people with disabilities, disability and state benefits.

Definition of persons with disabilities
Blindness
Deafness or severe hearing impairment
Physical disabilities
Intellectual or learning disabilities
Psychological or emotional condition
Chronical illness
Other

Table 10.1: Definition of a person with Disability

(For the descriptions, go to "Alternative text for images" page 217)

Data Collection

Face-to-face interview and questionnaire were used to collect the data. This method was chosen because of the duration of the survey (approximately 20 minutes). The questionnaire comprised items that had some social desirability bias associated with them. Social desirability bias is when in some circumstances, respondents may be tempted to give the socially desirable response rather than describe what they actually think, believe or do.

Results

This section describes the results of the survey under the following headings: knowledge of disability and general attitudes, education, employment, relationships, access to buildings and public facilities, level of comfort living with people with disabilities, State benefits and awareness of disability related organizations/legislation/ initiatives.

	Percent 2015
Intellectual (e.g. mental handicap – Down Syndrom)	75%
Physical disability	60%
Visual difficulties	51.7%
Mental health difficulty (mental illness – depression, schizophrenia)	45%
Elder disabilities	43.3%
Hearing loss	41.7%
Long-term illness (e.g. diabetes, dialysis)	26.7%
Addiction	25%
HIV/AIDS	18.3%
Total n = 400 (2015)	

Table 10.2: Illnesses, conditions or disabilities (N=400)

(For the descriptions, go to "Alternative text for images" page 218)

According to Table 10.2, the highest frequency is found for mental handicap with 75% and physical disability with 60%. Physical disability is the second most commonly cited attitude of the community towards the disabled. However, in 2001 and 2006 surveys, physical ability and mental handicap were ranked as the first and second most frequently cited, respectively. Furthermore, AIDS with 18.3%, addiction with 25% and long-term illnesses with 26.7% frequency have been the lowest frequency disabilities in society's attitude towards disabled people.

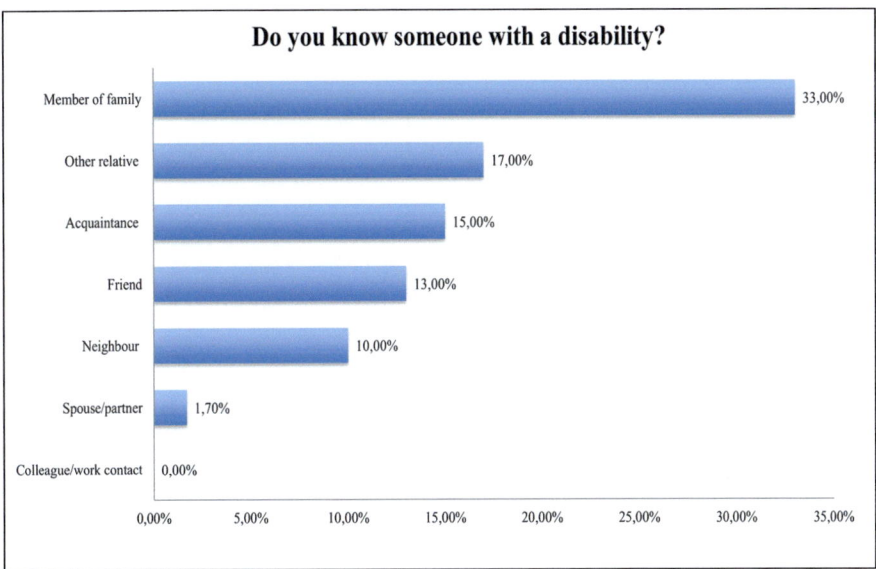

Figure 10.1: Percentage of respondents that knew someone with a disability

(For the descriptions, go to "Alternative text for images" page 218)

According to Figure 10.1, the highest frequency of familiarity with people with disabilities was found in familiarity with disabled people among the members of the family 33%, and close relationships,17% while the lowest frequency was found for partners, 1%, neighbors, 10% and friends, 13% respectively.

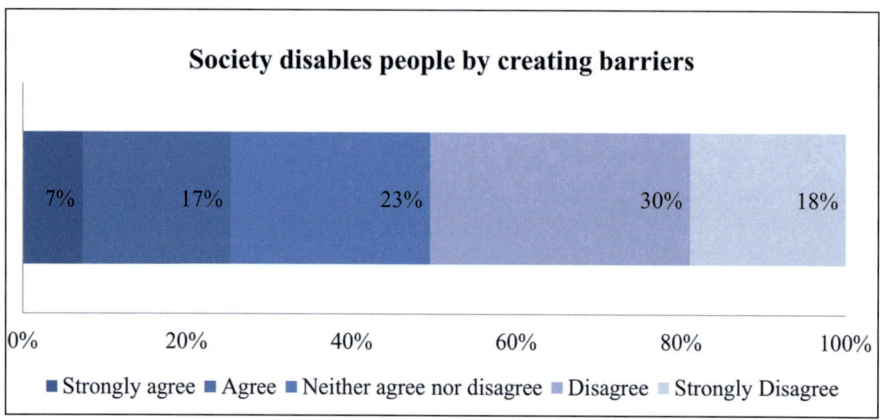

Figure 10.2: Level of agreement with the statement 'it is society which disables people by creating barriers'

(For the descriptions, go to "Alternative text for images" page 219)

According to Figure 10.2, 48% of the sample reported that disability would restrict people in the community, about 7% did not agree at all, and 17% did not agree that disability would not severely restrict people in the community.

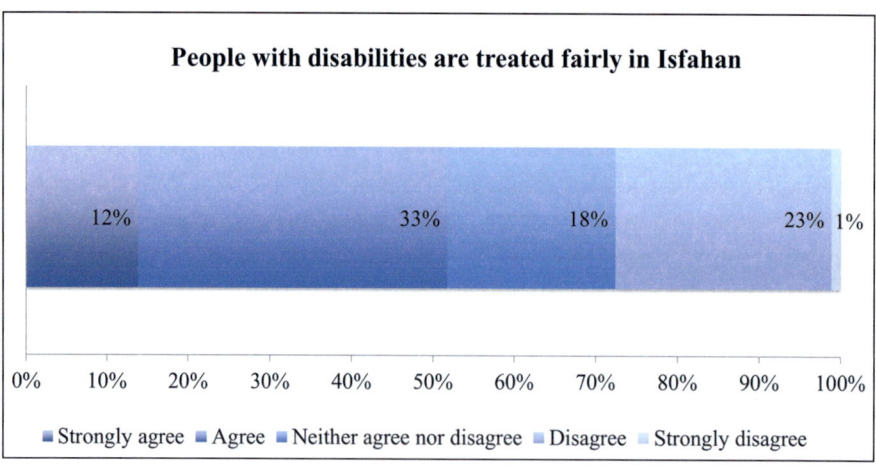

Figure 10.3: Level of agreement with the statement 'people with disabilities are treated fairly in Isfahan society

(For the descriptions, go to "Alternative text for images" page 219)

Hamid Nasiri Dehsorkhi et al.

The results of Figure 10.3 indicated that 24% of sample believed people with disabilities are well treated, 45% do not agree that with people with disabilities are well treated, and 18% did not have any opinion in this regard.

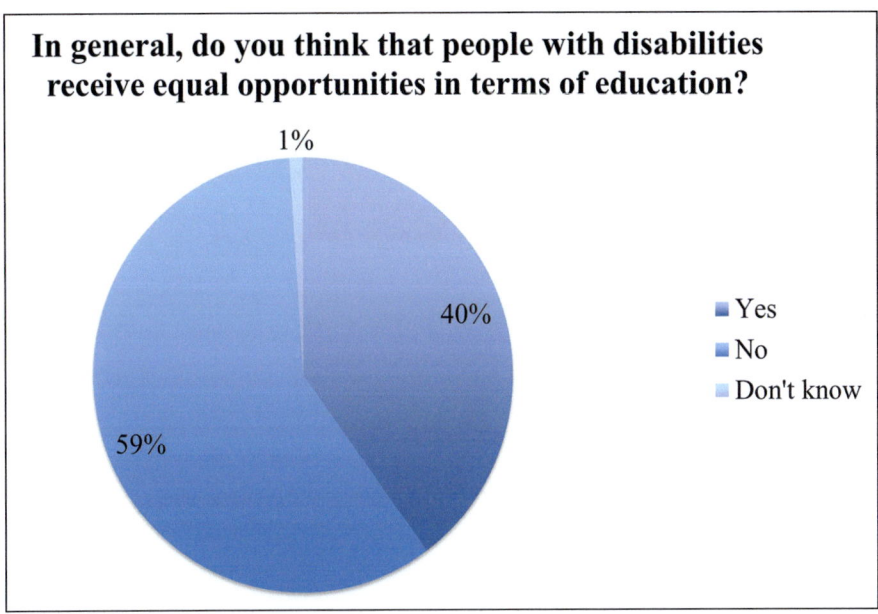

Figure 10.4: Do people with disabilities receive equal opportunities in terms of Education?
(For the descriptions, go to "Alternative text for images" page 219)

According to Figure 10.4, 59% of sample believe that people with disabilities have enough opportunities to educate and 40% of the people disagree that people with disabilities have enough opportunities to educate in society, and 1% of the respondents have no opinion in this regard.

The results shows that 57% of the sample would like their children to be classmate with peers with vision and hearing and peers with mental and learning difficulties, and 28% would like their child to be classmate with physically disabled peers and 43% of the sample do not want their children to be classmate with physically disabled children.

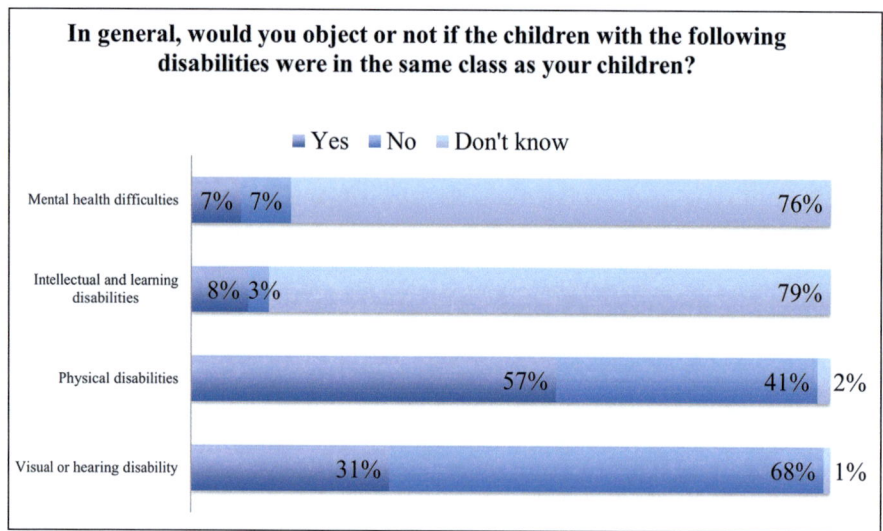

Figure 10.5: Object or not if children with disabilities were in the same class as your child (if you had a child) for different disability types

(For the descriptions, go to "Alternative text for images" page 220)

The results of Figure 10.5 indicated that about 79% of the sample had no idea that their children would be classmate with peers with learning disabilities and mental problems, and 57% would like their children to be classmate with peers with physical disabilities, and 31% would like their children to be classmate with hearing and visually impaired peers. In general, the most frequent statement found in the above table was having no idea about being classmate with people with disabilities.

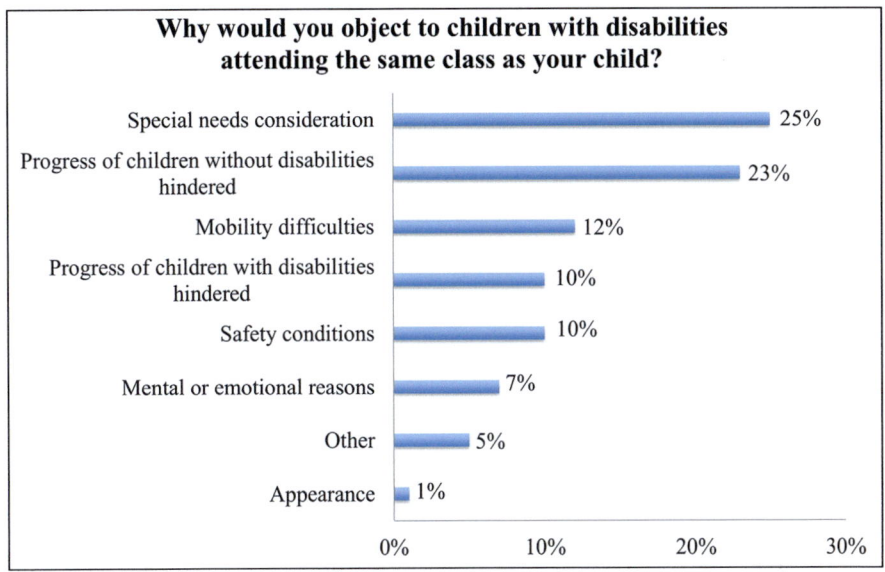

Figure 10.6: Reason for objection to children with disabilities in the same class as your child

(For the descriptions, go to "Alternative text for images" page 220)

Figure 10.6 reveals that the main reasons for parents' disagreement with educating normal and disabled children together are the specific needs of these children, 25% and being a barrier to the growth of normal children, 23%. Moreover, the following reasons were stated by the sample: motor problems, 12%, barriers to the growth of disabled children, 10%, emotional reasons, 7%, other reasons, 5%, and finally, appearance, 1% respectively.

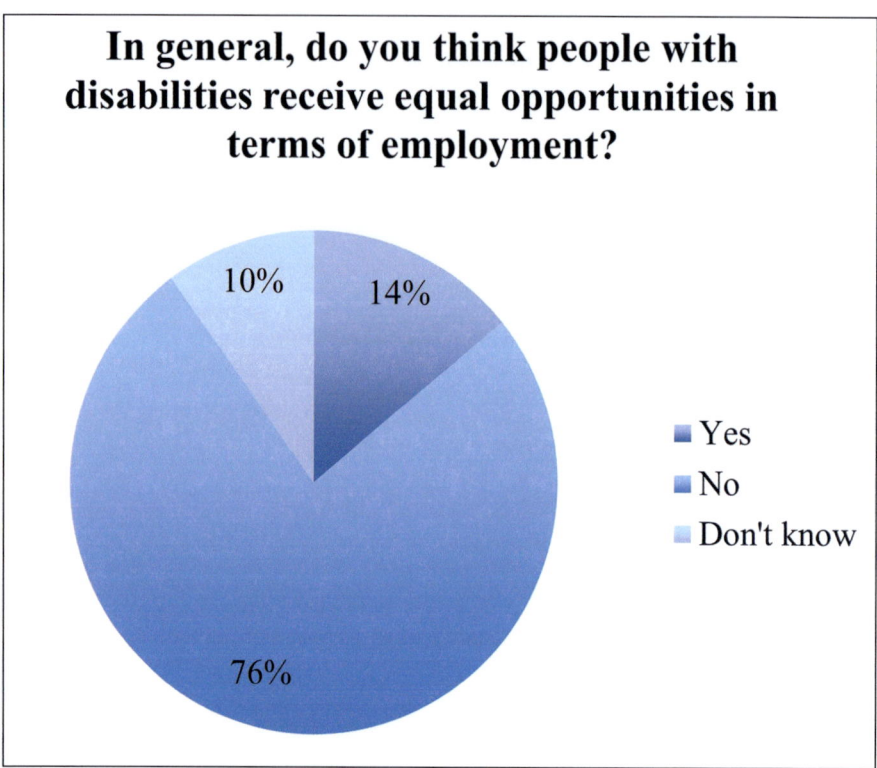

In general, do you think people with disabilities receive equal opportunities in terms of employment?

10% 14%

76%

- Yes
- No
- Don't know

Figure 10.7: Disability and equal opportunities in terms of employment
(For the descriptions, go to "Alternative text for images" page 221)

The results of the recent study revealed that 76% of the sample disagreed with the statement that disabled people can get equal opportunities for jobs, and 14% agreed that disabled people can get equal opportunities for jobs, and 10% did not have the any opinion in this regard.

Hamid Nasiri Dehsorkhi et al.

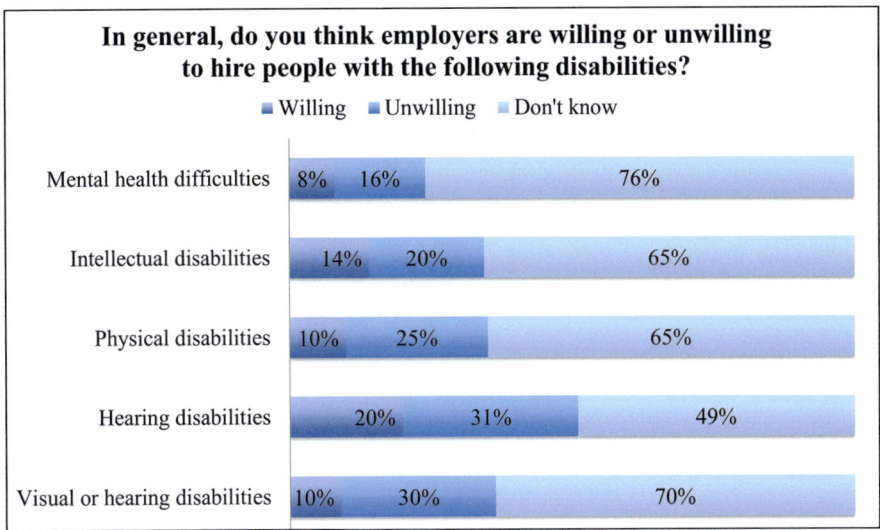

Figure 10.8: Willingness of employers to hire people with disabilities for different disability types
(For the descriptions, go to "Alternative text for images" page 221)

According to Figure 10.8, in most cases, employers do not have any idea about hiring disabled people. Considering visual and hearing disabled, 30% are not willing to hire them and only 10% agree. Considering physical problems, only 10% of the sample were inclined to hire people mental problems, 14% were inclined to hire people with psychological problems and 8% were inclined to employ people with mental problems.

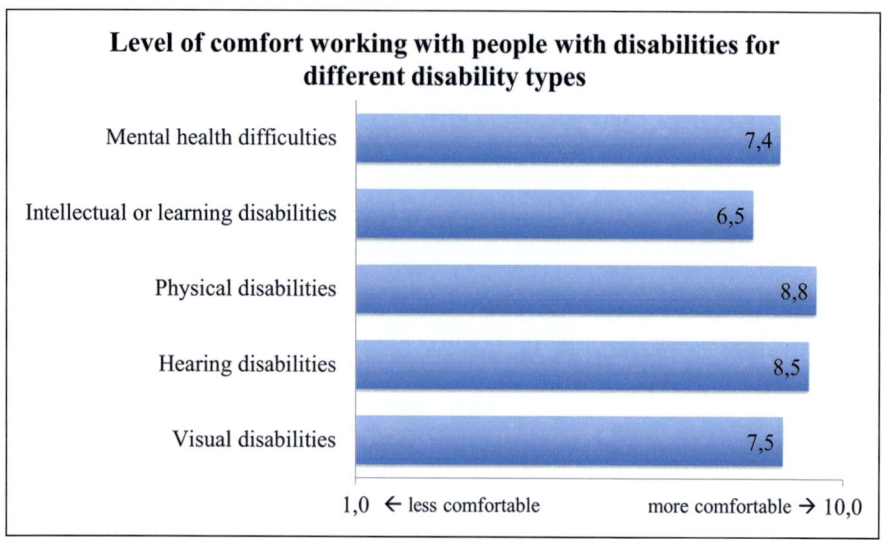

Figure 10.9: Level of comfort working with people with disabilities for different disability type
(For the descriptions, go to "Alternative text for images" page 222)

The results of the present study indicated that those who want to work with people with disabilities have the most preferences and ease of cooperation with a physical disability, 88% and hearing impairment, 85%, and the least preference and comfort was with mentally handicapped people, 65% and mental problems, 74%.

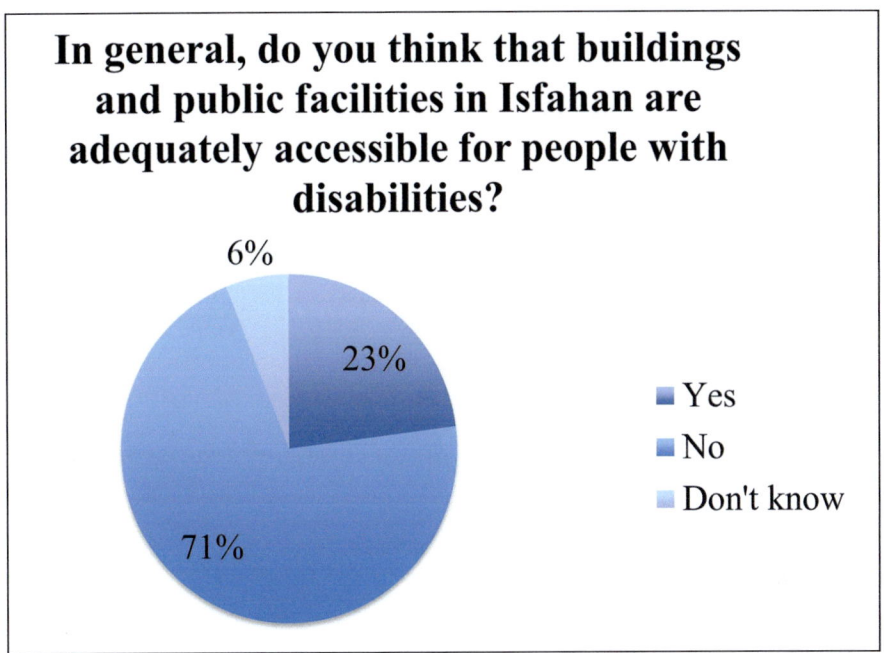

Figure 10.10: Accessibility of buildings and public facilities in Isfahan for people with disabilities
(For the descriptions, go to "Alternative text for images" page 222)

According to Figure 10.10 on adequate access to buildings and facilities, the results of Figure 10.11 reveal that 71 % of the respondents had negative opinions on this issue, and 23 % agreed on the appropriateness of buildings and facilities, and 6% of the sample had no information in this regard.

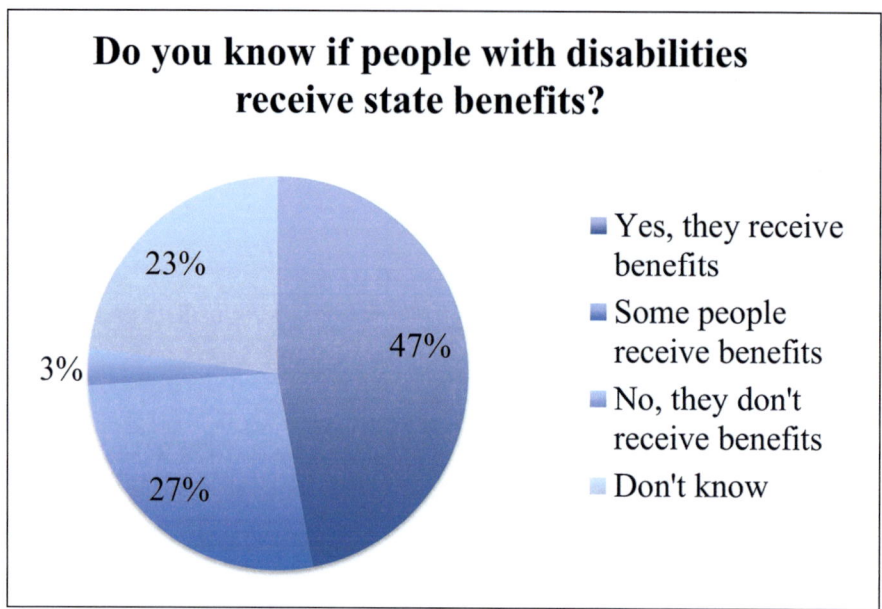

Figure 10.11: Knowledge of state benefits received by people with disabilities

(For the descriptions, go to "Alternative text for images" page 223)

According to Figure 10.11 on how to receive state benefits, 47% of the respondents believed the disabled receive aids and benefits, 23% believed that some of the disabled receive these services and 3% said they do not receive state benefits. 23% of the respondents had no information in this regard.

Discussion

According to the results of the present study, the disability from the view point of the present survey participants was mental, physical, visual, old age, hearing, and eventually addiction and AIDS, respectively. Therefore, it seems that the reason for these differences is to be considered in more accurate surveys on disability attitudes. According to Figure 10.2, the percentage differences in the sample, considering the difficulties and barriers of the community in relation to the disabled people, is due to the proportion of the previous results in the agree or disagree sections, and this is due to the lack of understanding of the disabled problems and difficulties.

Hamid Nasiri Dehsorkhi et al.

According to Figure 10.3, 33% of the sample believed that people with disabilities received free services, while 23% opposed it, and this response conflict might indicate a lack of understanding of the disabled difficulties.

Figure 10.4 significantly emphasizes that 59% of the sample do not believe in equal opportunities for the education of the disabled. On the other hand, the results significantly indicates the inclination of the sample to the inclusion of the disabled in education, while when a clearer question about inclusion in education was asked from the respondents in Figure 10.5 (whether they agree or not), the majority of respondents had no ideas about disorders, and this is again the case with employers and employment.

In general, it is necessary to increase the sample size and pay more attention and have a more realistic look at this issue in future studies.

References

1. Maurya, A. & Parasar, A. (2017). Attitudes toward Persons with Disabilities: A Relationship of Age, Gender, and Education of Students. International Journal of Indian Psychology, Vol. 4, (4), DIP:18.01.112/20170404, DOI:10.25215/0404.112

2. Grames, M. & Leverentz, C. (2010). Attitudes toward persons with Disabilities: A Comparison of Chinese and American Students. Journal of Undergraduate Research XIII.

3. Deal, M. (2006). Attitudes of Disabled People towards other Disabled People and Impairment Groups Doctoral Thesis, City University London (Health Care Research Unity, School of Nursing and Midwifery.

4. Olson, J. M., & Zanna, M. P. (1993). Attitudes and attitude change. Annual Review of Psychology, 44, 117-154.

5. Parashar, D., Chan, F., & Leierer, S. (2008). Factors influencing Asian Indian graduate students. Rehabilitation Counseling Bulletin, 51(4), 229-239.

6. Antonak, R. F., & Livneh, H. (1988). Measurement of attitudes towards persons with disabilities. Disability and Rehabilitation, 22, 211-224.

7. Cook, D. (1992). Psychological impact of disability. In R. M. Parker & E. M. Szymanski (Eds.), Rehabilitation counseling basics and beyond (249-272).

11 Feasibility of using mathematical and physical principles in evaluation the disabled-specific orthoses: A scientific report
(Mohammad Hossein Ebrahimi, Ali Mohammadi)

Introduction

Disabilities have become remarkable health problem causing an increasing cost to whether societies or families who are supposed to look after their patient. Surgical treatments are known as invasive and inclusive treatments aiming to treat the patients using instruments. Postsurgical consequences are generally difficult to overcome by the patients. Therefore, conservation treatment approaches are preferred to be used instead of invasive treatments. Amongst the disabilities-related treatments, the orthoses are well-known and are widely used in the clinical world. Disabled patients may use these orthoses for a long time to reduce either the incidence of their diseases or to control of the diseases progression. Although it is not quite convenient to wear those orthoses for long time, the benefits of orthoses compared to invasive treatments have been agreed by clinicians (1).

The amount of recovery achieved by orthoses is dependent on various factors including the orthoses type, the location of implementation, the time period of use and the severity of the disability incidences. Patients with different level of severities are likely to wear the same orthoses with the same treatment plan since there is no available method to distinguish the patients effectively without any interventions (2). Mathematical and Physical principles can provide us with that information which cannot be measured without intervention. The recovery achieved by the orthoses is measured after a period of time, while this recovery can be predicted via those approaches. This possibility of using these methods in prediction of the effectiveness of orthoses can be taken into account in designing the most proper patient-specific orthosis (2-4). Finite Element Analysis is wildly use to predict some variables like forces, stresses or deformations acting within a living tissue. These variables are difficult to measure unless we use some implants to measure (5-7).

Scoliosis is spinal curvature deformation causing musculoskeletal disabilities for the patients suffering from this disease. Surgical treatment is preferred to be performed if the orthoses are not effective enough in achieving spinal curvature correction (8). The orthoses are therefore the most common used treatment

Mohammad Hossein Ebrahimi & Ali Mohammadi

clinically. Various orthoses like Boston brace, Rosenberg and Miami have been used for those kind of patients suffering from degenerative scoliosis (9,10). Milwaukee is commonly used orthosis which works according to transverse loads applied on the ends of the scoliotic curves (11). The problem is referred to uncertainties of how to use the orthoses which is patient-specific. Clinically the physicians attempt to predict the amount of forces and their location based on their clinical experiences to gain the effective curvature correction needed. The physicians are convinced that this approach cannot be considered as an error-free treatment approach (12, 13).

Another example of those kind of orthoses is Scottish Rite orthoses which is used for Legg Calve Perthes Disease. When the blood supply of femoral head is disconnected with no reason, the cartilage and then the bone start to degenerate resulting in the joint flexion-extension and abduction-adduction angle alternation (2). That disease is mostly affecting the children between 5 to 10 years old and can cause irreversible severe disabilities for the children (14). The treatments aim to decrease the applied load on femoral head via putting the femur in some abduction-adduction angles. Although the effectiveness of these orthoses has been reported, the patients-specificity in choosing the rotational angles has not been studied extensively. Therefore, by the means of considering the patients-specificity in the orthoses used, we can train the disabled children to use their orthoses more effectively and more efficiently (3, 15).

In this scientific report we aim to assess two studies evaluated the effectiveness of orthoses through the mathematical or physical approaches.

Materials and Methods

Three main methods are used typically to estimate the biological factors acting within the living tissue. They can be employed either independently or combined together to have more realistic estimation.

1.   Motion capture system

The motion capture system consists of high speed cameras to track the patients motion, the faceplates to measure the ground reaction force and the reflecting markers to facilitate the motion tracking by the cameras. The patients musculoskeletal body can be modeled via scaling the defaults skeletal system by some factors. OpenSim is an open access musculoskeletal analysis software developed by the Stanford University. The inverse Kinematics is performed to calculate the joints angles and moments using the motion captured and the force measured by the devices. Then this kinematics data is exported to an optimization process to estimate the muscles and joints forces throughout the gait cycle.

2.   Three dimensional modeling of the body segments

Three dimensional model of the body segments can be produced using the patient-specific CT scans or MR images. The images are exported to Mimics software to do the segmentation of the region of interest. The material properties like the modulus of elasticity and the density can be estimated either by the gray values of the CT scans or by the literature values. Then this 3D body is ready for further analysis.

3.   Finite Element Analysis

Finite Element (FE) is a mathematical method which is able to estimate the stresses and the deformations while considering the applied force, boundary conditions and the material properties of the medium. The 3D model of the body segment created by Mimics based on CT and MR images is exported to Abaqus which is FE-based software. The material properties are assigned and the meshes are generated. The Abaqus software can give the stresses, strains and the deformations distribution in the medium that is necessary for further analysis of the living tissue segments.

Results and discussion

In this scientific report, we aimed to investigate the studies recently done, to evaluate the feasibility of using the mathematical methods in pre-surgery treatments like orthoses. In order to have a patient-specific body geometry and body motion some experiments need to be done beforehand.

In the first study, two children subjects suffering from the Musculoskeletal disease called LCPD were employed. The motions were captured using the motion capturing system and the analysis was performed. The Kinematic and the kinetics data show no significant changes in the applied forces on the hip joint. This means that the Scottish Rite Orthoses does not have direct effect on decreasing the applied force in those subjects. Additionally, it seems to be necessary to take the special needs of each patient into account for designing the patient-specific orthoses so that the orthoses are able to decrease those forces applied on the joints. In addition, when the hip joint is put in some degrees of abduction-addiction angles, the containment area of femoral head and the Acetabulum does not increase necessarily whereas the orthosis aims to increase the containment area. This is also another indicator of insufficient performance of those orthoses. Moreover, the stresses distributed in the femoral head does not indicate any increase or decrease while we are aiming to decrease the stresses on the femoral head so that the healing process can facilitate. All aforementioned reasons show low performance of Scottish Rite Orthoses is in disabled children (16).

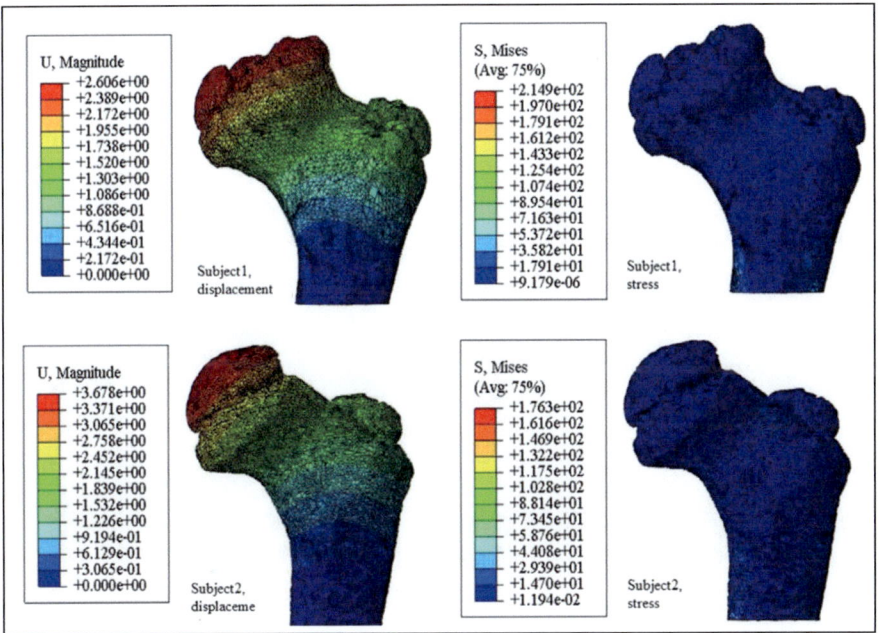

Figure 11.1: The stress distribution on the femoral head of the subjects with LCPD

(from Karimi et al. 2016)

(For the descriptions, go to "Alternative text for images" page 223)

In the second study, a degenerative scoliotic subject was assessed. The three dimensional model of the whole vertebrae column in addition to intervertebral discs were modeled using the patient's specific CT scans. Then the material properties were assigned. The three points Milwaukee orthosis was modeled as three set of distributed forces, on the two end sides and curvature and on the middle of curve. According to the clinical values, forces from 10 to 70 Newton were selected and curvature correction achieved using each forces were measured through finite element simulation. It was quantitatively observed that the most efficient correction is achieved through 70 Newton force. Although there are some limitations that can affect the reliability of this estimation, it seems to be feasible to predict the curvature correction through those kind of methods (17).

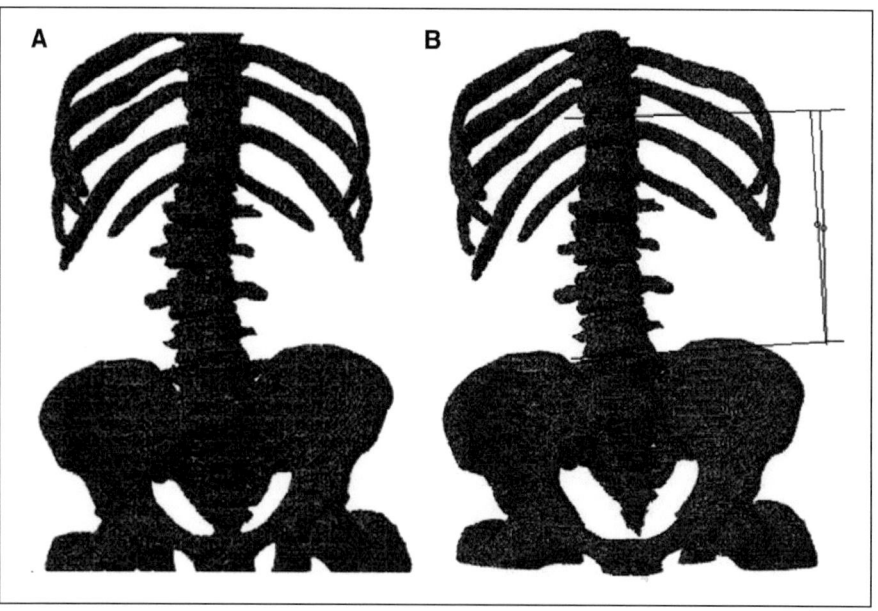

Figure 11.2: The curve correction obtained (a) without orthosis (b) with orthosis
(from Karimi et al. 2016)
(For the descriptions, go to "Alternative text for images" page 223)

Mohammad Hossein Ebrahimi & Ali Mohammadi

Conclusion

Conservative treatments are preferred due to having fewer consequences compared to surgical treatments. Orthoses are well-known conservative treatments used for variety of disabilities. The results of investigated studies show that the new engineering and mathematical methods are able to help physiotherapists and clinicians to evaluate the effectiveness of the orthoses in advance. Although there are variety of factors limiting the use of non-automated engineering methods in these disabled patients, it seems that it is feasible to have valuable estimations of how the orthoses can work on special patient with no interventions.

References

1) Brouwer, R.W., Jakma, T.S., Verhagen, A.P., Verhaar, J.A. and Bierma-Zeinstra, S.M., 2005. Braces and orthoses for treating osteoarthritis of the knee. *Cochrane Database Syst Rev, 1*(1).

2) Karimi, M.T. and McGarry, T., 2012. A comparison of the effectiveness of surgical and nonsurgical treatment of legg-calve-perthes disease: a review of the literature. *Advances in orthopedics, 2012.*

3) Martinez, A.G., Weinstein, S.L. and Dietz, F.R., 1992. The weight-bearing abduction brace for the treatment of Legg-Perthes disease. *JBJS, 74*(1), pp.12-21.

4) Meehan, P.L., Angel, D. and Nelson, J.M., 1992. The Scottish Rite abduction orthosis for the treatment of Legg-Perthes disease. A radiographic analysis. *JBJS, 74*(1), pp.2-12.

5) Chen, W.P., Ju, C.W. and Tang, F.T., 2003. Effects of total contact insoles on the plantar stress redistribution: a finite element analysis. *Clinical Biomechanics, 18*(6), pp.S17-S24.

6) Cheung, J.T.M. and Zhang, M., 2008. Parametric design of pressure-relieving foot orthosis using statistics-based finite element method. *Medical engineering & physics, 30*(3), pp.269-277.

7) Syngellakis, S., Arnold, M.A. and Rassoulian, H., 2000. Assessment of the non-linear behaviour of plastic ankle foot orthoses by the finite element method. *Proceedings of the Institution of Mechanical Engineers, Part H: Journal of Engineering in Medicine, 214*(5), pp.527-539.

8) Merola, A.A., Haher, T.R., Brkaric, M., Panagopoulos, G., Mathur, S., Kohani, O., Lowe, T.G., Lenke, L.G., Wenger, D.R., Newton, P.O. and Clements III, D.H., 2002. A multi-center study of the outcomes of the surgical treatment of adolescent idiopathic

scoliosis using the Scoliosis Research Society (SRS) outcome instrument. Spine, 27(18), pp.2046-2051.

9)   Aulisa, A.G., Mastantuoni, G., Laineri, M., Falciglia, F., Giordano, M., Marzetti, E. and Guzzanti, V., 2012. Brace technology thematic series: the progressive action short brace (PASB). Scoliosis, 7(1), p. 6.

10) Grivas, T.B., Rodopoulos, G.I. and Bardakos, N.V., 2008. Night-time braces for treatment of adolescent idiopathic scoliosis. Disability and Rehabilitation: Assistive Technology, 3(3), pp.120-129.

11) Blount, W.P., Schmidt, A.C., Keever, E.D. and Leonard, E.T., 1958. The Milwaukee brace in the operative treatment of scoliosis. JBJS, 40(3), pp.511-525.

12) Zaborowska-Sapeta, K., Kowalski, I.M., Kotwicki, T., Protasiewicz-Fałdowska, H. and Kiebzak, W., 2011. Effectiveness of Cheneau brace treatment for idiopathic scoliosis: prospective study in 79 patients followed to skeletal maturity. Scoliosis, 6(1), p.2.

13) Weiss, H.R., Werkmann, M. and Stephan, C., 2007. Correction effects of the ScoliOlog-iC®„Chêneau light" brace in patients with scoliosis. Scoliosis, 2(1), p.2.

14) Wynne-Davies, R. and Gormley, J., 1978. The aetiology of Perthes' disease. Genetic, epidemiological and growth factors in 310 Edinburgh and Glasgow patients. Bone & Joint Journal, 60(1), pp.6-14.

15) Curtis, B.H., Gunther, S.F., Gossling, H.R. and Paul, S.W., 1974. Treatment for Legg-Perthes disease with the Newington ambulation-abduction brace. JBJS, 56(6), pp.1135-1146.

16) Karimi, M.T., Mohammadi, A., Ebrahimi, M.H. and McGarry, A., 2017. Evaluation of the magnitude of hip joint deformation in subjects with avascular necrosis of the hip joint during walking with and without Scottish Rite orthosis. Medical engineering & physics, 40, pp.110-116.

17) Karimi, M.T., Ebrahimi, M.H., Mohammadi, A. and McGarry, A., 2017. Evaluation of the influences of various force magnitudes and configurations on scoliotic curve correction using finite element analysis. Australasian physical & engineering sciences in medicine, 40(1), pp.231-236.

IV Experiences and Research: Hamburg

12 Accessibility to Education and Therapy for Juvenile Refugees with Disabilities in Hamburg

(Frauke Meyer)

In Transition from Secondary School to Vocational Education and Training (VET) in Hamburg

In Germany compulsory education is for all juveniles up to the age of 18, regardless their dis*abilities, nationalities, ethnicities, religions, resident or marital status.[1] For that reason, secondary school leavers under the age of 18 have to continue their education either at high school or in vocational education and training system (VET). VET is in Germany traditionally separated in two strands:

1. Fulltime VET at vocational training schools (e.g. some care professions, chemical and pharmaceutic assistants, housekeeping)
2. VET in dual system, i.e. training on the job in a company on the labour market and vocational education at vocational school

VET in dual system is the most prominent way to get vocational education and to access the labour market.

Scholars in fulltime VET need to find a convenient school place after secondary school, whereas the future vocational trainees in dual system must find a company willing to employ them. While fulltime VET at vocational schools demands

---

[1] Some years ago, compulsory education was not foreseen in every Federal State. Even today different regulations concerning refugee's start of school exist in the Federal States (e.g. in Hamburg, Bremen, Berlin, Schleswig- Holstein and Saarland refugees start school immediately after arriving, whereas they start in Bavaria and Thuringia after three and in Baden-Wurtemberg only after six month in Germany.

---

at least a lower, but in general a higher secondary school diploma[2], access to VET in dual system is in theory possible without any school diploma. But in fact, companies are looking for their future employees when offering vocational training. Because of changes in production, work places where less qualified persons traditionally worked were reduced or require higher technical skills. Furthermore, personal and social skills became more importance due to the implementation of teamwork. Therefore, most branches prefer nowadays well educated juveniles with high social and personal skills, i.e. they mainly choose trainees with good results in higher secondary diploma or with high school graduation. Only a few branches, mainly handicrafts, accept trainees with good results in lower secondary school diploma. Secondary school leavers with bad results in diploma, without any diploma or with personal and/ or social problems rarely find a school or a training place in VET. For that reason, all Federal States of Germany invented different educational programs or actions aiming to manage the transition from secondary school to VET, to broaden personal and social skills as well as to offer the possibility to pass secondary school exam or to improve existent diploma. Vocational preparation classes are one of these educational programs for minor school leavers in transition from secondary school to VET.

While education falls under the sovereignty of the Federal States (Bundesländer), 16 more or less different transition systems with different vocational preparation programs exist in Germany. In the following I focus the transition system of the City and Federal State of Hamburg, especially the vocational preparation classes for dis*abled juveniles with(out) flight experiences.

---

[2] The German education system select traditionally after the fourth grade into three different secondary school levels: 1) Hauptschule ("main school"), 2) Real- or Mittelschule ("Middle School"), 3) Gymnasium (High School). Nowadays, most of the Federal States put Haupt- and Realschule together to one secondary school offering the former diploma on the level of Haupt- and Realschule. For example, the Stadtteilschule (quarter or community school) replaces the former Haupt- and Realschule. Scholars can reach the Erster allgemeinbildender Schulabschluss (ESA; first secondary school diploma) which is on a lower level or the Mittlerer allgemeinbildender Schulabschluss (MSA; middle secondary school diploma) which is on a middle level.

Frauke Meyer

Hamburg reformed its transition system in 2012 due to PISA[3] results and established all-day-schooling in dual system for preparatory classes. These classes offer two or three days training per week directly in a company on the labour market and three or two days education at school. The aim is to give scholars a realistic insight of different professions and work in companies, but also contacts to potential vocational training places and new learning experiences. Furthermore, work practice oriented education should be offered as well as skills requested for a vocational training should be developed. Lessons should meet the needs of every pupil. Therefore, teachers have to provide different approaches to certain content and to include different learning levels. The scholars themselves have to take responsibility for their own learning processes and their success, so teacher's tasks include coaching single learning steps or processes and considering pupils how to reach their objectives.

After one year in vocational preparatory class the juvenile should build up a perspective regarding his/her future, concrete: s*he should find a vocational training place, a job, a high school or another preparation for vocational training.[4] If scholars find a vocational training place in dual system or a place in an educative action for vocational preparation during the running school year they can leave preparatory classes. Scholars complete preparatory classes with a certificate of the vocational preparation school.[5] Besides, scholars with corresponding results have the possibility to pass secondary school exam on the two different

---

[3] Program to International Student Assessment (PISA). Germany got since the beginning of PISA comparate [*das Wort gibt es im Englischen, meine ich, nicht wirklich*] to other European States bad results concerning the reading, orthografic and scientific outputs of primary and secondary scholars. PISA pointed out that these results mainly emerge due to the high selectivity of the German education system and that selection functions via ethnicity and class. Even if this has been described by critical educational researchers, the German Federal States only started reforms of their educational systems after getting the international PISA ranking.

[4] Different actions are offered and financed by the German State (e.g. BvB: Berufsvorbereitende Bildungsmaßnahmen/ Educative Actions for Vocational Preparation; EQ: Einstiegsqualifizierung/ Start Qualification) or by the Free and Hanseatic City of Hamburg (QuAs: Qualifizierung und Arbeit für Schulabgänger/ Qualification and Work for School Leavers)

[5] The certificate has almost no value on the labour market.

---

levels existing in Germany: First school diploma (low level)[6] and middle school diploma (middle level) (HIBB o.J. a). Even if the School Authority of Hamburg announces that every scholar leaves preparatory classes with a certificate (HIBB o.J. a), we have to take into account that the certificate of vocational preparation school has almost no value on the labour market and that the lower secondary school diploma is less valuable, too. Scholars often start in vocational preparatory classes of what different researchers called "in-transition carrier": they go across different preparation programs or actions and end up without vocational training or workplace. If Hamburg's reformed preparatory classes will break down that effect has still to be seen, but project managers counselling school leavers tend to suppose in a first evaluation of preparatory classes in dual system that 50% instead of the former 9-15% of juveniles in transition get into regular vocational training and labour market after following a one year preparatory class (Gehrke 2017: 168). But Gehrke notes on the basis of qualitative interviews she did with juveniles that such a success does not automatically mean quality and sustainability of the transition (ibid.). Whereas some of the interviewed juveniles felt pushed by the counselling managers or pedagogues to VET's they didn't like or want, others are still struggling with their bad living and/ or health conditions, so that cancellations of VET are quite probably. In addition, 50% of juvenile school leavers rest in transition system after one year, so that we may assume that many barriers to VET or labour market still exist after reforming the transition system in Hamburg. But the transition system itself contributes to separation and exclusion, even if inclusion aimed to be developed in transition and VET since 2009.

Vulnerable juveniles like young refugees with disabilities question strongly accessibility and inclusion of Hamburg's transition system, because of their special needs, learning presumptions and living conditions.

---

[6]   Work or a vocational training place is hard to find with a secondary school diploma on a lower level. The diploma leads often to vocational training in handicrafts (e.g. baker, plumber, and mason) or to services like sales assistant, housekeeping, care assistant.

Frauke Meyer

Juvenile Refugees with Disabilities in Preparatory Classes for Vocational Training in Hamburg

Even if the State Parliament of Hamburg decided in 2009 to guaranty inclusive education in order to fulfil the UN-Convention on the Rights of Persons with Disabilities, most of the scholars with disabilities are still educated in special schools.[7] These concerns also VET. In theory, all VET including preparatory classes are open for juveniles with disabilities. If needed, scholars with disabilities may order school and/ or work assistance. They also have the right to extend their learning period in order to avoid disadvantages (vgl. HIBB o.J. b).

Single inclusive vocational preparatory classes are established since 2014 at 15 of the 32 vocational schools in Hamburg in the framework of an ESF-founded pilot project (HIBB o.J. c) So it can be stated that inclusive preparatory classes are not yet regular, even if scholars with disabilities have the right to enter every class.[8] The same is true for VET, which should be inclusive, but in fact, secondary school leavers with disabilities rarely find a company providing them a vocational training in dual system. Access to fulltime VET may seem easier for persons with disabilities, but VET scholars with disabilities in regular programs are rare as well. Only three vocational schools offer fulltime running preparatory classes for juveniles with mental or physic disabilities, one vocational school is specialised on juveniles with special educational needs and/or psychic disabilities and another focuses blind and visually impaired juveniles (HIBB o.J. d). Complementary, social institutions for persons with disabilities held sheltered workshops and different programs for integration into the labour market.

Other special preparatory classes focus juvenile migrants and refugees. Migrants and Refugees entering Germany in an age between 16 to 18 years are in general sent directly to transition system, despite of their own educational or work

---

[7] That results from lacks in financial and human resources, but also from barriers concerning the accessibility of schools and rooms (most schools don't have ramps or lifts, bathrooms, recreation rooms or playgrounds accessible for scholars with disabilities) and from missing special equipment as well as therapeutic rooms for certain needs.

[8] It should be noted that some severe disabilities do not allow learning and education in a common sense, so that education and learning means rather care. Also teachers who are able to offer inclusive education in VET schools are still rare.

---

projects, their knowledge, competences or interests. This clearly shows the selective German school system. It also shows the continuing separation of migrants and refugees from "German" scholars as well as the de facto continuing separation between disabled and abled scholars.

Preparatory classes for migrants[9] run two years in dual system, because of the need to learn German. Juveniles who are illiterate or only alphabetized in non-Latin languages first enter to one-year running alphabetisation classes and then reach the two-year preparatory classes for migrants. While most schools separate refugees from learners in one-year preparatory classes, a few schools tried out to educate young migrants, e.g. refugees in their second year and scholars in one-year preparatory class together. If these schools had inclusive preparatory classes, they included also juveniles with disabilities. However, what is about young refugees with disabilities in that separated transition system?

Until recently, refugees with disabilities were not focussed in transition system. Now, a pilot project addressing vocational training schools where juvenile migrants with special educational needs and/ or disabilities (ESF Hamburg 2017) are educated in preparatory classes for migrants, started. The project aims to assure that disabilities and special educational needs are recognized by the teachers, adequate support is given to the scholar and disadvantages are compensated. Besides, the project offers coaching and qualification for teachers (ibid.).

The aim to assure that disabilities and special educational needs are recognized may be irritating at a first glance. Is it not a teacher's professional responsibility to observe briefly his/ her scholars capacities, learning approaches and behaviour, to question his/ her learning and living conditions and meet his/ her needs? Indeed, it is, but most of the teachers in preparatory classes are not well experienced with special education, needs of scholars with disabilities, needs and/ or living conditions of juvenile refugees. VET teachers are generally qualified in subjects related to a certain profession. Therefore, they rarely know how to diagnose special educational needs or disabilities and how to support scholars with special needs. The same can be stated for their knowledge in how to teach the different subjects (e.g. mathematics, preparation to an internship) to scholars

---

[9] The term „migrant" means here all persons entering Germany from a foreign country, including refugees.

Frauke Meyer

who are just starting to learn German as a second language. VET schools hired quickly German as second language lectures in autumn 2015 due to the arrival of about 2000 young refugees. Nevertheless, these lecturers are mostly not qualified in special needs education as well. Work-related subjects are often not their specialisation, too. The few special educational teachers at VET schools are not always qualified in German as a second language and they are rarely trained to be sensitive to migration and flight. Overall, obligatory courses in VET teacher's (further) education are missing in the four intersectional fields – pedagogics of flight and migration, didactic of German as second language, special education and diagnostic under flight circumstances. That lack in teachers (further) education leads – as the following examples will show – to ignorance of refugee's special needs or disabilities, but also to miss-diagnostics of learning impairments and mental disabilities. Insofar, the pilot project Inclusive Preparatory Classes for Migrants (ESF Hamburg 2017) does well with the aim to assure that special needs and disabilities are recognised.

During my cooperation with teachers of vocational training schools in the framework of a project where we are developing educational material for juvenile refugees in preparatory classes I experienced several times, that teachers notice some impairments only after some month in class (e.g. because of their observation that someone takes regularly medicaments, is motoric conspicuous, is often subject to mood swings or often complains about stomach ache or headache. Sometimes, teachers do not realise impairments at all even though these impairments are obvious. One of the scholars in a preparatory class could hardly walk because of a malposition of his legs. He needed walking aids urgently. But his teacher realized that need only after six month in class, because that scholar was always sitting and stayed during recreation usually in the classroom.

If teachers notice disabilities or impairments in preparatory classes for migrants, it is not always clear for them to whom they may address in order to assure that the scholar will get the needed aids or therapies: should they address the social workers in refugee domiciles, the social workers or psychologists at school (if existent) or should they act by themselves? To solve that kind of problem a good interdisciplinary cooperation between teachers, social workers and psychologists in and outside of school is necessary.

On the contrary, it also happens due to the lack of flight and migration sensi-tive teacher's training that impairments of learning and/ or speech or even mental and psychic diseases are diagnosed too quickly. Scientific papers refer thereon since decades (Thielen 2011, Bednarz-Braun/ Heß-Meining 2004). I noticed that kind of rapid diagnostics also during my work with teachers in AvM-classes: Teachers and directory staff of different schools told me that refugee's learning preconditions remember to scholars with severe learning impairments or mental disabilities. Upon request they explained that scholars with flight experiences would be quickly unfocused, would not react to the subject matters in a conven-ient way and would promptly forget all they learned the next day.

Those "symptoms" refer on the one hand to the linguistic situation: learning in a second language is really exhausting. Especially beginners get quickly tired because they are not yet able to filter or understand audible information without giving much thought. What beginners do is to translate (almost) every word, in order to become able to give sense to a sentence. They are not yet able to antici-pate the sense of longer sentences as more proficient speakers of a language will do. On the other hand, the above mentioned "symptoms" refer to the difficult living conditions of juvenile refugees in Germany. Many of these juveniles are permanently stressed and stress is in general not beneficial for learning as neu-roscientific reports point out since a long time (Schwabe et al. 2011). Stress can result out of the following:

- Uncertainty during asylum procedure and due to suspension of deporta-tion ("Duldung"): May I stay in Germany?
- Experience of deportations in asylum domiciles
- Living in a shared or youth residence (no or almost no private sphere, inexist-ent room for learning, high noise level, nocturnal disturbance, sleep deficit)
- Living without parents, brothers and sisters, friends
- Anxiety and/ or care for relatives (in Germany and in the home country), eventually grief over the loss of relatives and/ or friends
- Management of all-day-living besides of school, concretely:
  - Administration work and several dates in different authorities (im-migration authority, social authority, employment office, job centre, school authority)

- Organisation of health/ care/ medical or therapeutic aids (more administration work and dates in authorities)
- Preparation for school (but: sleep deficit due to high noise level and shared rooms in asylum domiciles, feelings of sorrow, grief, anxiety)
- Precarious financial situation (refugees only get a „pocket money" in the first 15 months after arrival, then they touch social benefits; AsylbwLG; SGB II or X); need to earn money (reimbursement of flight expenses, financial support for relatives in transit- or home countries), but no working permit and for minors necessity to visit school
- Building up one's own future (but: would that future be in Germany?)
- Domestic work (shopping, cooking, doing laundry)
- Spending leisure time (but how to come along with a small budget?)
- Living adolescence and transition phases due to adolescence without parental or familiar support and guidance

Effective and focused learning under such conditions is for most of the juvenile refugees not possible. Forgetfulness, poor concentration and supposed disinterest as well as high absenteeism result from living conditions of juvenile refugees. In 2003, a juvenile refugee said in an interview: "You cannot learn with such a problem" (Schroeder 2003, p. 237) and meant at that time especially the legal situation, under which persons with a suspension of deportation (Duldung) had no access to the labour market. The legal situation changed, but the uncertainty if one can stay in Germany, the precarious financial situation, the difficult housing situation and the associated psychic loads remained.

Educational staff which is not aware about these living conditions tend quickly to misinterpretations concerning he recognised needs, competences, knowledge, the will to learn (German or any other subject at school), to integrate, to start a VET or to find a job.

If VET schools have up to three different educational experts in preparatory classes – VET teacher, German as second language teacher and special educational teacher – and sometimes additionally also school social workers, school and/ or work assistants and school psychologists, one may suppose that the different professions could give each other collegial advice or build up educational teams in order to close their eventually professional lacks. But even though preparatory classes for migrants started in dual system in February 2016, neither an interdisciplinary pedagogical concept nor an official educational plan describing objectives and fixing obligatory contents exists. Department heads at different VET schools told me that due to organisational and financial reasons as well as to staff shortage, they can rarely realise team teaching. Another factor is that VET teachers are often not trained to work in teams, so that department heads willing to establish team teaching have sometimes to deal with doubts, fears and resistance of their colleagues.

Thus, juvenile refugees and migrants with or without disabilities in vocational preparatory class are for instance more or less educated upon the ideas of each teacher, school or educational team. Another quite unclear point is how the interlocking between training in a company and education at school functions. The official concept of preparatory classes for migrants provides that German lessons at school should be interlocked with work-based language needs in the concrete company of each scholar (HIBB 2015). Therefore, instruction of work-based German is foreseen during practical training. Unfortunately, training for in-company instructors where they can develop professional skills concerning language learning on the work-place is not obligatory. The scholars are supervised during their training periods in companies by vocational teachers or educational assistants who should give individual support. Teachers and educational assistants may be able to train German on the job, but as I pointed out above, most of the vocational teachers are not experts in German as second language. Furthermore, neither teachers nor educational assistants have enough time to manage supervision *and* teaching German on the job. They only get one hour per week per scholar for both tasks. Therefore, we can suppose that German on the job is not systematically and regularly taught. As an evaluation of preparatory classes for migrants is still outstanding, the question how the interlocking of German on the job and German lessons at school works cannot be answered.

Refugees with special needs or disabilities have the right to a work assistant during their internships (HIBB o.J. c). Work assistance for persons with disabilities is well established in Hamburg since 1992. It is doubtful, however, if work assistants are well prepared to assist young refugees, i.e. beginners in German as second language and in often very precarious living conditions with all the impacts that may have on learning and working during an internship. If work assistants train persons with disabilities for example to apply for new tasks after finishing the just given task they have to be aware that it could be necessary to train also *how* the person can apply and what can be the supposed answer.

Refugee's access to diagnostics, therapeutic and medical aids
Refugee's health screenings, which are obligatory done just after arrival in Germany disabilities, notably those that are not immediately discernible, are not recorded systematically. This is particular true for mental and psychic impairments (Metzner et al. 2016, p. 642). Diagnostic instruments in refugee's languages or in German as second language are rare and less developed (Metzner et al. 201: 648). An equivalent diagnostic, therapeutic and/ or pedagogical work is hard to realise under these circumstances.

Special learning material is as well not always adapted for scholars starting to learn German as second language. For example, learning material for blind and visually impaired German as second language learners has been developed or adapted punctually by certain institutions for blind persons (e.g. SFZ Chemnitz o.J.), but is not widely spread. The same is true for young refugees with other sensitive disabilities or mental impairments.

Refugees needing therapeutic and/ or medical aids have to deal with different barriers. A first and very hard barrier is adult refugee's exclusion from full medical and social services in the first 15 months after arriving in Germany. Only those with acute symptoms of illness or ache have the right to medical care and treatments (§ 4 sentence 1 AsylbwLG). This also includes psychiatric medical treatments, but not psychotherapy. However, all refugees may receive therapy, tools, care and services to participate in daily-life, if such a support is necessary to secure livelihood and health (§ 6 AsylbLG). However, office staff in social authorities, not medicines or therapists, will finally decide if such a necessity is given.

§ 6 AsylbwLG regulates inter alia the rights of vulnerable refugee groups, among them minor refugees. Minors have the right to every medical or therapeutic treatment from the very first day of their stay in Germany. Nevertheless, social authorities in Hamburg refused regularly to overtake the costs for minor

---

refugee's psychotherapy arguing that a psychiatric-medical treatment would be sufficient until they get access to full medical and social services in the 16ᵗʰ month after their arrival in Germany (PtK Hamburg 2016). Only in duly substantiated cases, minor refugees got access to short-term psychotherapies with a maximum of 25 meetings in their first 15 months in Germany (KVHH 2015). The German Government clarified in July 2016 that permits of psychotherapy and psychosocial aid for refugees do not fall under the social authorities' discretion. The authorities are urged to permit at least the costs for short-term therapy, i.e. up to 25 meetings (Deutscher Bundestag 2016, p. 3). Thereby (not only) minor refugees get officially a better access to short-term psychotherapy. But in its report on treatment of refugee's post-traumatic stress disorders the scientific service of German Government still points out that the question if psychotherapy is essential for secure health during the first 15 months after arrival is seen very controversial (Deutscher Bundestag Wissenschaftliche Dienste 2017, p. 38). Only persons with a residence permit according to § 24 AuslG (temporary protection) have the irrevocable right to psychotherapies in the first 15 months (ibid., p. 39). It can be supposed that refugees still have the mentioned difficulties to access medical and (psycho-) therapeutic aid in the first 15 months (see also BPtK 2017).

From the 16ᵗʰ month after arrival all refugees regardless their resident status have access to full medical and therapeutic treatment (§ 2 AsylbwLG). But barriers are not fully broken down. While some barriers appear due to legal lacks and monolingual-monocultural orientation of many medicines and therapists in Germany, others results from discretion of social authorities and their bureaucratic work processes.

If minor refugees with psychic problems finally get financed a psychotherapy they are confronted with the fact, that very few therapists in Germany have knowledge of languages spoken by refugees. Therapists as well as clients rely on psychological trained professional interpreters. However, those interpreters are rare and in general, they are not employed in psychotherapeutic centers, clinics or surgeries. For that reason, refugees depend on the decision of reimbursing interpreter's costs by social authorities. Refugees who speak almost well German also depend on that decision, because emotional situations can often be easier and better described in mother tongue than in a foreign language. A binding rule for interpreter's reimbursing in psychotherapy with multilingual clients does not exist and a foreseen passage in the so-called Integration-law has been cancelled (BPtK 2016, p. 8). Therefore, minor refugees are depending on the discretion of social authorities. These refer in cases of refusal to the German Social Law (Sozialgesetzbuch, SGB) where German is mentioned as the only official language and argue that persons receiving social benefits – as refugees do from the 16th months after arrival – should be proficient in German, because if not, they won't be able to apply for social benefits. Ergo, they should be able to do psychotherapy in German (Metzner et al. 2016, p. 647). If the social authorities refuse interpreters, therapy cannot be carried out.

Even if minors have better chances compared to adults to get reimbursed interpreter's costs (ibid. p. 648), therapists or psychotherapeutic clinics cannot be sure that the costs are really reimbursed. That uncertainty in connection with the additional bureaucratic work for applying for refugee's therapy and interpreters is one of the reasons why youth psychotherapeutic clinics refuse long-term hospital admittance of young refugees (Mogk 2015, p.21). Clinic staff as well as registered therapists is doing additional work already during diagnostics: the existent instruments are not adapted to juveniles without or with poor German knowledge. Subsequently, staff needs to invent creativity, in order to adapt the needed instruments ad hoc. Therefore, more time for diagnostics is needed, but also knowledge in multi-linguistic or foreign language and culture sensitive diagnostics (Metzner et al. 2016, p. 648). The latter is as just mentioned seldom. Sometimes these lacks of knowledge unsettle therapists, for instance regarding the success of an interpreted psychotherapy or the possibility to integrate juvenile refugees into group therapy sessions in youth psychiatric hospitals (Mogk 2015, p. 24).

(Minor) Refugees have not only difficulties to obtain needed psychotherapeutic aid and/ or the needed interpreters, but also very obviously needed aids due to their disabilities or chronical illness. Different institutions for persons with disabilities from Berlin documented in 2014 under the title "(No) future. Minor refugees with disabilities – Human rights violation in Berlin" several cases where authorities refused medical beds, convenient wheel chairs or therapeutic inlays to young refugees with an unsecure resident permit. Family members of young refugees with disabilities and their supports even had to struggle for hygiene articles like diapers. Sometimes authorities appropriated finally the applied aids, but with such a delay that the child or juvenile had just grown out (Global Village e.V. et al. 2014). Persons with disabilities who do not know well the German bureaucratic system and their rights get quickly lost in between different authorities, paperwork and incomprehensible refusals if they do not get professional support or advice.

Required Changes
Cities like Hamburg have a good infrastructure concerning information centers for refugees as well as for persons with disabilities, but both strands worked in most German cities until 2016 more or less independently. For that reason, expertise in counselling and including refugees with disabilities to education and labour market is not really poor in Hamburg, but expertise of both strands – refugee's counselling on the one hand and advice for persons with disabilities on the other hand – need to be interlocked and put together. Even if in the last two years several projects advising and teaching refugees with disabilities have been developed in Hamburg (e.g. the project ZuFlucht of the Lebenshilfe Hamburg; see: *https://zf.lhhh.de/*) as well as a guidebook for counselling refugees with disabilities (passage gGmbH 2017), lots of outstanding exist, for example the adaptation of educational and diagnostic material for German as second learners with different impairments. But also accessibility to counselling centers for refugees, classrooms and refugee's housing has to be assured.

Apart from this, training and further education programs for medical, therapeutic and educational staff should develop flight and migration sensitiveness for the different professions. For example, psychotherapists should be trained on working with professional interpreters and to deal with multilingual situations during therapy. Medicines, therapist and educational staff should learn how to recognize flight specific psychic impairments. Medicines doing the health screening after refugee's arrival should be sensitive for disabilities, impairments and chronicle illness and should know to whom refugees with disabilities should address.

The different educational staff in schools should not only be trained to recognize disabilities and psychic impairments, but also in adapting or developing diagnostic and educational material which meets the intellectual, mental, physic and psychic needs of each scholar. Cooperation, collegial advice and exchange between different institutions and professions need to be broadened. Imaginable

Frauke Meyer

are round table, but also trainings and further education addressing the different professions. The separation between counselling institutions for persons with disabilities on the one and institutions for refugees on the other hand should terminate and inclusive institutions providing advice and support should be build up. It is absolutely necessary that experts from both strands work in those institutions together.

Finally yet importantly, it is quite necessary to break down the legal barriers. Refugees need regardless their recent or future resident permit access to medical and therapeutic aid from their first day in Germany. Therefore, the regular health screenings of refugees should include diagnostics of mental, psychic, physic, motoric and sensitive impairments. This would help to offer quickly the needed help and to implement convenient education.

Until law does not change, the German State Governments should give at least instruction to their employees in social authorities to appropriate medical and therapeutic aid if that need has been diagnosed by therapists or medicines.

References

Bednarz-Braun, I., Heß-Meining, U. (2004). Migration, Ethnie und Geschlecht. Theorieansätze – Forschungsstand – Forschungsperspektiven. Schriften des Deutschen Jugendinstituts, Wiesbaden: VS.

Berlin Global Village e.V., MenschenKind, Lebenshilfe Berlin, HVD Berlin-Brandenburg (2014): (K)eine Zukunft. Flüchtlingskinder mit Behinderungen. Menschenrechtsverletzungen in Berlin, zuletzt geprüft am 25.10.2017.

Brune, M., & Fischer-Ortmann, J. (2014). Erfahrung mit Trauma. In M. Gag & F. Voges (Hrsg), Inklusion auf Raten. Zur Teilhabe von Flüchtlingen an Ausbildung und Arbeit, (S. 205-218). Münster: Waxmann.

Bundespsychotherapeutenkammer (BPtK) (2016). Entwurf eines Integrationsgesetzes. Bundestagsdrucksache 18/1615, Stellungnahme Bundespsychotherapeutenkammer vom 01. Juli 2016. *http://www.bptk.de/uploads/media/20160714_2016-07-01_STN_BPtK_Integrationsgesetz.pdf*. Zugegriffen: 22. Juli 2016.

Bürgerschaft der Freien und Hansestadt Hamburg, Drucksache 21/3203 vom 08.03.2016, Inklusion von Flüchtlingen: Können Flüchtlinge mit Behinderung(en) inklusiv am Leben in den ZEA und Folgeunterkünften in Hamburg teilnehmen?

Bürgerschaft der Freien und Hansestadt Hamburg, Drucksache 21/7872 vom 07.02.2017, Stellungnahme des Senats zu dem Ersuchen der Bürgerschaft vom 11. November 2015 „Schulabschluss und Ausbildungsvorbereitung für jugendliche Flüchtlinge". In: URL: *https://hibb.hamburg.de/wp-content/uploads/sites/33/2015/10/21-7872.pdf (30.10.2017)*

Deutscher Bundestag (2016). Verbesserungen der gesundheitlichen und psychosozialen Versorgung von Geflüchteten zur Umsetzung der EU-Aufnahmerichtlinie. Schriftliche kleine Anfrage und Antwort der Bundesregierung. (Vorabfassung vom 04. Juli 2016). *http://dipbt.bundestag.de/doc/btd/18/090/1809009.pdf*. Zugegriffen: 30.10.2017.

Deutscher Bundestag Wissenschaftliche Dienste (2017). Psychotherapeuten – Behandlung von Traumafolgestörungen. Insbesondere Fortbildung, Kostenübernahme bei der Behandlung von Flüchtlingen sowie Versorgung, zuletzt geprüft am 30.10.2017.

Deutscher Bundestag: Drucksache 18/9009, zuletzt geprüft am 30.10.2017.

ESF (Europäischer Sozialfond) Hamburg (2017). AvM-dual & inklusiv. In: URL: *http://www.esf-hamburg.de/projekte-neu/8558868/ausbildungsvorbereiten-fuer-migranten/*, zuletzt geprüft am 30.10.2017

Gag, M. & Weiser, B. (Hrsg.): Leitfaden zur Beratung von Menschen mit einer Behinderung. In: URL: *http://www.fluchtort-hamburg.de/artikel/news/leitfaden-zur-beratung-von-menschen-mit-einer-behinderung-im-kontext-von-migration-und-flucht/*, zuletzt geprüft am 30.10.2017

Gehrke, A.-M. (2017). Nobody should get lost. Reflections on the Youth Employment Agency in Hamburg as a Social Policy Measure against Youth Poverty. In: Schroeder, J./ Seukwa, L.H./ Voigtsberger, U. (ed.): Soziale Bildungsarbeit – Europäische Debatten und Projekts. Social Educational Work – European Debates and Projects, (pp 159-120). Wiesbaden: Springer VS

HIBB (Hamburger Institut für Berufliche Bildung) (2015). Ausbildungsvorbereitung für Migranten (AvM-dual). Download paper on: URL: *https://hibb.hamburg.de/bildungsangebote/berufsvorbereitung/berufsvorbereitungsschule/bildungsangebote-fuer-migrantin-nen-und-migranten/*

HIBB (Hamburger Institut für Berufliche Bildung) (o.J. a). Duale Ausbildungsvorbereitung (Av-Dual). In: URL: *https://hibb.hamburg.de/bildungsangebote/berufsvorbereitung/berufsvorberei-tungsschule/die-dualisierte-ausbildungsvorbereitung/*, zuletzt geprüft am 26.10.2017.

HIBB (Hamburger Institut für Berufliche Bildung) (o.J. b). ESF-Projekt „dual & inklusiv". In: URL: *https://hibb.hamburg.de/schulentwicklung/efs-projekt-dualinklusiv/*, zuletzt geprüft am 26.10.2017.

HIBB (Hamburger Institut für Berufliche Bildung) (o.J. c). Inklusive Ausbildungsvorbereitung (AV) für junge Menschen mit und ohne Behinderungen. In: URL: *https://hibb.hamburg. de/bildungsangebote/berufsvorbereitung/bildungsgaenge-fuer-junge-menschen-mit-behinderungen/inklusive-ausbildungsvorbereitung-av-fuer-junge-menschen-mit-und-ohne-behinderungen/*, zuletzt geprüft am 30.10.2017.

HIBB (Hamburger Institut für Berufliche Bildung) (o.J. d). Bildungsgänge für junge Menschen mit Behinderungen. In: URL: *https://hibb.hamburg.de/bildungsangebote/berufsvorbereitung/ bildungsgaenge-fuer-junge-menschen-mit-behinderungen/*, zuletzt geprüft am 30.10.2017

Kassenärztliche Vereinigung Hamburg (KVHH) (2015). Anlage 1 zur Vereinbarung zwischen der AOK und der FHH zur Übernahme der Krankenbehandlung für nicht Versicherungspflichtige gegen Kostenerstattung nach § 264 Abs. 1 SGB V. *http://www.kvhh.net/ media/public/db/media/1/2015/08/671/telegramm_31_2015_sondertelegramm_auszug. pd*, zuletzt geprüft am 30.10.2017.

Lebenshilfe Hamburg: In: URL: *https://zf.lhhh.de/*, zuletzt geprüft am 26.10.2017.

Metzner, F., Reher, C., Kindler, H., & Pawils, S. (2016). Psychotherapeutische Versorgung von unbegleiteten und begleiteten minderjährigen Flüchtlingen und Asylbewerbern mit Traumafolgestörungen in Deutschland. *Bundesgesundheitsblatt – Gesundheitsforschung – Gesundheitsschutz, 5*, (S. 642-651).

Mogk, C. (2015). „Erst dann kann ich sicher sein…" Psychiatrische und psychotherapeutische Versorgung junger Flüchtlinge und ihrer Familien am Beispiel der Flüchtlingsambulanz Hamburg. *soziale psychiatrie, 3*, (S. 20-24).

Psychotherapeutenkammer (PtK) Hamburg (2016). Psychotherapie für psychisch erkrankte Flüchtlinge muss genehmigt werden. h*ttp://www.ptk-hamburg.de/aktuelles/nachrichten/9242987.html*, zuletzt geprüft am 30.10.2017.

Schroeder, J. (2003). „Man kann nicht lernen mit so einem Problem." Auswirkungen der Lebenslagen auf die Bildungskarrieren. In: U. Neumann, H. Niedrig, J. Schroeder & L.H. Seukwa (Hrsg.): Lernen am Rande der Gesellschaft. Bildungsinstitutionen im Spiegel von Flüchtlingsbiografien, (S. 237-262). Münster: Waxmann.

Schwabe, L. et al. (2011). Stress effects on memory: An update and integration. *Neuroscience Biobehaviour Revue, 36*, (S. 1740-1749).

Sehzentrum (SFZ): Integrationskurs Chemnitz für blinde und sehbehinderte Migranten, zuletzt geprüft am 26.10.2017.

Thielen, M. et al. (Hrsg.) (2013). Prekäre Übergänge. Erwachsenwerden unter den Bedingungen von Behinderung und Benachteiligung, Bad Heilbrunn: Klinkhardt.

13　Depression among asylum seekers in Germany

(Negin Shah Hosseini)

Introduction

In the current day and age, ever fewer people are able to live in peace on our earth. Almost daily, the latest conflicts lead to major crises. Indeed, over the past two decades, the number of forcibly displaced people grew exponentially from 33.9 million in 1997 to 65.6 million in 2016. The sharp increase between 2012 and 2015 was mainly due to the conflicts in Syria, Iraq and Yemen as well as in sub-Saharan Africa including Burundi, the Central African Republic, the Democratic Republic of Congo, South Sudan, and Sudan. Conflicts and civil wars are leading a growing number of people to flee their homes out of necessity and fear but also in the hope of a better life, and to resign themselves to an uncertain future (UNHCR, 2017).

The situation of refugees, who have arrived in so-called 'safe countries' after overcoming countless difficulties and applied for asylum, will not immediately improve. Complex and lengthy asylum procedures further complicate the situation for many asylum seekers.

Who exactly is classified as an "asylum seeker" in Germany? Asylum seekers are persons, who request entry and protection (e.g. from political persecution) in a foreign country. After applying for asylum, asylum seekers begin a recognition procedure that is often extremely protracted. Unlike refugees, who are able to begin working immediately, asylum seekers and tolerated persons are not permitted to work in the first three months after their arrival. This work ban is then lifted, provided the asylum seeker is no longer living in state accommodation (Proasyl, 2017). Asylum seekers must also live in the collective accommodation they are assigned to. They have no say in where they are accommodated. Once their application has been recognised, they are designated a "person with refugee status" or a "person entitled to asylum". The German Federal Office for Migration and Refugees (*Bundesamt für Migration und Flüchtlinge*, BAMF) has received a total of 151,057 initial applications so far in 2017. During the same period in 2016, 643,211 initial application were submitted. This corresponds to a 76.5% decrease in applications compared to the previous year. In September 2017, the most initial applications were submitted by citizens of Syria (21.4%), Iraq (13.0%) and Turkey (6.8%) (BAMF, 2017).

Compared to other migrants, asylum seekers and refugees are particularly disadvantaged on a number of fronts: before arriving in the new country, they have often experienced various stressful incidents, such as armed conflicts, persecution, poverty or natural disasters. Moreover, their 'emigration' was involuntary and they face a variety of integration difficulties in the new country. They also do not have the option of returning to their home country. Their cultural background often differs considerably from the culture in the new country, too. It is therefore perhaps unsurprising that this group is particularly vulnerable and the prevalence of psychological impairments is high (cf. Müller et al., 2012). In previous scientific studies, very different prevalence rates of depression were reported among asylum seekers. In addition, comparatively more studies have looked at post-traumatic stress disorders (PTSD) among asylum seekers and see depression as more of a comorbid medical condition or consequence. The number of studies that investigate depression in asylum seekers is therefore still extremely limited (Turrini et al., 2017). Moreover the findings from studies on refugees cannot necessarily be applied to asylum seekers for, as previously mentioned, this group differs from refugees in a number of fundamental points. This article will therefore provide an overview of depression and the factors influencing this among asylum seekers, and also suggest necessary support requirements.

Factors influencing depression among asylum seekers

Post-traumatic stress disorders (PTSD) and major depression are the most prevalent psychiatric disorders reported among asylum seekers. Depending on the study, the prevalence rates vary widely, whereby they are reportedly as high as 86% for PTSD and 81% for depression (Lindert et al., 2008). The diverging prevalence rates for depression among asylum seekers can be explained by methodological factors on the one hand and individual risk factors on the other. With regard to the methodology, Steel et al. (2009) concluded that the sample size and quality (e.g. non-probabilistic sampling) as well as the diagnostic instruments used influence the prevalence rates. Studies that used non-random sampling, smaller sample sizes, and self-assessments also tended to lead to higher prevalence rates. Classification systems categorize depressive illnesses (Latin deprimere = press down) as affective (or mood) disorders. Depression manifests as changes in mood as well as cognitive, somatic and motor symptoms. Depressive disorders are among the most common mental illnesses (Berking & Rief, 2012). A depressed mood or increased irritability, loss of interest or pleasure, low energy or increased fatigue count among the key symptoms of depression (ICD-10). But what factors actually cause asylum seekers to become depressed? Is it the circumstances in the new country that lead to a depressive disorder or are asylum seekers already suffering from depression when they arrive? Steel et al. (2009) considered this question in their study. Miller et al. (2002) propounded that depression among asylum seekers can be attributed to exile-related stressors. The continuous fear of deportation, the work ban, discrimination and uncertainty about the future are factors believed to trigger depression in asylum seekers. Moreover, traumatic experiences in the home country or while fleeing can exacerbate the symptoms of depression. The "dose-effect relationship" is referred to here, according to which the risk of illness increases the more potentially traumatic events were experienced (cf. Steel et al., 2002). In their study of Cambodian refugees, Mollica et al. (1998) examined the dose-effect relationship of traumatic events and symptoms of depression and PTSD. They discerned a link between the number of traumatic events experienced and symptoms of depression. A number of studies investigated different protection and risk factors influencing the prevalence of symptoms of depression. Bhugra (2003) considered depression among migrants from different perspectives and developed a hypothetical model. According to this model, diverse factors play a role during different phases of migration that can lead to depression. If migrants are psychologically or biologically vulnerable to the development of depression, their migration is associated with different negative emotions such as grief, and they face a variety of conflicts in the new country while they feel isolated and alienated, these factors can lead to depression. Different factors are mentioned in the literature that may intensify the symptoms of depression among asylum seekers. The loss of extended family or separation from family and friends, critical life events, a low level of education and poor physical health are just a few examples of situations believed to lead to depression (cf. Assion et al., 2010; Pumariega et al., 2005). Bhui et al. (2003) established a link between pre-migration factors and symptoms of depression and anxiety in their study of the psychiatric symptoms displayed by Somali refugees and migrants in the UK. They identified cumulative pre-migration trauma as a risk factor for depressive states and anxiety. Specific traumatic events such as food shortages or being lost or alone during a war situation are associated with higher levels of depressive symptoms in Somali refugees and lead to anxiety more often. The situation is similar among Afghan migrants. Scholte et al. (2004) determined in their study that traumatic events experienced during a war can lead to depression. One further factor influencing symptoms of depression is the degree of social isolation and support. The impact of the former could be established in a longitudinal study of East German migrants. The study investigated how unemployment and social support affect the mental health and well-being of migrants. The authors were able to determine that the level of depression was highest among the migrants, who were unemployed and had less social support. The prevalence of depression was lower among the migrants who were unemployed but had better social support. This study makes the major impact of social isolation and social support on symptoms of depression clear (Schwarzer et al., 1993).

The role of social support is particularly apparent in "collective cultures" in which people are considerably emotionally dependent on one another and the need to belong is very pronounced. Social support gives people a sense of security, safety and acceptance. A lack of social support is particularly difficult for those originating from such cultures. In their study, Abu-Ras and Abu-Bader (2009) investigated different predictor factors for depression and PTSD among Arab and Muslim Americans in the wake of the terrorist attacks of 11 September 2001. They came to the conclusion that symptoms of depression were more prevalent among those who reported little or no social support.

However, certain protective factors reduce the likelihood of symptoms of depression developing among asylum seekers. Contact with their own cultural community and living with families from a similar culture are just a few of the factors that can help to keep depression at bay. The duration of the stay also appears to influence the symptoms of depression: the longer asylum seekers spend in the new country, the fewer symptoms of depression they display (cf. Jenkins et al., 1991). The relationship between the expectation of self efficacy and depression among migrants is important, for example. During their time in the new country, migrants are subject to a variety of stressors and conflicts. The example of language skills was used to illustrate the impact of the expectation of self efficacy on their mental health. Limited language skills leave migrants feeling frustrated and incompetent in different encounter situations. This in turn leads to experiences of stress that can have a lasting detrimental effect on psychiatric health (cf. Rahrakhshan, 2007). In their study, Sulaiman-Hill and Thompson (2013) explored the impact of perceived self efficacy on the psychological well-being of Afghan and Kurdish refugees. This proved better among refugees with high efficacy beliefs.

Psychotherapeutic care for asylum seekers

It was explained in the previous section that asylum seekers are a group at high risk of developing a psychiatric disorder. Moreover, a variety of factors were mentioned that have been found to influence the prevalence of symptoms of depression. According to past studies, psychosocial interventions have produced positive outcomes in asylum seekers (Tribe et al., 2017). But what possibilities actually exist to treat asylum seekers with psychiatric disorders? According to the German Asylum Seeker Benefits Act (*Asylbewerberleistungsgesetz*, AsylbLG), the necessary treatment for mental illnesses is only provided in specific cases. § 6 para. 2 AsylbLG states that:

"Persons granted a residence permit as per § 24 para. 1 of the Residence Act (Aufenthaltsgesetz, AufenthG) who have special needs, such as unaccompanied minors or persons who have undergone torture, rape or other serious forms of psychological, physical or sexual violence, shall be provided with the required medical or other assistance."

According to the German Act on the Acceleration of Asylum Procedures (*Asylverfahrensbeschleunigungsgesetz*, AsylVfBG) agreed in October 2015, asylum seekers are entitled to an electronic health card. The latter were actually introduced in Hamburg and Bremen some time ago. Other federal states, such as North Rhine-Westphalia, only began issuing asylum seekers with an electronic health card in recent months. In other federal states, asylum seekers only receive a health card from a health insurance company after fifteen months of uninterrupted residence in Germany. Prior to this, they are issued with a treatment certificate (*Behandlungsschein*). However, a health card does not mean that asylum seekers are granted full statutory health insurance privileges. Countless restrictions apply – regarding the provision of psychotherapeutic treatment, for example. Only a limited amount of short-term treatment is granted following an expert assessment. The expenses associated with long-term psychotherapy are not normally covered (Wächter-Raquet, 2016) and the interpreter costs are not reimbursed either. As a consequence, the language barrier can mean that psychotherapy is not even possible in the first place. It is for this reason that the German Association of Psychosocial Centres for Refugees and Victims of Torture (BAfF e. V.) and other facilities working in this field play a decisive role. However, it should be mentioned here that they mostly only exist in major cities. Mewes et al. (2016) investigated the barriers to the psychotherapeutic treatment of asylum seekers. In their study, they focused specifically on licensed psychotherapists. A survey revealed that the majority of this group were only moderately willing to offer psychotherapy to asylum seekers, whereby the commissioning of an interpreter was considered the main obstacle.

According to the BAfF's treatment report (2016), access to needs-oriented health and psychosocial treatment for refugees remains extremely limited on the structural level. For this reason, equal access to the health system, language mediation and support for client empowerment processes constitute important steps in the provision of care for asylum seekers (ibid).

Conclusions

Given the current situation in the different countries in which serious conflicts prevail, it should be assumed that the influx of people forced to leave their countries will not abate. The mental health of refugees and asylum seekers is one of the aspects receiving only scant attention. What is the mental state of the people arriving in "safe countries"? How much trauma have they experienced in their home countries and while fleeing? How should mental health care be provided and psychological disorders be treated? These considerations often get lost among the many bureaucratic and administrative aspects. It is therefore vitally important for theory and practice to be developed in tandem. Interdisciplinary research into the situation of asylum seekers is moreover necessary to be able to draw on the findings in the current debates on the situation of asylum seekers and to better adapt the support system accordingly (Sieberer & Machleidt, 2015). Culture-sensitive psychotherapy, intervention and prevention programmes must also be developed to enable asylum seekers to receive more appropriate treatment. In addition, the existing support structures need to be expanded – by offering regular consultation hours in preliminary reception centres and residences, for example – to allow psychological disorders to be detected early on. It is also extremely important for the staff of such facilities to be made aware of psychiatric disorders and to have the opportunity to participate in supervisions. Only then is intervention possible at an early stage (Assion et al., 2016).

Past studies have shown that asylum seekers' residency status has an impact on their mental health. Heeren et al. (2016) concluded in their study that uncertain residency status increases the risk of a psychiatric disorder. It is therefore essential that asylum seekers, who are vulnerable to psychiatric disorders or already suffering from these due to the difficult life situations they have experienced, are granted appropriate and easy access to the care system. Changes to the legislation are thus necessary, which among others also take the mental health of asylum seekers into account.

References

Abu-Ras, W., & Abu-Bader, S. H. (2009). Risk Factors for Depression and Posttraumatic Stress Disorder (PTSD): The Case of Arab and Muslim Americans Post-9/11. *Journal of Immigrant & Refugee Studies*, 7(4), 393-418.

Assion, H. J., Bender, M., Koch, E., & Pollmächer, T. (2016). Flüchtlinge in Not – Fachverbände und Kliniken sind gefordert:Psychiatrische und psychotherapeutische Hilfe frühzeitig anbieten. *Psychiatrische Praxis*, 43(2), 116-119.

Assion, H., Stompe, T., Aichberger, M., & Calliess, I. (2010). Depressive Störungen. In M. Machleidt, & A. Heinz, *Praxis der interkulturellen Psychiatrie und Psychotherapie*. 321-330. Munich: Elsevier, Urban & Fischer.

Berking, M., & Rief, W. (2012). *Klinische Psychologie und Psychotherapie für Bachelor*. Heidelberg: Springer.

Bhugra, D. (2003). Migration and depression. *Acta psychiatrica Scandinavica*, 108 (418) 67-72.

Bhui, K., Abdi, A., Abdi, M., Pereira, S., Dualeh, M., Robertson, D., Sathyamoorthy, G. & Ismail, H. (2003). Traumatic events, migration characteristics and psychiatric symptoms among Somali refugees. Preliminary communication. *Social Psychiatry and Üsychiatric Epidemiology*, 38(1), 35-43.

Bozorgmehr, K., Mohsenpour, A., Saure, D., Stock, C., Loerbroks, A., Joos, S., & Schneider, C. (2016). Systematische Übersicht und „Mapping" empirischer Studien des Gesundheitszustands und der medizinischen Versorgung von Flüchtlingen und Asylsuchenden in Deutschland (1990-2014). *Bundesgesundheitsblatt – Gesundheitsforschung – Gesundheitsschutz, 59(5)*, 599-620.

Dilling, H. (2011). *Internationale Klassifikation psychischer Störungen.* Berlin: Huber.

Federal Ministry of Justice and Consumer Protection (Bundesministerium der Justiz und Verbraucherschutz, BMJV). (n.d.). § 6 AsylbLG. [online] Available at: *https://www.gesetze-im-internet.de/asylblg/__6.html.* Last accessed 27 October 2017.

Federal Office for Migration and Refugees (Bundesamt für Migration und Flüchtlinge, BAMF). (2017). Aktuelle Zahlen zu Asyl. [online] Available at: *http://www.bamf.de/SharedDocs/ Anlagen/DE/Downloads/Infothek/Statistik/Asyl/aktuelle-zahlen-zu-asyl-september-2017. pdf?__blob=publicationFile.* Last accessed 27 October 2017.

German Association of Psychosocial Centres for Refugees and Victims of Torture (*Bundesweite Arbeitsgemeinschaft der Psychosozialen Zentren für Flüchtlinge und Folteropfer, BAfF e. V.*). (2016). Versorgungsbericht. [online] Available at: *http://www.baff-zentren.org/wp-content/uploads/2017/02/Versorgungsbericht_3-Auflage_BAfF.pdf.* Last retrieved 12.10.17.

Heeren, M., Wittmann, L., Ehlert, U., Schnyder, U., Maier, T., & Müller, J. (2016). Psychopathologie und Aufenthaltsstatus. *Forum der Psychoanalyse,* 32(2), 135-149.

Jenkins, J. H., Kleinman, A., & Good, B. J. (1991). *Cross-cultural studies of depression.* In J. Becker & A. Kleinman (Eds.), Psychosocial aspects of depression. 67-99. Hillsdale, NJ: Lawrence Erlbaum Associates.

Lindert, J., Brähler, E., Wittig, U., Mielck, A., & Priebe, S. (2008). Depressivität, Angst und posttraumatische Belastungsstörung bei Arbeitsmigranten, Asylbewerbern und Flüchtlingen. *Psychotherapie Psychosomatik Medizinische Psychologie,* 58, 109-122.

Mewes, R., Kowarsch, L., Reinacher, H., & Nater, U. (2016). Ansatzpunkte zur Verbesserung der psychotherapeutischen Versorgung von Asylsuchenden. *Psychotherapie, Psychosomatik, Medizinische Psychologie,* 66, 1-8.

Miller, K., Weine, S., Ramic, A., Nenad, B., Bjedic, Z., Smajkic, A., & al., (2002). The Relative Contribution of War Experiences and Exile-Related Stressors to Levels of Psychological Distress Among Bosnian Refugees. *Journal of Traumatic Stress,* 15(5), 377-387.

Mollica, R. F., McInnes, K., Poole, C., & Tor, S. (1998). Dose-Effect relationships of trauma to symptoms of depression and post-traumatic stress disorder among Cambodian survivors. *British Journal of Psychiatry,* 173(6), 482-488.

Moss-Morris, R., Weinman, J., Petrie, K., Horne, R., Cameron, L. & Buick, D. (2002). The Revised Illness Perception Questionnaire (IPQ-R). *Psychology & Health,* 17(1), 1-16.

Müller, B., Hasse, M., Kreienbrink, A., & Schmid, S. (2012). *Klimamigration. Definitionen, Ausmaß und politische Instrumente in der Diskussion.* Berlin: Bundesamt für Migration und Flüchtlinge.

Proasyl. (2017). Available at: *https://www.proasyl.de.* Last accessed 12 October 2017.

Pumariega, A. J., Rothe, E., & Pumariega, J. B. (2005). Mental health of immigrants and refugees. *Community Mental Health Journal,* 41 (5), 581-597.

Rahrakhshan, M. (2007). *Das psychische Befinden von iranischen Migranten in Deutschland. Zur Bedeutung des Attributions- und Bewältigungsstils bei der Auseinandersetzung mit akkulturativem Stress.* Dissertation. Hamburg: Universität Hamburg.

Scholte, W. F., Olff, M., Ventevogel, P., de Vries, G. J., Jansveld, E., Cardozo, B. L. & Gotway Crawford, C. (2004). Mental health symptoms following war and repression in Eastern Afghanistan. *JAMA,* 292(5), 585-593.

Schwarzer, R., Hahn, A., & Jerusalem, M. (1993). Negative Affect in East German Migrants: Longitudinal Effects of Unemployment and Social Support. *Anxiety, Stress, and Coping,* 6, 57-69.

Sieberer, M., & Machleidt, W. (2015). Seelen ohne Heimat: Zur Situation von Asylsuchenden in Deutschland. *Psychiat Prax, 42,* 175-177.

Steel, Z., Chey, T., Silove, D., Marnane, C., Bryant, R. A., & van Ommeren, M. (2009). Association of Torture and Other Potentially Traumatic Events With Mental Health Outcomes Among Populations Exposed to Mass Conflict and Displacement. *JAMA,* 302(5), 537-549.

Steel, Z., Silove, D., Phan, T., & Bauman, A. (2002). Long-term effect of psychological trauma on the mental health of Vietnamese refugees resettled in Australia: a population-based study. *Lancet,* 360(9339), 1056-62.

Sulaiman-Hill, C. M., & Thompson, S. C. (2013). Learning to fit in: an exploratory study of general perceived self efficacy in selected refugee groups. *Journal of Immigrant and Minority Health, 15(1),* 125-131.

UNHCR – The UN Refugee Agency. (n.d.). Available at: *http://www.unhcr.org/globaltrends2016/.* Last accessed 12 October 2017.

Tribe, R. H., Sendt, K. V., & Tracy, D. K. (2017). A systematic review of psychosocial interventions for adult refugees and asylum seekers. *Journal of Mental Health,* (9), 1-15.

Turrini, G., Purgato, M., Ballette, F., Nosè, M., Ostuzzi, G., & Barbui, C. (2017). Common mental disorders in asylum seekers and refugees: umbrella review of prevalence and intervention studies. *International Journal of Mental Health Systems,* 11, 1-14.

Wächter-Raquet, M. (2016). *Einführung der Gesundheitskarte für Asylsuchende und Flüchtlinge. Der Umsetzungsstand im Überblick der Bundesländer.* Gütersloh: Bertelsmann Stiftung.

14　Trauma in Mentally Disabled People

(Farid Mosharaf Dehkordi)

Introduction

Due to unfavourable family and social circumstances, people with mental disabilities often suffer from mental and psychological disorders more frequently. These include anxiety, depression, schizophrenia, bipolar disorder, borderline personality disorder, manic depression, personality disorders, trauma, etc.

In Germany, which has one of the best health systems for psychiatric patients after Switzerland, there is still a huge difference between the treatment of people with and without disabilities suffering from mental disorders though. One third of the offices of psychiatrists and psychologists do not cater for people with sensory impairments, who are deaf or blind, or have a visual impairment or physical disability. Psychologists are unsure how to deal with disabled people with mental disorders. They are uncertain what to do with them and do not know how to work in this area. There are just two rehabilitation clinics in Germany for blind and deaf people suffering from mental and psychological disorders (Heil, 2017, p. 11).

These unfavourable conditions are even worse when it comes to people with a mental disability or mental and physical disabilities. In most courses on behavioural therapy and psychoanalysis for children, adolescents and adults, psychologists receive absolutely no training on how to work with mentally disabled people.

Disabled children tend to suffer more harassment than non-disabled children, and almost one in four people with disabilities in Germany are sexually harassed by adults or other children during their childhood (Schröttle, 2012). In order to understand the needs and desires of mentally disabled people, specialization and training in communication skills are required. (Hennicke, 2011; Vogel, 2012).

Traumatic disorders have been discussed in greater depth in the fields of education, psychology and psychiatry since the arrival of war immigrants from Libya, Iraq, Afghanistan and especially Syria, and the arrival of more than 890,000 migrants in Germany and over one million migrants in Europe in 2015. However, it should be noted that traumatic disorders are a new topic that has only been included in the International Statistical Classification of Diseases and Related Health Problems (ICD10) of the World Health Organization (WHO) for about twenty years now. Very little research has been conducted into the treatment of people with mental disorders suffering from traumatic disorders. One of the main reasons for this is that people with disabilities cannot report on their experiences.

Trauma

In Latin and medicine, "trauma" means wounds and injuries caused by an external factor (e.g. an accident/incident). In psychology, this term refers to an incident in which all anti-stress systems become ineffective and freeze, leaving the person unable to combat stress or escape from it, which in turn causes them to enter a state of shock.

When early humans were faced with wild animals, their biological system acted in one of three ways to deal with this stressful situation: fight, escape or enter an excessive state of fear and stress (shock). In the latter situation, all of their stress management systems were in fact rendered ineffective and they were then eaten by the wild animals like tigers.

Today, we see these three mechanisms in another form. When a person takes their driving test, for example, it can be seen that s/he may pass or fail the test (fight mechanism), quit the exam before it takes place (escape mechanism) or even enter such a state of stress that s/he cannot react and fails the exam (shock mechanism).

Trauma can generally be divided into the following categories:

- **Shock trauma:** A person enters a state of shock due to an unfortunate and unexpected incident, such as an accident, the death of a loved one, rape, torture, etc.
- **Secondary trauma:** This type of trauma often occurs in people working in helper professions, such as firefighters, police officers, doctors, psychologists, social workers, etc. The person is actually a witness to the incident and is not directly involved.
- **Transgenerational trauma:** A generation transfers its trauma to another generation. For example, a generation that has experienced a war does not understand the next generation and therefore hurts and abuses it.
- **Social trauma:** An unfortunate incident occurs for a group of people and causes a collective trauma, e.g. a flood, earthquake, bombing, plane crash, etc.

Farid Mosharaf Dehkordi

- **Developmental trauma:** A child's development is damaged; the child's emotions and needs (e.g. for security, peace, etc.) are ignored.

When talking about trauma in Post-Traumatic Stress Disorder (PTSD), the following symptoms can occur, which are described in detail in the tenth revision of the International Statistical Classification of Diseases and Related Health Problems (ICD10):

- Remembering the subject that caused the trauma, nightmare, flashbacks (one of the most important symptoms for the diagnosis of trauma).
- Experiences of partial amnesia.
- Symptoms of trauma can often manifest one week after the incident and rarely after six months.
- Emotional symptoms such as insomnia, increased tantrums, concentration disorders, emotional intolerance.
- Isolation and avoidance behaviour (avoiding emotions or traumatic stimulants). Repeated traumatic incidents reflected and reconstructed in children's games, which are often accompanied with unexpected behaviour, anger and mania.

Other disorders accompanying PTSD include depression, anxiety disorders, alcoholism, and drug abuse. They are often coupled with side effects such as suicide attempts; drug use (particularly alcohol); medicine consumption, refraining from expressing thoughts and feelings; and exaggerating security, fear and pessimism.

In a comprehensive study carried out in the United States (ACE Study; Felitti, 2001), it was clearly seen that trauma patients are more likely to suffer from liver or lung cancer, alcoholism, and/or sexual harassment, and have a tendency toward sexual violence or are themselves often sexually harassed.

Miserable experiences, multiple mental and psychological pressures, and a lack of proper analysis, abilities and necessary resources to deal with these problems can later lead a person to suffer trauma when combined with other unfortunate incidents and sometimes even just a minor incident. Not all disasters cause PTSD though – it depends on the person's attitude and his/her mental and psychological experiences.

The cause of PTSD in patients is about 80% due to torture, 50% due to rape, 25% due to war and accidents, and 15% due to physical illness (Siol, Flatten & Wöller, 2001)

The trauma is more severe in those who are familiar with the person or group that causes their trauma. Hence, the trauma is more severe in those who have been raped or tortured than those whose trauma is caused by a natural disaster, flood, earthquake or war. Their trust in humans is diminished due to having been hurt directly by humans. They are pessimistic and avoid treatment (occupational therapy, psychotherapy, physiotherapy, etc.) because – from a psychoanalytical perspective – they believe that they are being treated by the very people who hurt them.

Most specialized staff and parents of mentally disabled people only notice the mental disability after a relatively long time. For example, in children with autism in the United States (a field in which significant progress has been made compared to other countries), autism is often diagnosed at the age of around five and a half years. (Howlin & Asghavian, 1999, p. 834).

According to Klauß, some parents know that their child will be disabled before it is born. Others notice their child's disability only months or years after their birth. They are suddenly shocked by this event. The burden falls on the family. The family initially does not want to accept the child's disability. It is difficult to understand it. The hopes and wishes of the family are destroyed.

The family now faces a difficult task. At this time, nobody knows or can tell what the frame of mind of the family is (Klauß, 1999, p. 63).

The child's primary requirements of warmth, care, love and belonging that must be satisfied are fulfilled through the physical contact, support, attention and warmth of the parents.

A healthy bond between the child and their parents will empower the child to overcome the crisis in their life. Specifically, psychoanalysts claim that individuals without any bond with their parents and dependent on them are the most difficult patients to treat.

Some parents with a disabled child do not have a real affinity for the child and this worsens the conditions for trauma in the disabled child.

Biologically, when a person is in a state of stress, information is transmitted from the amygdalae to the prefrontal cortex (Fig. 1) where it is interpreted and analysed on the emotional, intellectual and sensory levels, and stimulus is then provided in response. However, in situations where a person is in danger (e.g. experiences a traumatic incident), the amygdalae react automatically as a reflex, and respond to the stimulus. No analysis is then performed by the prefrontal cortex.

(It is for this reason, for example, that some people jumped from the windows of higher floors in panic during the 9/11 attacks in New York.)

This reaction by the amygdalae makes it conditional and possible to act as a reflex in the same conditions or when someone remembers an unpleasant incident (triggered by a smell, shape or sound). It then causes a flashback that leaves the person in a state of shock.

Trauma disrupts the brain system. As previously mentioned, trauma causes the system to be physically and psychologically disrupted (isolation, insomnia, irritability, lack of concentration, etc.).

Treatment of trauma patients with mental disabilities

One of the most important treatment measures is for the person to be taken to a safe place. For example, the patient is removed from the battlefield or from the environment in which s/he has been sexually abused, and is then treated.

The next most important treatment measure once the person is in a safe place is for their daily life to be returned to normality. Trauma patients often find themselves isolated and are unable to regulate their lives (in terms of hormones, an excess of stress hormones are expressed and, as a result of their activity, the traumatised person are overloaded and overperform, or their activity is less than normal). In this regard, social workers play an important role in the training on how to deal with trauma patients.

Once the structure of daily life has somehow been restored and life becomes more stable, if the disabled person is interested in domestic animals, these can be very helpful in structuring life and in giving motivation to live, as animals need constant and regular care [author's experience[.

The most common methods of movement therapy are Eye Movement Desensitization and Reprocessing (EMDR), movement therapy, relaxation therapy (particularly Imagination and Progressive Muscle Relaxation (PMR)) and Trauma Focused Cognitive Behavioural Therapy (TF-CBT).

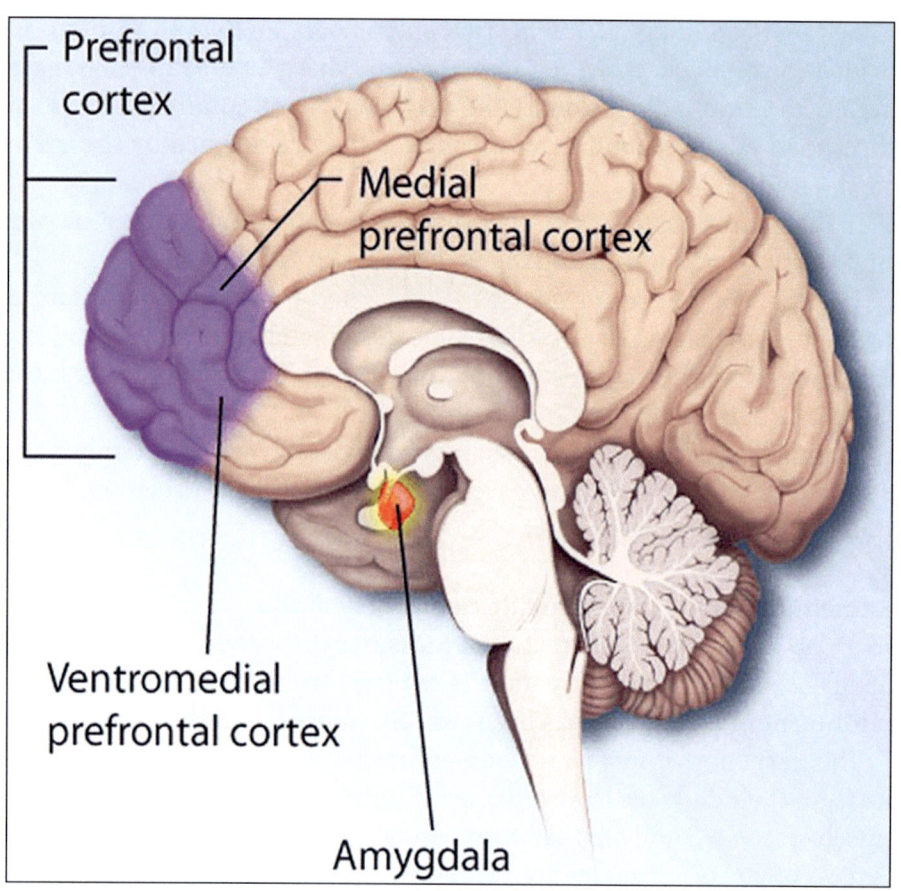

Figure 14.1: The limbic system of the human brain

(For the descriptions, go to "Alternative text for images" page 224)

References

Artman, L.K. & Daniels, J. A. (2010). Disability and psychotherapy practice: Cultural Competence and Practical Tips. Professional Psychology: Research and Practice, 41 (5), 442-448.

Barol, B.; Seubert, A. (2010). Stepping Stones: EMDR Treatment of Individuals. With Intellectual and Development Disabilities and Challenging Behavior. In: Journal of EMDR Practice and Research, 4, 156-169.

Farid Mosharaf Dehkordi

Becker, M. (2001). Sexuelle Gewalt gegen Mädchen mit geistiger Behinderung. Daten und Hintergründe. Heidelberg: Winter.

Brandis-Stiehl, C. von (2001). Wenn die Sehkraft schwindet: Ein Ratgeber für sehgeschädigte Menschen und ihre Angehörigen. Stuttgart: Urachhaus.

Bungart, P. (2005). Sexuelle Gewalt gegen behinderte Menschen. Der Schutz Behinderter durch das Sexualstrafrecht. Frankfurt am Main: Mabuse-Verlag.

Copeland, W.E.; Keeler, G.; Angold, A. & Costello, E.J. (2010). Posttraumatic stress without trauma in children. In: American Journal of Psychiatry, 167, 1059-1065.

Esbensen; A.J.; Benson, B.A. (2006). A prospective analysis of life events, problem behaviours and depression in adults with intellectual disability. In: Journal of Intellectual Disability Research, 4, 248-258.

Focht-New, G.; Clements, P.T; Barol, B.; Faulkner, M.J. & Service, K.P. (2008). Persons with developmental disabilities exposed to interpersonal violence and crime: strategies and guidance for assessment. Perspectives in Psychiatric Care, 44 (1), 3-13.

Heil, C. (2017): Psychotherapeutische Arbeit mit Menschen mit Körper- und Sinnenbehinderungen. In: Psychotherapeuten Journal 16 (1), 11-18.

Hennicke, K. (2011). Praxis der Psychotherapie bei erwachsenen Menschen mit geistiger Behinderung. Marburg: Bundesvereinigung Lebenshilfe.

Hosemann, E. (2000). Gegenübertragungsprobleme bei der psychoanalytischen Behandlung sichtbar körperlich behinderter Patienten. In U. Streeck (Ed.): Das Fremde in der Psychoanalyse, Gießen.

Howlin, P. & Asghavian, A. (1999). The diagnosis of autism and Asperger syndrome: findings from a survey of 770 families. In: Developmental Medicine and Child Neurology 41, 834-839.

Klauß, T. (1999). Ein besonderes Leben: Was Eltern und Pädagogen von Menschen mit geistiger Behinderung wissen sollten. Heidelberg: Winter.

Loschen, E., Fletscher, R., Stavrakaki, C., First, M. (Eds.) (2007). Diagnostic Manual-Intellectual Disability (DM-ID): A Clinical Guide for Diagnosis of Mental Disorders in Persons with Intellectual Disability. New York: NAAD.

Lingg, A., Theunissen, G. (2008). Psychische Störungen und geistige Behinderungen: Ein Lehrbuch und Kompendium für die Praxis. Freiburg: Lambertus.

Perkonigg, A.; Kessler, R.C.; Storz, S., Wittchen, H.-U. (2000). Traumatic events and post-traumatic stress disorder in the community: prevalence, risk factors and comorbidity. Acta Psychiatrica Scandinavica, 101(1), 46-59.

Schröttle, M., Hornberg, C., Glammeier, S., Sellach, B., Kavemann, B., Puhe, H., and Zins-meister, J. (Ed.) (2012): Lebenssituation und Belastungen von Frauen mit Beeinträchtigungen und Behinderungen in Deutschland. Kurzfassung Berlin: Bundesministerium für Familie, Senioren, Frauen und Jugend.

Shapiro, F. (1989). Efficacy of the Eye Movement Desensitization procedure in the treatment of traumatic memories. In: Journal of Traumatic Stress, 2, 199-223.

Siol, T., Flatten, G., & Wöller, W. (2001). Epidemiologie und Komorbidität der Posttraumatischen Belastungsstörung. In: Flatten, G., Galley, N., Hofmann, A., Liebermann, P., Petzold, E.R., Siol, T., & Wöller, W. (Eds.), Posttraumatische Belastungsstörung: Leitlinie und Quellentext (p. 41-58). Stuttgart: Schattauer.

Yule, W. (2001). Posttraumatic stress disorder in the general population and in children. Journal of Clinical Psychiatry, 62 (Suppl 17), 23-28.

Tischler, L., Brand, S.R., Stavitsky, K., Labinsky, E., Newmark, R., Grossman, R., Buchsbaum, M.S., Yehuda, R. (2006). The relationship between hippocampal volume and declarative memory in a population of combat veterans with and without PTSD. Annals of the New York Academy of Sciences. 1071, 405-409. doi: 10.1196/annals. 1364.031

Vogel, V. (2012). Psychotherapie bei Menschen mit geistiger Behinderung. Marburg: Tectum Verlag.

Weiss, J.A., MacMullin, J., Waechter, R., Wekerle, C. (2011). Child maltreatment, adolescent attachment style, and dating violence: considerations in youths with borderline-to-mild intellectual disability. International Journal of Mentally Health Addict, 9, 555-567. doi: 10.1007/s11469-011-9321-x.

Werner, E.; Dawson, G.; Munson, J.; Osterling, J. (2005). Variation in early developmental course in autism and its relation with behavioral outcome at 3-4 years of age, In: Journal of Autism and Developmental Disorders 35, 3, 337-350.

Werth, I.; Sieprath, H. (2002). Interkulturelle Kommunikation zwischen Hörenden und Gehörlosen. Das Zeichen, 61, 360-364.

Wilhelm, M. (1996). Behindertenintegration und Sexualerziehung: Eine Studie zur schulischen Sexualpädagogik. Vienna: Wiener Universitätsverlag.

Wilken, U. (1980). Beruf – Freizeit und Behinderung. Bonn: Reha.

Farid Mosharaf Dehkordi

15 Supporting educational and coping processes in hospital schools of child and adolescent psychiatric units

(Tobias Hensel)

Current situation[10]

In recent decades, epidemiological studies and hospital statistics have shown continued growth in the number of children and adolescents in Germany suffering from a psychiatric disorder. Currently, 20.2 per cent of 3 to 17-year-olds are considered at risk of a mental illness. Psychiatric disorders not only cause a high level of psychological stress and additional health risks, but also other burdens such as negative impacts on family life and their social environment, learning difficulties, and reduced opportunities to participate in formal education or the labour market. Moreover, it is assumed that there will be an increasing demand for beds in child and adolescent psychiatric units (CAP) in the coming years (cf. i.a. Hölling et al. 2014: 807ff.; Myschker/Stein 2014: 416).

Pupils who are inpatients of CAP are unable to attend their normal school due to the institutional setting and restrictions of CAP. In order to provide continuous access to education, safeguard their right to education and fulfil their obligation to attend school, they attend hospital school. Children and adolescents usually have not recovered completely after hospitalisation. However, upon discharge from CAP, they are no longer in an environment sensitive to mental illness with round the clock therapeutic and pedagogical assistance. Concurrently, they have to face expectations and demands from the outside world e.g. from a mainstream school. The transition from CAP and hospital school back to mainstream education[11] therefore represents a major challenge for a large number of young inpatients. The risk of discontinuity in their educational biography not only exists after the onset of a psychiatric disorder before an inpatient stay but also following discharge from CAP. This is because the risk that reintegration will

---

[10] This article is an abridged, revised, and translated version of my article "'Bei denen ist erstmal gar nicht an Schule zu denken.' Unterstützung von Bildungs- und Bewältigungsprozessen in Klinikschulen in der Kinder- und Jugendpsychiatrie" (Hensel 2017).

[11] For better clarity, I will only use 'transition from CAP back to mainstream education' hereafter.

---

fail is particularly high among children and adolescents without a reliable and supportive environment. Based on their experiences, teachers consider the transition problematic. Pupils and parents also perceive the transition as "burdening and risky" (Weber/Welling/Steins 2010: 74), do not feel sufficiently prepared, and wish for specific support. Similar requests for professional support to help children and adolescents coping with the transition are made in relevant literature (i.a. Wertgen 2009).

Offers of support for coping processes as a task of hospital schools

From the perspective of transition research, transitions are "central turning points where questions of social participation and exclusion are decided sustainably for each individual" (Ahmed et al. 2013: 7).[12] The individual significance attributed to each particular transition depends on the subject's social environment, socialisation processes, and previous biographical experiences of transitions (e.g. school). If subjects are able to cope with transition demands, new problem-solving skills, development impetus, and stabilising identity formations can emerge from the transition. However, transitions do not only harbour opportunities and potential, but also risks and dangers. If the transition demands are too high or the subject cannot meet these because of their psychosocial circumstances, disorientation, destabilization, and psychological stress may result. Moreover, if in this context labelling subjects e.g. as 'special needs students', 'school refuser', 'mentally ill' and 'unteachable' by educational institutions becomes too powerful, and if these socially attributed identities are taken on by the subjects themselves (secondary deviance), transitions can ultimately result in discontinuity in educational biographies or even dropping out of school (cf. Kramer/Helsper 2013: 591f.).

These risks also exist in the transition from CAP back to mainstream education. If inpatients of CAP cannot cope with the demands of the transition, they are at higher risk of social exclusion, reduced social participation, and exposure to the structural constraints of the social state supply system and psychological healthcare system. If and the extent to which an inpatient's transition back to mainstream school is successful is seen as one prognostic factor for long-term social reintegration, regardless of the psychiatric disorder the pupil is suffering

---

[12] All quotes from German literature have been translated by myself.

Tobias Hensel

from. Hence hospital school education is one essential component of the CAP inpatient treatment concept for social reintegration and everyday resilience (cf. Krüger/Romer 2003: 251; Ricking/Schulze 2012: 16).

In light of the disadvantaged life situation of children and adolescents with psychiatric disorders and the challenging transition from CAP to mainstream education, the pupils must cope with different demands. Coping refers to "situations or incidents, that are perceived as burdening and demanding, differ from assumed normality, and usually involve action and behaviour requiring a major effort by the affected individuals" (cf. Mack 2008: 147). The concept of coping is of central importance in transition research and theory as analyses of transitions cannot focus exclusively on the structures of transition, but must take the perspectives and experiences of those going through the transition into account as well. Moreover, how the subjects cope with the demands of the transition and social processes of their capacity for action within the transition phase have to be considered (cf. Schröer 2013: 70). The coping concept has its origins in psychology and is applied in different subdisciplines of psychology, e.g. stress research (Lazarus/Folkman 1984) or developmental psychology (Filipp/Aymanns 2010). Due to its multiple and various applications, there is no coherent definition of coping. The social-pedagogical concept of coping is based on the psychological concept of coping, which focuses on the level of the individual. However, social pedagogy, which comprises aspects such as support for coping processes in personal development, individual crises, and precarious life situations, expands the concept of coping with the perspective of social conditions for coping (cf. Mack 2008: 146ff.). Based on the assumption that critical life events result from crises of integration and integrity associated with problems relating to the social structure, coping is seen as "striving for the subjective ability to act in life situations in which the psychosocial balance – in the interaction with self-esteem, social recognition, and self-efficacy – is at risk" (Böhnisch 2012: 47).

Even though precarious life situations, critical life events and the associated demands of subjects to gain the ability to act are social conditions of education and influence individual educational processes and their organization (cf. Mack 2013: 124), schools are not tasked with helping children and adolescents to cope with these demands either in their traditional role as educational institution or in their legal requirement or societal ascription of function (Fend 1980). On the contrary, schools expect pupils to cope with their specific life situation and day-to-day (school) life for themselves and delegate the task of supporting coping mechanisms to other disciplines or institutions such as social pedagogy or CAP (cf. Mack 1999: 280).

However, education during times of medical or mental crisis, which is oriented towards the special needs of their pupils and aims for social integration, has to take at least two points into consideration: firstly, the transition from CAP back to mainstream education can be challenging and sometimes a major turning point in the further educational biography. And secondly, most children and adolescents with mental illness are in a precarious health and life situation. Thus, hospital schools cannot assume successful coping performances of their pupils, but have to be open to the demands each child and adolescent has to cope with. Learning will not be possible and the risk of a failed transition will increase otherwise. This means that hospital education cannot restrict itself to the institutional educational task of school because (unlike the concept of coping) the concept of education does not include the ability to manage day-to-day (school) life in a disadvantaged life situation (cf. Mack 1999: 21).

In the following, I shall therefore consider the question of how the educational task of hospital schools can be expanded with the task of providing pedagogical support for pupils' coping mechanisms. I shall apply Mack's (1999) theoretical model regarding the relation between education and coping, which refers to the social-pedagogical concept of coping and expands the school pedagogy debate on pupils in precarious life situations with the concept of coping. I shall begin by describing Mack's three relations between education and coping in order to then apply them to hospital school education based on data from qualitative interviews conducted with hospital teachers for my PhD[13] along with relevant specialist literature.

---

[13] For my PhD, I analyse the transitions of adolescents back into mainstream education following inpatient treatment at CAP. I conducted interviews for this, among others with educational experts at hospital schools and affiliating schools involved in the transition as well as with adolescents who have already completed the transition.

Tobias Hensel

1) Coping as a purpose of education

Assigning education the purpose of overcoming precarious life situations and biographical burdens in the spirit of successful coping performance initially seems like wishful pedagogical dreaming that cannot be fulfilled by institutionalised education. However, as I show in the two subsequent relations, educational offers can create opportunities for coping processes, though it can only be discerned in hindsight whether education processes have successfully enabled coping (cf. Mack 1999: 287). Moreover, coping also depends on further factors over which schools have no influence, such as the social environment and therapeutic care given after discharge from hospital. Mack (1999) therefore concludes that education *may* help to enable coping processes (cf. ibid.: 287).

In this relation, I try to show that hospital schools contribute to initiating education and coping processes due to their structural orientation and their presence in daily life of CAP. In the two relations considered in (2) and (3), I will discuss teaching organisation and goals regarding education and coping.

For many children and adolescents who have experienced school-related failures, with several changes of school or extended periods of absence before admission to CAP, hospital schools are "often the final port of call in the education system" (Wertgen 2012: 227). They can therefore fill a "serious gap" (ibid.) in the provision of education for mentally ill pupils at high risk of school dropout. They provide access to educational services according to the individual needs, are oriented to the pupils' special circumstances, and reduce performance pressure due to their exemption from the mainstream education curriculum. Hospital schools essentially lay the foundations for the initiation of coping processes through education that other school educational programmes are unable to. However, creating the foundations for coping processes is not only necessary because of the special life and health situations of the pupils, but also because of the transition from CAP back to mainstream education. The formal responsibility of hospital schools for children and adolescents undergoing inpatient treatment starts with admission to CAP and ends with their discharge. Therefore, if the patients are still of compulsory schooling age, the transition from CAP back to mainstream education is structurally predetermined. Even though the school authority regulations and special education guidelines in most German states do not task hospital schools with supporting reintegration (cf. Fesch/Müller 2014: 53), experts for child and adolescent psychiatry (i.a. Krüger/Romer 2003) and hospital school education (i.a. Bleher/Hoanzl/Ramminger 2014) claim that preparing for the transition and helping pupils to cope with the demands of the transition is in fact a key task of hospital schools. "Hospital school education aims to facilitate the most comprehensive and sustainable school rehabilitation and reintegration possible" (Wertgen 2009: 308). As a consequence, hospital school education must focus on helping pupils to cope with the upcoming transition. This not only includes helping them to catch up with the school curriculum of their normal class, offering academic career advice, and organising reintegration, but also fostering problem-solving skills that can help pupils to react appropriately to stress and burdens. My empirical data shows that other than therapy that focuses on dealing with illness and the associated problems, hospital schools also set demands that relate to educational contexts and situations that the pupils have to meet. In this way, children and adolescents can be supported with educational offers to develop and use coping strategies (see the following relations).

Furthermore, hospital schools can help to initiate coping behaviour by being present in CAP life. By offering education at hospital, patients can experience school as part of daily life and feel that they are taken seriously as pupils despite their difficult situation. Thus, hospital schools establish normality to some extent that may help patients to cope with burdening life circumstances and develop new life perspectives (cf. Frey 2008: 142; Bleher/Hoanzl/Ramminger 2014: 277f.). At the same time, by preparing organisational and school subject-related aspects of the transition, hospital schools focus on reintegration and contribute to a normalization of the living condition (cf. Wertgen 2009: 309). Hospital schools thereby promise a future, which seems for many children and adolescents to be jeopardised or even lost given the massive limitations due to illness and partly existential threats (cf. Hoanzl et al. 2009: 407). "School is a principle of hope because as long as school and education continue, life goes on and goals are still achievable" (Hilff 1997:164). According to coping research, hope can be a starting point for coping behaviours as it relates to holding on to aspirations, which may provide impetus for a change of state. Moreover, in difficult life situations, hope can counteract thoughts of resignation and lead to positive evaluations of critical events (cf. Filipp/Aymanns 2010: 281). If hospital schools offer hope and help their pupils to keep theirs, they can help to foster coping processes.

2) Coping as a condition of the possibility of education

Education and coping make different demands of both the subjects and the pedagogical offers (cf. Mack 2008: 152). Mack (1999) considers education and coping as two mutually dependent components of an individual's development: not coping with demands, (development) tasks, or problems affects educational processes. Conversely, impaired educational processes in turn influence coping behaviour and strategies. Coping demands that emerge from biographical events like a mental illness and the accompanying secondary effects can be so high that education in the traditional understanding of formal education is not possible. Instead, primary needs must first be satisfied, problems mitigated, and the individuals disburdened. However, coping with these burdens is at the same time part of education in the sense of education towards becoming an autonomous subject capable of action (cf. ibid.: 286). Mack concludes that school as an educational institution has to support their pupils' coping efforts. "As such, school support for coping is an essential condition for the possibility of education" (ibid.).

Psychiatric disorders and therapeutic treatment result in special pedagogical needs that must be taken into account in educational offers for children and adolescents in inpatient and day-care treatment. Initially, many pupils need a lot of attention, encouragement, and a feeling of acceptance before they are able to open up to school-based learning processes (cf. Wertgen/Scheid 2014: 22). Establishing positive relationships between teachers and pupils and within learning groups is therefore an essential part of the pedagogical work of hospital teachers in order to initiate educational processes. A positive relationship between teachers and pupils is certainly also an important precondition for successful learning in mainstream schools. However, due to the experiences of negative, in part traumatic incidents or relationship breakdowns that many mentally ill pupils have had, positive relationships are often of greater importance in hospital school (cf. Hoanzl et al. 2009: 410). Through relationship building, pupils should gain the feeling that they are important and taken seriously. At the same time, they can (re)learn social interaction with regard to closeness, distance and boundaries (Hilff 1997) as well as social and cooperative learning skills (see relation 2.3). By building trust and mutual appreciation, attempts are not only made to initiate educational processes but at the same time also opportunities for coping (cf. Frey 2008: 139; Warzecha 2003: 264). "Being well integrated socially and knowing that one is surrounded by people one can trust in difficult times is a central resource for dealing with burdening life events" (Filipp/Aymanns 2010: 264). One of the core functions of social support is to make the further process of difficult situations foreseeable, reduce insecurities, and point out possibilities for action (cf. Ibid.: 249). Hence relationship building should above all help pupils with a high absence rate, who have mainly had negative experiences of school, or who cannot cope with their everyday life without help due to their illness to gradually re-establish contact with education and school. Moreover, being slowly introduced back to educational offers by enabling positive learning experiences and learning successes is an important foundation for the further educational process. Because – at least in recent times – many inpatients of CAP have not experienced much success with regard to their academic performance and developed correspondingly low self-esteem (cf. Frey 2008: 139). According to the concept of applying self-efficacy to pedagogical fields of action, optimistic self-efficacy expectations are a basic condition to handle and cope with challenging demands (cf. Schwarzer/Jerusalem 2002: 36). The expectation of self-efficacy is considered a "subjective certainty to be able to cope with new or difficult situations based on one's own skills" (ibid.: 35) Therefore, it seems pedagogically reasonable to support self-efficacy expectations, especially among children and adolescents who have to cope with high demands. This concept links to Bandura's (2001) social cognitive theory, which suggests that motivational, emotional, actional and cognitive processes are controlled by subjective convictions. According to Bandura, experiences of self-efficacy are among others possible through feelings of success and the perception of one's own emotional excitement (see relation (3)). Mediating successes can be motivating for pupils if they recognise that their qualifications increase and they are able to achieve something for themselves (cf. Schwarzer/ Jerusalem 2002: 35ff.). Experiences of success can primarily be supported by setting short-term goals because these seem to be manageable and more achievable with personal effort. In this way, the subjects can experience a gradual increase in their skills, which is essential for developing and stabilising belief in one's own self-efficacy. Furthermore, supporting coping strategies is among others conducive to the development of self-efficacy expectations (see relation (3)) (cf. ibid.: 42ff.). My empirical data shows that hospital schools apply the concept of self-efficacy to their educational programme by attempting to set tasks that are orientated to individual needs and learning capabilities in order to mediate successful learning experiences. The emotional consequences of critical events can be reduced and individual interpretations of coping demands gradually transformed by reinforcing self-esteem and confidence in one's own abilities (coping as an iterative process) in order to lay the foundations or create resources for emotion- and problem-focused coping behaviour (cf. Filipp/Aymanns 2010: 148, 252).

3) Coping as part of education

Coping with everyday life during critical events or precarious life situations requires skills and qualifications to be able to act, which are acquired throughout educational processes. Thus education not only contributes to coping if considered as a process for imparting and acquiring (cf. Mack 1999: 286f.). By including matters relevant to everyday life in (school) education, "coping with daily life becomes tangible as a specific form of emancipation and individuation" (Mack 1999:21).

Therefore, in order to build confidence for coping with difficult situations, it is necessary to acquire skills and qualifications to bring demands under cognitive control and develop the capacity to act. The resulting expectations of self-efficacy may alleviate the emotional excitement before or while coping with difficult situations and reinforce coping skills (cf. Schwarzer/Jerusalem 2002: 45).

The pedagogical task of schools is to impart subject matter and qualifications. Hospital schools are required to organise teaching in such a way that pupils are able to catch up on the subject matter of their normal class following discharge, even after several months of absence from school. As suggested in the first relation, sufficient academic performance is important for the transition, however reintegration often requires further skills too (cf. Wertgen 2009: 309). Hence the pupils of hospital schools cannot be considered without taking their illness and their previous experiences of education into account (cf. Hoanzl et al. 2009: 405f.). Furthermore, my interviews with hospital schoolteachers revealed that gaining qualification in school subjects is certainly an important task of teaching. However, due to the pupils' special life situations, this is of secondary importance compared to imparting skills that enable pupils to participate in class and to cope with the demands of the transition and day-to-day school life. As mentioned in relation 2.2, beside setting short-term goals, supporting the development of coping strategies is an essential pedagogical task for improving self-efficacy. Burdens and critical events are dealt with on different levels of consciousness. Therefore, coping includes both unintentionally controlled and intentional actions (emotion- and problem-focused coping strategies) (cf. Filipp/ Aymanns 2010: 132). Transferred to educational offers, the acquisition of work and learning techniques, metacognitive skills, and problem-solving capabilities on the one hand and dealing with oneself on the other are of prime importance with regard to intentional action (cf. Schwarzer/Jerusalem 2002: 4ff.). Especially for children and adolescents who have not attended school for a longer period, the initial aim of hospital education is for them to (re)learn how to work continuously in a concentrated manner, follow rules, and develop cooperative learning and methodical skills (cf. Frey 2008: 139).

From a functional perspective, various types of social support are differentiated between, such as emotional and informational support. Emotional support relates to reinforcement of one's self-esteem and the feeling of acceptance through encouragement and assistance (see relation (2)) (cf. Filipp/Aymanns 2010: 241). Additionally, social learning and group work can foster pupils' awareness of others, self-perception and positive self-image, and at the same time counteract social isolation. By facilitating participation in smaller learning groups, feelings of security and stability can be encouraged and pupils prepared for participation in larger learning groups (cf. Frey 2008: 135ff.; Fesch/Müller 2014: 56f.). Informational support refers to enhancing knowledge about difficult demands and critical events in order to learn how to judge and deal with them better (cf. Filipp/Aymanns 2010: 241). With regard to the aforementioned ability to deal with oneself, hospital schools support their pupils particularly in their active intellectual, emotional, and social confrontation with the illness and the hospital stay (cf. Wertgen 2009: 309). Relevant German literature on hospital school education often refers to providing opportunities for creative writing or publishing school newspapers, which should encourage constructive consideration of one's own illness. Thus, the children and adolescents can confront and reflect on their illness and resulting situation on a personal and factual level. Sensitive pedagogical support is necessary during this process, as this learning topic may trigger emotions or revive past conflicts (cf. Wertgen 2007: 84; Warzecha 2003: 263).

The examination of one's own situation also takes place during consultation processes in hospital school. The closer pupils come to discharge from hospital, the greater the fear of stigmatization outside CAP becomes the focus of many pupils. Moreover, children and adolescents who return to their former class at a mainstream school after a long period of absence or join an existing class are often the centre of attention of their classmates (cf. Wertgen 2009: 309ff.). Hospital schools make questions about how to deal with these situations and whether to go public with one's own illness the subject of consultations and lessons. Most of the hospital teachers interviewed reported that they advise pupils to be open about their illness. Regulation theory approaches consider coping with difficult life situations as overcoming disparities between the current situation and how things should actually be (actual-target discrepancy) on the mental and action levels (cf. Filipp/Aymanns 2010: 128). Hospital schools contribute to overcoming discrepancies of what is and what should be (in this case, overcoming the fear of rejection towards a confident approach in social situations) by accompanying pupils' examination of their own situation.

Conclusion

Psychiatric disorders result in critical events not only in terms of the health condition but also school and social integration. "As such, the aim of all rehabilitative measures in psychiatry is not only to restore health but also social integration and the preservation of quality of life despite the existing health impairments" (Clausen/Eichenbrenner 2016: 175). As a permanent fixture in inpatients' daily life in CAP, hospital school is an "essential pillar of the treatment concept" (Krüger/ Romer 2003: 251).[14] With its key task of pedagogical preparation for the transition from CAP to mainstream education, it contributes to both school rehabilitation and social integration. The associated requirement to combine educational offers with offers to support coping processes is described theoretically with Mack's (1999) model regarding the relation between education and coping. Coping can be a purpose as well as a condition or part of education.

The findings of my analysis show that hospital school education takes each of these relations into account. Coping can be fostered with educational offers directly (e.g. by imparting relevant competences such as problem-solving skills)

---

[14] Although hospital schools and CAP cooperate on an interdisciplinary level, hospital schools are not assigned a therapeutic task.

or indirectly (e.g. by building trust in one's own capabilities or social learning through group work). If coping processes help pupils to overcome their aversion to school and the related negative connotations or painful experiences, then offers to support coping may trigger educational processes. Furthermore, certain learning topics can initiate both educational and coping processes (e.g. pupils' critical examination of their own situation (education) ideally leads to a change in their life situation (so coping)).[15]

Although the presentation of the three relations of education and coping may give the impression of a chronological order, their transfer to hospital education shows that educational and coping processes can take place either simultaneous, successively or in parallel to one another. According to Mack, education and coping are therefore in a dialectic relationship (cf. 2008: 151f.). Ultimately, the children's and adolescents' needs determine which relation(s) of education and coping is or are salient in the given classroom situation. In addition, educational offers and offers to support coping have to be combined across locations and profession boundaries: as I have shown, on the one hand pupils' coping needs, which are obviously also treated in a clinical-therapeutic context, cannot be ignored *per se* in hospital school education. Especially since educational processes can be triggered by meeting these coping needs. On the other hand, the learning topics and classroom situations of hospital schools' educational offers may help to initiate coping processes, which can then be adopted and supported by the CAP. Social skills and feelings of self-esteem and confidence in coping with the demands of the transition and day-to-day (school) life outside of the CAP can be proactively mediated by the hospital school and consolidated by the CAP – or vice versa. Fostering coping processes among inpatients of child and adolescent psychiatric units is thus neither limited to individual professions nor to locations such as CAP (therapy, care on hospital wards) or hospital school (teaching). Rather it must be set up as an overarching multimodal treatment concept across all disciplines and locations. The focus of CAP is therefore on recuperation, whereas the remit of hospital school is education.

---

[15] In practice, it is not always possible to draw a clear line between educational and coping processes. Therefore, my transfer of Mack's theoretical model on teaching practices in hospital schools is mostly an ideal-typical analysis.

Tobias Hensel

References

Ahmed, Sarina; Pohl, Axel; Schwanenflügel, Larissa von; Stauber, Barbara (Eds.) (2013): Bildung und Bewältigung im Zeichen von sozialer Ungleichheit. Theoretische und empirische Beiträge zur qualitativen Bildungs- und Übergangsforschung. Weinheim: Beltz Juventa.

Ahmed, Sarina; Pohl, Axel; Schwanenflügel, Larissa von; Stauber, Barbara (2013): Bildung und Bewältigung im Kontext sozialer Ungleichheit – Einleitung. In: Sarina Ahmed; Axel Pohl; Larissa von Schwanenflügel and Barbara Stauber (Eds.): Bildung und Bewältigung im Zeichen von sozialer Ungleichheit. Theoretische und empirische Beiträge zur qualitativen Bildungs- und Übergangsforschung. Weinheim: Beltz Juventa, p. 7-16

Bandura, Albert (2001): Social Cognitive Theory: An agentic perspective. In: *Annual Review of Psychology* 52, p. 1-26.

Bleher, Werner; Hoanzl, Martina; Ramminger, Edit (2014): Die Ungehaltenen halten. Ausgewählte Unterstützungssysteme/-angebote für psychisch kranke Kinder und Jugendliche aus sonderpädagogischer Sicht. In: *Sonderpädagogische Förderung heute* 59 (3), p. 272-293.

Böhnisch, Lothar (2012): Sozialpädagogik der Lebensalter. Eine Einführung. 6th revised edition. Weinheim, Basel: Beltz Juventa.

Clausen, Jens; Eichenbrenner, Ilse (2016): Soziale Psychiatrie. Grundlagen, Zielgruppen, Hilfeformen. 2nd revised and extended edition. Stuttgart: Verlag W. Kohlhammer.

Coelen, Thomas; Otto, Hans-Uwe (Eds.) (2008): Grundbegriffe Ganztagsbildung. Das Handbuch. 1st edition. Wiesbaden: VS Verlag für Sozialwissenschaften.

Ertle, Christoph (Ed.) (1997): Schule bei kranken Kindern und Jugendlichen. Wege zu Unterricht und Schulorganisation in Kliniken und Spezialklassen. Bad Heilbrunn: Klinkhardt.

Fend, Helmut (1980): Theorie der Schule. Munich: Urban & Schwarzenberg.

Fesch, Katharina; Müller, Thomas (2014): Schule für Kranke in Deutschland. Zur heterogenen Situation der Bundesländer im Umgang mit psychisch erkrankten Kindern und Jugendlichen. In: *Zeitschrift für Heilpädagogik* (2), p. 50-59.

Filipp, Sigrun-Heide; Aymanns, Peter (2010): Kritische Lebensereignisse und Lebenskrisen. Vom Umgang mit den Schattenseiten des Lebens. 1st edition. Stuttgart: Verlag W. Kohlhammer.

Flitner, Elisabeth; Ostkämper, Frodo; Scheid, Claudia; Wertgen, Alexander (Eds.) (2014): Chronisch kranke Kinder in der Schule. Stuttgart: Verlag W. Kohlhammer.

Frey, Hermann (2008): Was ist eine Schule für Kranke? In: Gisela Steins (Ed.): Schule trotz Krankheit. Eine Evaluation von Unterricht mit kranken Kindern und Jugendlichen und Implikationen für die allgemeinbildenden Schulen. Lengerich: Pabst Science Publ, p. 128-154.

Hensel, Tobias (2017): »Bei denen ist erstmal gar nicht an Schule zu denken«. Unterstützung von Bildungs- und Bewältigungsprozessen in Klinikschulen in der Kinder- und Jugendpsychiatrie. In: Joachim Schroeder and Louis Henri Seukwa (Ed.): Soziale Bildungsarbeit mit jungen Menschen. Handlungsfelder, Konzepte, Qualitätsmerkmale. Bielefeld: transkript Verlag, p. 183-208.

Hilff, Günter (1997): Zwischen Distanz und Nähe - aus der Arbeit mit Schülern der Sekundarstufe in einer kinder- und jugendpsychiatrischen Klinik. In: Christoph Ertle (Ed.): Schule bei kranken Kindern und Jugendlichen. Wege zu Unterricht und Schulorganisation in Kliniken und Spezialklassen. Bad Heilbrunn: Klinkhardt, p. 161-180.

Hinne-Fischer, Jutta (Ed.) (2007): Schule und Klinik. Beiträge zur Pädagogik bei Krankheit. Eine Festschrift der Alfred-Adler-Schule. Alfred-Adler-Schule. Berlin: LIT Verl.

Hoanzl, Martina; Baur, Werner; Bleher, Werner; Thümmler, Ramona; Käppler, Christoph (2009): Unterricht in psychiatrischen Klinikschulen. In: Günther Opp and Georg Theunissen (Ed.): Handbuch schulische Sonderpädagogik. Bad Heilbrunn: Klinkhardt, p. 404-411.

Hölling, Heike; Schlack, Robert; Petermann, Franz; Ravens-Sieberer, Ulrike; Mauz, Elvira (2014): Psychische Auffälligkeiten und psychosoziale Beeinträchtigungen bei Kindern und Jugendlichen im Alter von 3 bis 17 Jahren in Deutschland – Prävalenz und zeitliche Trends zu 2 Erhebungszeitpunkten (2003-2006 und 2009-2012). Ergebnisse der KiGGS-Studie – Erste Folgebefragung (KiGGS Welle 1). In: *Bundesgesundheitsblatt - Gesundheitsforschung - Gesundheitsschutz* 57 (7), p. 807-819.

Hospital Organisation of Pedagogues in Europe (HOPE) (Ed.) (2010): Das kranke Kind – Aufgehoben im Netzwerk zwischen Pädagogik und Medizin. Proceedings of the 7th HOPE Congress 2010 in Munich. Available online at *http://hope2010munich.eu/berichte/HOPE_Tagungsband-m.pdf*, last accessed on 26.08.2015.

Jerusalem, Matthias; Hopf, Dieter (Eds.) (2002): Selbstwirksamkeit und Motivationsprozesse in Bildungsinstitutionen. Weinheim and Basel: Beltz Verlag (Zeitschrift für Pädagogik, 44th supplement).

Kramer, Rolf-Torsten; Helsper, Werner (2013): Schulische Übergänge und Schülerbiographien. In: Wolfgang Schröer, Barbara Stauber, Andreas Walther, Lothar Böhnisch and Karl Lenz (Eds.): Handbuch Übergänge. Weinheim: Beltz Juventa, p. 589-613.

Krüger, Detlev; Romer, Georg (2003): Schule in der Kinder- und Jugendpsychiatrie: Eine Herausforderung an die Erziehungswissenschaft. In: Birgit Warzecha (Ed.): Heterogenität macht Schule. Beiträge aus sonderpädagogischer und interkultureller Perspektive. Münster: Waxmann, p. 251-257.

Lazarus, Richard S.; Folkman, Susan (1984): Stress, appraisal, and coping. New York: Springer.

Mack, Wolfgang (1999): Bildung und Bewältigung. Vorarbeiten zu einer Pädagogik der Jugendschule. Weinheim: Dt. Studien-Verl.

Mack, Wolfgang (2008): Bewältigung. In: Thomas Coelen and Hans-Uwe Otto (Eds.): Grundbegriffe Ganztagsbildung. Das Handbuch. 1st edition. Wiesbaden: VS Verlag für Sozialwissenschaften, p. 146-154.

Mack Wolfgang (2013): Bildung und Bewältigung bei prekären Übergangsprozessen. In: Sarina Ahmed, Axel Pohl, Larissa von Schwanenflügel and Barbara Stauber (Eds.): Bildung und Bewältigung im Zeichen von sozialer Ungleichheit. Theoretische und empirische Beiträge zur qualitativen Bildungs- und Übergangsforschung. Weinheim: Beltz Juventa, p. 122-139.

Myschker, Norbert; Stein, Roland (2014): Verhaltensstörungen bei Kindern und Jugendlichen. Erscheinungsformen - Ursachen - hilfreiche Maßnahmen. 7th revised and extended edition. Stuttgart: Kohlhammer.

Opp, Günther; Theunissen, Georg (Ed.) (2009): Handbuch schulische Sonderpädagogik. Bad Heilbrunn: Klinkhardt.

Ricking, Heinrich; Schulze, Gisela C. (Ed.) (2012): Schulabbruch. Ohne Ticket in die Zukunft. Bad Heilbrunn: Klinkhardt, Julius.

Ricking, Heinrich; Schulze, Gisela C. (2012): Schulabbruch - Eine Zukunftsfrage. In: Heinrich Ricking and Gisela C. Schulze (Ed.): Schulabbruch. Ohne Ticket in die Zukunft. Bad Heilbrunn: Klinkhardt, Julius, p. 12-21.

Schroeder, Joachim; Seukwa, Louis Henri (Eds.) (2017): Soziale Bildungsarbeit mit jungen Menschen. Handlungsfelder, Konzepte, Qualitätsmerkmale. Bielefeld: transkript Verlag.

Schröer, Wolfgang (2013): Entgrenzung, Übergänge, Bewältigung. In: Wolfgang Schröer, Barbara Stauber, Andreas Walther, Lothar Böhnisch and Karl Lenz (Eds.): Handbuch Übergänge. Weinheim: Beltz Juventa, p. 64-79.

Schröer, Wolfgang; Stauber, Barbara; Walther, Andreas; Böhnisch, Lothar; Lenz, Karl (Eds.) (2013): Handbuch Übergänge. Weinheim: Beltz Juventa.

Schwarzer, Ralf; Jerusalem, Matthias (2002): Das Konzept der Selbstwirksamkeit. In: Matthias Jerusalem and Dieter Hopf (Ed.): Selbstwirksamkeit und Motivationsprozesse in

Bildungsinstitutionen. Weinheim and Basel: Beltz Verlag (Zeitschrift für Pädagogik, 44th supplement), p. 28-53.

Steins, Gisela (Ed.) (2008): Schule trotz Krankheit. Eine Evaluation von Unterricht mit kranken Kindern und Jugendlichen und Implikationen für die allgemeinbildenden Schulen. Lengerich: Pabst Science Publ.

Warzecha, Birgit (Ed.) (2003): Heterogenität macht Schule. Beiträge aus sonderpädagogischer und interkultureller Perspektive. Münster: Waxmann.

Warzecha, Birgit (2003): Unterricht, Bildung und Erziehung in der Kinder- und Jugendpsychiatrie. In: Birgit Warzecha (Ed.): Heterogenität macht Schule. Beiträge aus sonderpädagogischer und interkultureller Perspektive. Münster [i.a.]: Waxmann (November-akademie, 3), p. 259-267.

Weber, Pia Anna; Welling, Verena; Steins, Gisela (2010): Die Nachsorge von schulabstinenten Kindern und Jugendlichen: Die Relevanz einer sozialpsychologischen Perspektive. In: Hospital Organisation of Pedagogues in Europe (HOPE) (Ed.): Das kranke Kind – Aufgehoben im Netzwerk zwischen Pädagogik und Medizin. Proceedings of the 7th HOPE Congress 2010 in Munich, p. 74-78.

Wertgen, Alexander (2007): Schülerzeitungsarbeit an der Alfred-Adler-Schule, Städt. Schule für Kranke, Düsseldorf. In: Jutta Hinne-Fischer (Ed.): Schule und Klinik. Beiträge zur Pädagogik bei Krankheit. Eine Festschrift der Alfred-Adler-Schule. Berlin: LIT Verl, p. 84-109.

Wertgen, Alexander (2009): Auf den Übergang kommt es an! Pädagogisch begleitete Schulrückführung als Angebot der Schule für Kranke für Schüler nach einem Psychiatrieaufenthalt. In: *Zeitschrift für Heilpädagogik* (8), p. 308-316.

Wertgen, Alexander (2012): Welchen Beitrag können Schulen für Kranke zur schulischen Reintegration von Kindern und Jugendlichen mit schulvermeidendem Verhalten leisten? In: *Zeitschrift für Heilpädagogik* 63 (6), p. 224-230.

Wertgen, Alexander; Scheid, Claudia (2014): Chronisch kranke Schüler/innen - ein thematischer Abriss. In: Elisabeth Flitner, Frodo Ostkämper, Claudia Scheid and Alexander Wertgen (Eds.): Chronisch kranke Kinder in der Schule. Stuttgart: Verlag W. Kohlhammer, p. 17-25.

16 Inclusive School without Barriers (InkluSoB) – A service centre at Universität Hamburg

(Marie-Luise Schütt, Manfred Steger)

Abstract

With the ratification of the UN Convention on the Rights of Persons with Disabilities (CRPD), Germany is obligated to implement inclusive structures throughout the entire education system. As a main consequence, pupils with special needs have the general right to attend a mainstream school. This increases the heterogeneity of pupils in mainstream schools. In the future, Germany needs teachers who can deal with this heterogeneity in the classroom. With the primary intention of optimizing the existing teacher education system, the German Federal Ministry of Education and Research (BMBF) launched the Quality Initiative for Teacher Education in August 2015. This article gives some insights into the Inclusive School without Barriers (InkluSoB) project forming part of the main ProfaLe project[16] based at Universität Hamburg. The main aim of ProfaLe (and especially the action area of inclusion) is to identify the professional competence of future teachers in inclusive schools and to provide concrete offers to train this professional competence on a university level.

Starting point

In the main process to determine the necessary competencies of future teachers, the definition of inclusive education is essential. In 2007, Vernor Muñoz, the UN Special Rapporteur on the Right to Education, declared that: *"Inclusive education acknowledges that every child has unique characteristics, interests, abilities and learning needs and that those learners with special education needs must have access to and be accommodated in the general education system through a child-centred pedagogy. Inclusive education, by taking into account the diversity among learners, seeks to combat discriminatory attitudes, create welcoming communities, achieve education for all as well as improve the quality and effectiveness of*

---

[16] The ProfaLe project on professional teaching to promote subject-based learning under changing social conditions is supported by the Federal Ministry of Education and Research (BMBF) within the Quality Initiative for Teacher Education.

---

education of mainstream learners" (GA 2007, 6). In this definition, Vernor Muñoz referred to one essential point that is needed when implementing inclusive structures: every pupil – with or without disabilities – must have access to the general education system. Schools are required to eliminate barriers that might deprive qualified persons with disabilities of the opportunity to succeed in school. In fact, an inclusive school must be an accessible school. In Germany, Kersten Reich highlighted that accessibility is one important requirement for achieving an inclusive school system (Reich 2014, 235).

Accessibility is a guiding principle of the UN CRPD. According to the UN CRPD, accessibility means that *"to enable persons with disabilities to live independently and participate fully in all aspects of life, States Parties shall take appropriate measures to ensure to persons with disabilities access, on an equal basis with others, to the physical environment, to transportation, to information and communications, including information and communications technologies and systems, and to other facilities and services open or provided to the public, both in urban and in rural areas. These measures, which shall include the identification and elimination of obstacles and barriers to accessibility, shall apply to, inter alia:*

a)   *Buildings, roads, transportation and other indoor and outdoor facilities, including schools, housing, medical facilities and workplaces;*
b)   *Information, communications and other services, including electronic services and emergency services"* (UN 2006/2008, Art. 9).

The principle of accessibility is relevant to all areas of implementation of the UN CRPD. In this definition, it becomes obvious that accessibility means more than access to the physical environment.

With the help of two examples, the importance of accessibility in the context of school will be demonstrated. First, learners with special needs must have access to the learning materials. Teachers have to select learning materials that are accessible for all children. If the teacher copies a worksheet repeatedly, the contrast of the task description will be reduced. Low contrast makes it difficult for all learners to read the task on the worksheet. In particular, the task is not legible for learners with a visual impairment. In addition, blind learners are unable to use the paper worksheet and thus have no chance to obtain the information. These

Marie-Luise Schütt & Manfred Steger

learners are dependent on receiving an electronic or Braille version of the worksheet. Secondly, videos are used in many classes to develop knowledge. In order to be accessible to learners with a hearing impairment, the videos need subtitles and/or captions. These are also extremely helpful for children with German as their second language.

Further examples of the meaning of accessibility in the school setting are summarized in the paper by Schroeder and Degenhardt (2016, 9).

Accessibility and Universal Design

Schroeder & Degenhardt point out that *"[i]solated strategies for enhancing accessibility and inclusion for people with disabilities are insufficient"* (Schroeder & Degenhardt 2016, 16). Instead of using isolated strategies, they propose following the Universal Design (UD) approach. *"'Universal Design' means the design of products, environments, programmes and services to be usable by all people, to the greatest extent possible, without the need for adaptation or specialized design. 'Universal Design' shall not exclude assistive devices for particular groups of persons with disabilities where this is needed"* (UN 2006/2008, Art. 2). By applying the idea of UD in the field of education, some further developments become possible that support inclusive school structures. One concept in the field of education, which is based on the UD framework, is the Universal Design for Learning (UDL) that was developed at the Center for Applied Special Technology (CAST) in the 1990s. David Rose and Anne Meyer, the main developers of the concept of UDL, said that it is possible to transfer the main idea of UD to build learning environments for all pupils. UDL provides *"rich supports for learning and reduces barriers to the curriculum while maintaining high achievement standards for all"* (UDL 2018).

The scientific background of the concept of UDL is based on neuroscience research. Every learner is equipped with three types of networks: a recognition network, a strategic network and an affective network (cf. Table 16.1 on the principles of UDL). These networks differ from learner to learner. As a result, the teacher must create learning opportunities that address the different types of learners. The learning task should therefore include alternatives to make it accessible and applicable for students with different backgrounds, learning styles, abilities, and disabilities. Finally, learning opportunities that take the heterogeneity of the learners into account reduce the need for adaptation for learners with special needs.

Recognition network	Strategic network	Affective network
"What" of learning	"How" of learning	"Why" of learning
Present information and content in different ways	Differentiate the ways that students can express what they know	Stimulate interest and motivation for learning
Principle 1 **Multiple means of representation**	Principle 2 **Multiple means of action and expression**	Principle 3 **Multiple means of engagement**

Table 16.1: Overview of three UDL principles

To illustrate this effort by using the idea of UDL in the inclusive school setting, the selected examples need to be expanded. Not only learners with a visual impairment will benefit from an electronic version of the worksheet, for example. In addition, learners without a disability, who are auditory learners, can also benefit. An accessible, electronic version of the worksheet makes it possible for the learning task to be read out at the computer – and this supports auditory learners. To summarise, paying attention to the special characteristics of learners with disabilities can optimise the participation of all learners. In this context, the concept of UDL must be focused on, as the idea of UDL offers many possibilities to achieve an accessible learning environment.

The InkluSoB service centre

The theoretical background shows that future teachers must familiarise themselves with the meaning of accessibility for implementing inclusive school settings. Therefore, knowledge of the concept of UDL must be imparted during the teacher training at university. Within the scope of the Quality Initiative for Teacher Education, these topics will be included in the curriculum of future mainstream and special needs education teachers. By founding a service centre called InkluSoB (Inclusive School without Barriers), future teachers will have the opportunity to consciously look at accessibility, Universal Design and other topics relating to the implementation of inclusive education. In the following, the steps for implementing the InkluSoB service centre within the Faculty of Education at Universität Hamburg will be presented.

Marie-Luise Schütt & Manfred Steger

1. Analysis of needs

A needs analysis was the essential starting point for development of the InkluSoB service centre. To gain an impression of the knowledge of future teachers (especially future mainstream school teachers) regarding accessibility and Universal Design, an online survey was conducted within the teacher training programme at Universität Hamburg. In October 2015, a mix of prospective teachers from a series of seminars were interviewed (n = 31). For example, the prospective teachers were asked the following questions:

- Do you know something about the accessibility of the physical environment in the classroom (using furniture in the classroom; designing the order and structure, acoustic conditions, lighting in the classroom)?
- Do you know something about producing accessible learning materials (e.g. verbalization of visual information; preparation of accessible videos, presentations, text materials)?

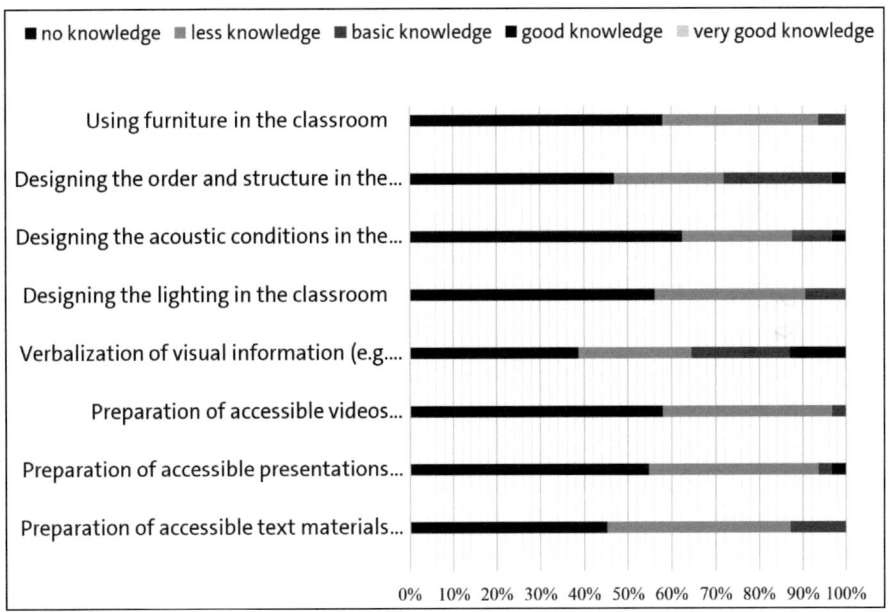

Figure 16.1: Knowledge about the accessibility of the physical environment and preparing learning materials

The majority of the respondents answered that they have no or minimal knowledge of accessibility. In the first part of the online survey, the respondents indicated their knowledge of designing accessible learning environments. Only 6% of the students interviewed declared that they had any knowledge about using furniture in the classroom. More than 90% stated that they have no or little knowledge of the design of lighting in the classroom. Around 90% also indicated that they have no or little idea about the acoustic requirements of classrooms.

In the second part of the survey, the students estimated their knowledge of the production of accessible learning materials. Similar results can be seen here. Specifically, around 80% of the students interviewed declared that they have no or little knowledge of creating accessible text documents. The percentage of students with no or little knowledge of producing accessible presentations with PowerPoint is even higher. Overall, the needs analysis revealed a lack of knowledge about accessibility. As a main consequence, offers in which future teachers can develop their expertise about realizing accessible learning environments and materials must be implemented in the teacher training programme.

2. Aims of InkluSoB

In summary, the analysis of needs has shown that the majority of students have no idea about designing an accessible learning environment and accessible learning materials. To develop their expertise in this field, the InkluSoB was launched in May 2016. InkluSoB has two main target groups: students and lecturers within the Faculty of Education. By involving the lecturers (as well as the administrative staff) within the Faculty of Education, it is possible to ensure that students experience accessible learning environments as early as possible. For example, trainee teachers receive accessible documents for studying teacher education. If students can experience this at the university on their own, it is easier for them to transfer their knowledge about accessibility and UDL to their future practice.

InkluSoB therefore has two main aims. Firstly, InkluSoB will determine the main accessibility problems for raising awareness about existing problems in inclusive classrooms. Secondly, InkluSoB will support future teachers and lecturers so as to improve their knowledge.

Marie-Luise Schütt & Manfred Steger

3. An overview of the InkluSoB measures

In the following, the important arrangements that are available at the InkluSoB service centre are presented. These arrangements will support the development of expertise. In general, they can be divided into two types of offers: permanent (1) and temporary offers (2).

1. Helpdesk at the Faculty of Education (Universität Hamburg)
   a. *Accessibility of classrooms* (instruments for identifying accessibility problems of the physical environments)
   b. *Peer-to-peer counselling project:* exchange about designing inclusive learning settings

2. Training offers at the Faculty of Education (Universität Hamburg)
   a. *Workshops* (e.g. on creating accessible videos and documents, making lectures more accessible)
   b. *Cooperation with courses/lecturers* (team teaching)

In terms of permanent offers, it is possible to borrow special instruments that can be used to check the accessibility of the learning environment. Specifically, students can borrow an acoustic analyser, which they can use to measure the acoustic conditions in the classroom. They learn how to use these instruments and to interpret the results in special workshops organised by the InkluSoB.

Since May 2017, the permanent offers include a peer-to-peer counselling service. The primary goal of this service is to facilitate an exchange between prospective special needs education teachers and prospective mainstream school teachers on the best possible solutions for learning situations in the inclusive school setting. Empirical studies show that cooperation between special needs education teachers and mainstream school teachers is one success condition for achieving inclusive school settings. The peer-to-peer-counselling supports cooperation at an early stage. Since June 2017, five master's students have been responsible for the counselling hours (once a week). They are special needs education students with diverse knowledge about disability (e.g. expert knowledge about hearing and visual impairments). In addition to the counselling hour, the students are responsible for furthering the concept of peer-to-peer counselling.

In terms of temporary offers, InkluSoB provides trainings at the Faculty of Education. Almost every month, students have the chance to participate in a workshop. These workshops are held in cooperation with other services at the Faculty of Education, such as the media centre. Students can develop their expertise about creating accessible videos, learning materials and presentations with PowerPoint during these workshops.

Example of a workshop: Smartpen

The principle of Universal Design also dominates the workshops. Not only knowledge about special devices, like speech output or Braille display, but also knowledge about universally-designed equipment is necessary. With regards to this matter, one component covered in the workshops is the possible use of smartpens in the inclusive classroom.

The Livescribe 3 Smartpen is a digital pen that allows accessible notes and audios (Livescribe 3 Smartpen 2018). The pen is equipped with a camera and a microphone. In this way, the smartpen captures everything that is written or spoken during lessons. It uses Bluetooth to send all notes and audio recordings to a smartphone or tablet. In the workshop, students learn how to use the smartpen. In addition, they can try out the smartpen and discover the possible uses in an inclusive school setting. The smartpen can support students with and without special needs. A student who prefers to listen more than to write can reduce the amount of writing. At home, the student can tap anywhere in their notes and the audio playback will play from that exact spot. This function is one example for supporting pupils with learning problems and auditory learners (Smartpen and Students with Learning Disabilities 2018).

In addition to the workshops, InkluSoB cooperates with courses. In contrast to workshops, which are entirely voluntary, mainstream school teachers are required to consider accessibility in schools during courses. This semester, Britta Lübke, who is a teacher of the didactics of biology, is collaborating with the InkluSoB on one lecture. As part of the lecture, students review the degree of accessibility of an extracurricular learning space (such as a museum, zoo or planetarium). This allows them to develop their expertise in the field of accessibility and to provide input on possible improvements for the extracurricular learning space.

Marie-Luise Schütt & Manfred Steger

In addition, prospective teachers can transfer their knowledge to other learning situations.

Conclusion

Overall, InkluSoB started off well with a range of different offers within the Faculty of Education at Universität Hamburg. Publicity (in the form of posters, a homepage and a Facebook group) helps to raise awareness for InkluSoB. Despite this, it will take time to become a fixed component of the service offers. Currently, only a minority of students know about the InkluSoB service centre. One of the next steps must therefore be to make InkluSoB more popular at Universität Hamburg. New workshops and cooperation with other partners (e.g. the Office of Affairs for Students with Disabilities or Chronic Diseases) will support this process. Additionally, continuous evaluation of the temporary and permanent offers is essential to achieve the highest possible quality. Students and lecturers will only use offers if they are of a high quality. All offers that are organized by InkluSoB will be evaluated by the Hamburg project ProfaLe (Quality Initiative for Teacher Education). Despite the good evaluation, the offers are mainly used by future special needs education teachers. Mainstream school teachers only occasionally take advantage of the offers. Concerning the educational policy goal of implementing inclusive structures in the whole education system, the training activities have to be extended. The offers must be used by future mainstream school teachers in the same way. If they take the basics of accessible text documents into account, a blind pupil can participate by using a Braille display. An adapted text document that might isolate the blind pupil is not necessary. One possible measure to increase the participation of mainstream school teachers would be to introduce official certificates from the Faculty of Education for all students who participate in the workshops. This would be an opportunity to promote the InkluSoB service centre and to increase the knowledge of future teachers about accessibility in schools.

References

GA – General Assembly (2007): Implementation of General Assembly resolution 60/251 of 15 March 2006 entitled 'Human Rights Council', The right to education of persons with disabilities, Report of the Special Rapporteur on the right to education, Vernor Muñoz, A/HRC/4/29, 19 February 2007.

Livescribe 3 Smartpen (2018): Overview; URL: *www.livescribe.com/en-us/smartpen/ls3*, last accessed on 22.01.2018.

Reich, Kersten (2014): Inklusive Didaktik: Bausteine für eine inklusive Schule. Weinheim: Beltz.

Schroeder, Joachim & Degenhardt, Sven (2016): Inclusive education and accessibility. Science to Policy Brief. Bonn: Deutsche Gesellschaft für internationale Zusammenarbeit (giz); URL: *www.giz.de/expertise/downloads/giz2016-inclusive-education-and-accessibility.pdf*, last accessed on 16.01.2018.

Smartpen and Students with Learning Disabilities (2018): How Smartpens Help Students with Learning Disabilities; URL: *www.livescribe.com/en-us/solutions/learningdisabilities*, last accessed on 22.01.2018.

UN - United Nations (2006/2008): Convention on the Rights of Persons with Disability (CRPD); URL: *www.un.org/development/desa/disabilities/convention-on-the-rights-of-persons-with-disabilities.html*, last accessed on 22.01.2018.

UDL – Universal Design for Learning (2018): What is UDL? URL: *http://udl-center.org*, last accessed on 22.01.2018.

17 Basic education for people with disabilities in Hamburg GRUND:BILDUNG research project: 2012-2015 [17]

(Uta Wagner)

Background

In Germany, basic education was for a long time a side topic in the debate on life-long learning. In terms of the consequences for education planning, reporting and monitoring, this is still very much the case. The term *basic education* describes a key area of adult education that includes the aspects of literacy, reading, writing, numeracy and digital skills. It also involves helping people with a low level of education to learn German as a second language. In work-related basic education, there are offers of further professional training in simple tasks as well as courses for low-skilled workers.

Particularly in the last decade, national and international research has increased the visibility of functional illiteracy as a social and pedagogical challenge. Empirical studies hint at the scale of this phenomenon in Germany: it can be assumed that every year, around 15% of young people leave the general education system without having gained confidence in literacy. Biographical reconstructions and participant analyses have yielded a very differentiated picture of the extremely heterogeneous life situations of people with a low level of education, many of whom live in socially unprivileged and culturally deprived environments and are in precarious employment.

From the end of 2012, we compiled and catalogued all of the current offers, providers, concepts and locations in Hamburg offering basic education. In spring 2015, we then concluded the compilation work for the time being to map and digitalise our findings in a *Basic Education Atlas* and publish this online in an information portal (*www.fs-grundbildung.de*).

Based on the research complemented with systematic surveys, interviews, visits to providers and document analyses, individual aspects of basic education

---

[17] This article was originally published in German in: Gag, Maren; Grotheer, Angela; Schroeder, Joachim; Wagner, Uta & Weber, Martina (Eds.): Berichte aus den Randbezirken der Erwachsenenbildung. Eine empirische Analyse der Hamburger Grundbildungslandschaft. Bielefeld: W. Bertelsmann Verlag 2016, p.99-116. It has been adapted, revised and translated into English for the present publication.

were investigated in terms of the access to these, the target group orientation, suitability and demand fulfilment and detailed in a *Basic Education Report*: beside education planning and monitoring, we considered the aspects of immigration and ethnicity, disability and inclusion, correctional facilities and forensic psychiatry, and different fields of social educational work in great depth (cf. Gag et al. 2015). It should be emphasised here that the reports presented merely provide a snapshot of the situation gained during the period investigated.

Term definitions
People living with a disability, impairment or serious chronic illness often face a variety of barriers, which complicate their participation in social life or even render it entirely impossible. Educational poverty or difficulty accessing educational offers can prove a hindrance, as (basic) education is undeniably a fundamental requirement for participation in society. Thus the German federal government's participation report on the life situations of people with disabilities in Germany (BMAS 2013) showed, for example, that half of 20 to 64-year-olds with a disability do not have any academic qualification or are only qualified to the minimum social standard (cf. BMAS 2013, p.111 and Solga 2005, p.17f). As a consequence, 19% of people with a disability (aged 30 to 64 years) do not have a vocational qualification – twice as many as their peers without a disability (cf. BMAS 2013, p.111).

In Germany, more than seven million people are considered severely disabled[18] (BMAS 2013, p.7 and p.60). At the end of 2013, there were 130,153 people with a severe disability living in the Hanseatic city. According to an older statistic, approximately 251,500 people with disabilities were living in Hamburg in 2008, of which 156,600 were considered severely disabled (cf. Free and Hanseatic City of Hamburg 2008, p.9).

This article examines how Hamburg is addressing this situation (at least with regard to the need for basic education) and which offers exist accordingly for adults with disabilities. It is particularly interested in whether these educational

---

[18] This is all of the people that the benefits office (*Versorgungsamt*) has issued with a disabled person's pass with a degree of disability of at least 50 (Statistics Agency for Hamburg and Schleswig-Holstein 2015, p.58).

Uta Wagner

opportunities are in fact suitable or whether shortcomings exist. The group of individuals described as *people with disabilities* must first be considered for this. Brief consideration of the term *disability* can provide clarity – though a uniform, generally-recognised definition does not actually exist for this category to date (cf. e.g. Dederich 2009, p.15). The opinion of what a disability is or who can actually be considered disabled among others depends on the discipline on which the opinion is based, such as medicine, pedagogy or psychology. Bleidick (1995) formulates his definition from a special needs education perspective:

"A person is considered disabled, when their physical, mental or psychiatric functions are impaired to such an extent that their immediate life or participation in social life is hindered." (Bleidick 1995, p.15; cited in Cloerkes 2007, p.4)

This definition is very broad, but includes an aspect that is very decisive in the context of basic education: a disability hinders participation in social life or renders it impossible. Book Nine of the German Social Code[19] (hereinafter SGB IX), which considers the *rehabilitation and participation of disabled persons* adopts a similar view:

"A person is disabled if their physical functions, mental capacity or psychological health are highly likely to deviate for more than six months from the condition which is typical for their respective age and whose participation in the life of society is therefore restricted. They are at risk of disability if a hindrance is to be expected." (§ 2 para. 1 SGB IX)

SGB IX came into force on 1 July 2001 and is oriented to the guidelines of the World Health Organization and the wording used in other European countries (Cloerkes 2007, p.4). This amendment to the law is particularly important in light of the reinforcement of the self-determination of those affected and improvements to the rehabilitation law (for information on this and development of the legal situation for people with disabilities in Germany, cf. e.g. Thomann 2012).

Educational offers for adults with disabilities are being established all across Germany, whereby organisations for people with disabilities are responsible for the majority of these. In the following, the basic education offers for people with

---

[19] The books of the social code regulate implementation of the principle of a social state in Germany. Thus SGB II regulates the basic benefits for jobseekers and SGB V-VII the statutory health, pension and accident insurance.

---

disabilities in Hamburg shall be examined. This examination shall be based on an in-depth review of the basic education offers for people with disabilities in Hamburg as well as on interviews with the staff at organisations for people with disabilities. The analysis will consider interviews conducted between April and November 2014 with staff from the different organisations, most of which are responsible for the field of basic education or for the development of adult education offers for people with disabilities.

Legal framework

The legal basis, legal entitlement to education of people with disabilities and educational requirements are embedded in Book Nine of the German Social Code (SGB IX) on the rehabilitation and participation of disabled persons and in the German Law on the United Nations Convention on the Rights of Persons with Disabilities, CRPD.

As previously mentioned, the group of people referred to as "people with disabilities" is defined in § 2 SGB IX. With regard to work-related basic education, particularly § 33 SGB IX in which the assistance for participation in working life is defined is decisive. According to paragraph 1:

"For the participation in work life, the required support shall be provided to sustain, enhance, establish or restore the earning capacity of persons with disabilities or persons at risk of becoming disabled, and to ensure their permanent participation in working life wherever possible." (§ 33 para. 1, SGB IX)

The corresponding support is then described in greater detail in paragraph 3: "In particular, the services shall include

1. assistance to retain or obtain employment, including activation and professional integration measures;
2. work preparation assistance, including basic training necessitated by the disability;
2a. individual workplace training as part of supported employment;
3. vocational adaptation and further training, including the obtaining of an educational qualification required to take part in the vocational adaptation or further training;
4. vocational training, including courses that are not predominantly school-based;

5. startup subsidies in compliance with Section 93 of Book III of the Social Code, provided by the rehabilitation providers as laid down in Section 6 (1), No. 2-5 of Book IX of the Social Code;
6. other forms of assistance to promote participation in working life in order to allow people with disabilities to obtain and remain in appropriate employment or selfemployment." (§ 33 para. 3 SGB IX)

The work preparation assistance mentioned in paragraph 3 no. 2 is not explained in any detail in the legal text. A glance at the supplementary notes provides clarity however:

"*Work preparation assistance* (no. 2) should enable those affected to learn a profession. Decisive for permanent participation in working life wherever possible are not the actual skills that exist, but rather the potential of those affected that can be tapped into with supporting aids. It is therefore a question of filling knowledge gaps and imparting basic skills without which the ensuing measures would not promise success." (Lachwitz *et al.* 2010, p. 321f, emphasis in the original)

Although it is not explicitly mentioned here, a legal right to work-related basic education is inferred indirectly here.

The subject of education is addressed in Article 24 of the Convention on the Rights of Persons with Disabilities, reaffirming the right to education provided for in Article 26 of the *Universal Declaration of Human Rights*. According to § 24 para. 1:

"States Parties recognize the right of persons with disabilities to education. With a view to realizing this right without discrimination and on the basis of equal opportunity, States Parties shall ensure an inclusive education system[20] at all levels and lifelong learning directed to:

---

[20] Striking here is the use of the adjective "integrative" in the German translation to describe the education system; the original English text uses the term "inclusive". Consideration of the terminology of these two terms would exceed the scope of this work, hence just a brief note here: on the etymological level, the two terms differ significantly. While inclusion derives from the Latin word *includere*, so "to include", integration originates from the Latin word *integrātus*, meaning "to make whole". In German, these terms are often used synonymously, though, in the sense of a process to improve the social participation of people with disabilities.

---

a) The full development of human potential and sense of dignity and self-worth, and the strengthening of respect for human rights, fundamental freedoms and human diversity;

b) The development by persons with disabilities of their personality, talents and creativity, as well as their mental and physical abilities, to their fullest potential;

c) Enabling persons with disabilities to participate effectively in a free society." (§ 24 para. 1, UN Convention on the Rights of Persons with Disabilities, CRPD)

Decisive in this context is that lifelong learning is also explicitly mentioned and the right to education therefore does not end with compulsory education but rather persists for a person's entire lifetime.

Basic education offers for people with disabilities in Hamburg

The courses offered are primarily aimed at people with a mental disability, learning impairment or psychiatric disorder. The life and living situations of the course participants is extremely heterogeneous. Most of them work, but there is also a growing number of senior citizens and people who currently do not (or no longer) work. The access threshold to the different programmes is very low. The courses are generally free, community-based and open to all interested parties. A programme published annually, flyer and recommendations from other participants or employees inform on the programme. Cooperation between the different organisations allows a broad range of offers for which the demand and quality are regularly reviewed.

The offers are primarily aimed at aspects like leisure activities such as cooking and music groups, to name just a few. In addition, there are courses focusing on basic and fundamental skills that can be used in a professional setting later on. These learning opportunities are located at the interface between fostering everyday skills and work-related basic education. They include telephone training as well as courses to further financial literacy and numeracy as well as to develop reading and writing skills, for instance.

No specific preconceived aims are worked towards within the educational setting. Instead, the courses are oriented to the extremely heterogeneous nature of the participants. The course instructors take the individual goals and capabilities of the respective participants as their starting point, and keep limitations and barriers in mind with the aim of overcoming these wherever possible.

The programmes of organisations for people with disabilities are financed by Hamburg's educational authority (*Behörde für Schule und Berufsbildung*) as well as through donations and association activities. The authorities provide a set budget and the organisations develop course offers accordingly.

Vocational training and (insofar as necessary for professional work) basic education are offered in the sheltered workshops for people with disabilities in Hamburg. However, these offers are only open to workshop employees. The educational opportunities therefore always go hand in hand with a concrete work position at a sheltered workshop and are therefore not freely accessible.

In recognition of the UN Convention on the Rights of Persons with Disabilities and with the aim of enhancing the social participation of people with disabilities, the organisations for people with disabilities recently intensified their cooperation with Hamburg's adult education centres.[21] The goal is to develop inclusive offers; the organisations for people with disabilities have been tasked with facilitating access to educational offers (also beyond their own courses).

In a first step, the adult education centres and organisations for people with disabilities are striving for mutual opening: people with disabilities should be given the opportunity to participate in the courses offered by adult education centres (elimination/overcoming of barriers) and people without disabilities should in turn be able to access courses offered by organisations for people with disabilities. Ongoing joint programmes were reviewed and developed further as necessary. The organisations for people with disabilities offered to share their specific expertise with the adult education centres, among others regarding the aspects of educational support and cooperative course management. Further development of this cooperation has further positive effects: the shared use of resources and facilities as well as the enhanced staffing possibilities not only enable significant expansion of Hamburg's adult education offers, but also broadening of the content. The cooperation with adult education centres involves overcoming the following barriers: mobility aspects must first be considered and any potential

---

[21] In Germany, adult education centres are non-profit establishments that primarily offer adult education and continuing education courses.

structural barriers (e.g. steps) overcome. One more decisive – and perhaps more inhibiting – factor is then the financing of such measures. The focus of the offers diverges quite considerably in some cases. Thus the courses offered by the adult education centres generally pursue a clear, common course objective. As previously mentioned, this is different in the learning setting of the organisations for people with disabilities. Support must also be provided for course instructors with little experience of working with people with disabilities and developed further.[22]

Course providers are facing with new situations in the shift to outpatient care.[23] The example of weekend courses was given here. Most course participants do not receive any assistance at the weekends, which means that they are unable to reach the course venue on their own. These are "in part also consequences of the growing scarcity of resources".

One group of individuals for whom very little support exists is those with severe multiple disabilities. This lack of support manifests itself in hindered access to courses as well as the often insufficient adaptation of the content of concepts.

Most of the courses are run by salaried staff whose qualifications correspond with the respective offer. They are frequently pedagogues, teachers or special needs education specialists.

Accessibility issues

If additional assistance and support is provided, adults with visual, hearing and speaking impairments, motor function disorders or physical disabilities are successfully able to participate in educational offers. To overcome perception, mobility and communication impairments, the structural, technical, medial and didactic-methodological conditions must be created in educational establishments and businesses to allow participants to learn as well as to work in businesses independently or with support despite their disability. It is actually relatively easy to set up *person-specific* workstations in companies in the mainstream labour

---

[22] According to the 2014 adult education centre statistics, the adult education centres in Hamburg offer a total of 7,724 course, whereby just 58 of these are provided in cooperation with other institutions (e.g. schools, ministries, clubs, companies or universities) (cf. Huntemann/Reichart 2014, p.28 and p.41ff).

[23] The outsourcing of inpatient care to outpatient residential services is meant here.

Uta Wagner

market as well as special facilities (vocational training and career development establishments, sheltered workshops for people with disabilities, activity day centres). Instruments such as work assistance or job coaching along with other integration aids (§ 54 SGB IX) can also effectively support participation in work life. However, this task is extremely challenging for all types of educational establishments striving for inclusion, as access with few barriers to learning, professional preparation and employment-promoting qualification must be established not just for individual impairments but rather across the board for *all* disabilities (cf. Schroeder 2015a).

From a special needs education perspective, a central task of literacy and basic education is therefore to facilitate "barrier-free" access to programmes, courses and training. Paragraph four of the German Act on Equal Opportunities for People with Disabilities (*Behindertengleichstellungsgesetz*, BBGG) dated May 2002 stipulates barrier-free, non-discriminatory access in terms of the design and use of rooms, media, information and communication tools as well as "other structured areas of life" – so courses and training offers, too. Not only wider doorways and user-friendly lifts are needed here, but also countless other measures (cf. Schroeder 2015a):

- Important technologies and measures for "barrier-free" learning are mobility with minimal hindrances so that all kinds of school buildings, classrooms, sports facilities, workshops, toilets, cafeterias and lifts are freely accessible to people with disabilities without having to negotiate any steps. The furniture in teaching rooms must be arranged in such a way that course participants with sensory impairments are still able to reach and find their folders, storage trays and work materials.
- It must be clarified how optimal intelligibility can be achieved in classrooms and group rooms, sports halls and cafeterias without any background noise, echoes or sound distortion (acoustic access). According to the two-sense principle, it must moreover be ensured that information is always available to at least two of the three senses of sight, hearing and touch: alarms should not only be presented as acoustic signals, but also as visual stimuli (e.g. traffic lights) so that they can be perceived by people with hearing impairments.

- Augmentative and alternative communication is the generic term used to describe all educational and therapeutic measures to enhance the communicative possibilities of people with limited or no speech capability. Examples include the introduction of image or symbol cards or communication boards for comprehension, the provision of touch talkers or the complementing of spoken language with the signing of key words.
- Programmes such as "Blindows" enable the barrier-free use of computers and the internet by translating the popular Windows interface into Braille or spoken language. Universal Design is an international concept that produces products, equipment, environments and systems that are inherently accessible to people of different abilities without the need for additional technology or adaptation, and therefore ensures simple, widespread and flexible usage.
- Educational materials can be made accessible. There are picture books and maps that can be felt, crayons that can be recognised by their colour and balls that can be heard. Whether printed on paper, in a digital format or on a Smart Board for download, all learning materials must be provided in an accessible format. Film material (e.g. videos) should have subtitles as a matter of principle not only when non-German speakers participate in the course, but also for people with a hearing impairment.

In special needs education, the field of rehabilitative measures is handled well. Such support technology is available in schools – and particularly in special needs schools. The need for comprehensive consideration of inclusion is not only a matter of whether society wishes to invest in making such technology and materials available in mainstream state schools, but whether they are also provided at adult education establishments. Throughout Germany, the regional education, support and advice centres offer mainstream schools comprehensive support for this. They set up workstations to cater to the specific needs of students with impairments and supply accessible lesson materials, advise teachers at mainstream schools and, where necessary, support students with impairments throughout their entire school career to ensure that they successfully complete their education. We are not aware of any similar intensive support for the adaptation, restructuring and inclusive opening of adult education establishments – at least not in Hamburg. If, however, as described above, less than sixty of the thousands of courses offered by the adult education centres cater to people with disabilities, it can be assumed that many of the literacy and basic education offers in the city in general will tend *not* to be accessible.

Desideratum: disability and migration

To date, the expert debate has not focused on one aspect affecting the living situations, level of education and above all educational barriers of people with a disability *and* a migration background.[24]

Experts criticise (cf. Kauczor 2004) that there are currently two distinct support structures for people with a migration background and people with disabilities. The overlap between migration and disability is not sufficiently taken into account: there are offers for migrants (e.g. advice on social welfare for migrants) on the one hand and support for people with disabilities on the other. While the professionals providing the former generally aren't trained to deal with questions relating to disability, there is a lack of knowledge on the subject of migration among the latter.

The German federal government's current participation report on the living situations of people with disabilities (BMAS 2013) included migration as a cross-cutting topic but conceded that only very scant data and information are available on this complex issue (cf. BMAS 2013, p.56). In Germany, 2.5 million people with a migration background have a disability – so every fifth adult with a migration background (ibid).[25] This figure does not tally with the anticipated proportion indicated in the 2011 national action plan:

"A strikingly low proportion of people with a migration background have an officially recognised disability. According to the data from the special evaluation of the 2005 microcensus, 7% of people with a migration background and 6.6% of foreigners have an officially recognised disability compared to 13% of people without a migration background. Among the people with severe disabilities, 5.2%

---

[24] "People with a migration background are people who have immigrated to Germany since 1950 and their descendants. The majority of these people, namely 8.8 million, had a German passport in 2011; 7.2 million were foreigners." (Federal Statistical Office, press release no. 326 dated 19 September 2012).

[25] In the participation report, a person is described as having a migration background if they immigrated to Germany themselves, they do not currently have German citizenship or at least one of their parents was not born in Germany (BMAS 2013, p.56).

---

have a migration background and 4.8% are foreigners – this is also significantly lower than the proportion of people without a migration background, which lies at 10.2%." (BMAS 2011, p.28)

The national action plan sees the reason for the low proportion of people with a migration background in the "fewer claims to offers for people with disabilities, beginning with the official recognition of a disability" (BMAS 2011, p.28f). The members of the coordination group have similar suspicions: the path to obtaining support is often long and complicated. The search for suitable offers is also frequently hindered by language barriers.

The national action plan therefore postulates: "The intercultural opening of information, support and care offers is thus an important cross-cutting task for establishments and associations." (BMAS 2011, p.29)

The participation report does not provide precise data on all of the areas of life covered (housing, education, work, leisure, etc.) for people with a migration background. It should moreover be noted that it mainly concentrates on adults of working age (18 to 64-year-olds). At the same time, the report gives a number of relevant statistics on schooling and education:

1. A disproportionately high number of people with a migration background and a disability do not have a vocational qualification (21% without a disability, 38% with a disability) (BMAS 2013, p.119).
2. The unemployment rate among people with a migration background and a disability is also disproportionately high (14% of men, 24% of women compared with 10% and 7% respectively for men and women without a disability) (ibid, p.142).
3. People aged 18 to 64 years with a disability and a migration background are far less likely to earn their own living (49% vs. 75%) (ibid, p.148).

The evidence is alarming. Whether the disadvantages in the field of education and the labour market as well as the greater dependence on the social welfare system can be attributed to the lack of basic education must be investigated further. The fact is, though, that considerable exclusions exist in social law in the interplay between the right of residence and disability. These must be scrutinised in future, as subgroups are otherwise denied access to basic education and lifelong learning (cf. Weiser 2016). For when it comes to migration, the funding and support defined in the German Social Code is dependent on the specific residence permit that a person holds. The entitlement to claim benefits for a disability (SGB IX) and social support for people with disabilities (SGB XII) are moreover linked to the disabled person's pass.

It is therefore not a case of the collective exclusion of migrants with disabilities from the social benefits defined in the German Social Code, but rather exclusions that arise from the respective residency status, individual stay duration and type of benefits. The benefits for people with disabilities pursuant to SGB XII (social welfare) are described as *integration assistance* (§§ 53 to 60 SGB XII). Integration assistance is subordinate, meaning that it is only granted when there is no entitlement to benefits from other sources. Many migrants with disabilities still aren't entitled to any integration assistance though.

Frings (2008) and Weiser (2016) describe countless other consequences of these legal exclusions: in most cases, migrant families have to pay to use the special family support services for households in which a child with disabilities lives (group offers, targeted individual care). The coverage of costs for hearing, visual and mobility aids, etc. is not guaranteed with all types of residence permits either. Legal exclusions for young migrants with disabilities moreover exist in the Child and Youth Welfare Act (SGB VIII). Entitlement issues also arise when it comes to assistance for adequate school education (§ 54 SGB XII), such as the day care facilities/centres for young people with disabilities offering remedial education and therapeutic support for children, youths and young adults with physical, mental or psychological impairments.

In-depth legal expertise must therefore urgently be developed in which the social law exclusions for the combined conditions of a migration background and disabilities are systematically identified and brought to the attention of the national, state and municipal levels.

Suggestions for improvements and wishes

The investigation outlined herein reveals striking differences between the opportunities for participation and the development needs in the literacy and basic education offers for people with disabilities in Hamburg. The statutory support instruments contain exclusions from entitlement to access to benefits, and the education system displays the parallel structure of target group-specific and so-called inclusive approaches typical for the field of disability work all across Germany.

The structure of the offers for "classic" – so target group-oriented – special needs education literacy and basic education is relatively broad, comprehensive and needs oriented. Tailored offers for continuing education for adults with disabilities link to a hitherto relatively closed system comprising general education special schools followed by work-related special facilities. Some of these educational offers are provided in cooperation with Hamburg's adult education centres, but most remain "segregated" in their organisational structures and concepts. Furthermore, due to a strong orientation to the special needs education dogma of individualisation, such offers are often not held in a group format and individual support instead dominates.

With the cooperation between different organisations for people with disabilities, there is a high-profile and established network in Hamburg that manages and develops the municipal adult special needs education and also takes care of literacy and basic education. However, one gets the impression that the range of disabilities are not addressed equally intensively: while there are a relatively large number of offers for people with learning impairments, mental disabilities and psychological disorders, more (and increasingly tailored) offers must be created for people with severe multiple disabilities, too. This is easier said than done though. For the educational offers for people with severe disabilities are characterised by the complex constellation of education and care (Klauß 2003, p.49): care is a *requirement* for education, as only when the physical needs have been met is access to educational development possible. Care is moreover a *reason* for education, whereby care activities can be linked to educational processes specifically in the fields of awareness and communication. And care requires *complementary* educational offers in all areas of life such as nutrition, daily life, the development of preferences, etc., which can be extended with learning and educational processes. Implementation of this educational antinomy is easier in special facilities, but should also be addressed in mainstream facilities.

In recognition of the UN Convention on the Rights of Persons with Disabilities and in appreciation of the attempts towards the most comprehensive social participation of people with disabilities possible, the efforts to develop,

Uta Wagner

implement, and maintain cooperative offers of organisations for people with disabilities and adult education centres should be intensified. In particular, the according necessary (financial) resources must also be made available. The Hamburg state action plan on implementation of the 2012 convention moreover states:

"Hamburg's educational authority (*Behörde für Schule und Berufsbildung*) is committed to expanding adult education for people with disabilities in cooperation with the authority for continuing education (*Amt für Weiterbildung*) and the city's adult education coordination group. It is increasingly considering how collaborative learning can be initiated in this field. Within this, it should be reviewed whether the task of inclusive learning can be integrated into the structuring of grants." (BASFI 2012, p.58)

As yet, there is still very little evidence of resolute implementation of the aims set out in the state action plan for the creation of accessible educational facilities. While countless adult education providers have ensured that there are lifts and ramps, the consistent elimination of acoustic, visual and linguistic barriers, equally consistent application of the building and design principles of Universal Design, and comprehensive digital accessibility cannot be discerned. In particular, there are scarcely any indications of a sustainable, disability-aware opening of adult education facilities not already traditionally forming part of the rehabilitation system.

There is a considerable need to act when it comes to people with disabilities and a migration background. In terms of institutional activities, the complex interdependencies between these two exclusion risks must first be taken into consideration more than they have been to date:

"A disability can be the result of migration; take refugees, for instance, who often develop a severe physical or mental impairment during their at times perilous escape. A disability can also be a reason for deciding to migrate, in the hopes of better or more affordable medical treatment and care elsewhere. A disability is often an obstacle to migration as only capable workers are successfully able to find a job. In some cases, a disability can justify a right to remain – if the country of origin does not offer at least as good access to medication as the country of exile." (Schroeder 2015)

Each of these constellations involves very different personal aims, which relate to the decision to emigrate or immigrate. The necessity and individual motivation to participate in (basic) education measures are also very hetero-geneous. An expert debate must be initiated in these two previously separate support structures (advice on social welfare for migrants and disability support) to consider the combined aspects of migration and disability and to take these into account more in basic education (cf. Gag/Schroeder 2015). The recommenda-tions for further development of the practical work and institutional structuring detailed in the joint declaration on intercultural opening and culture-sensitive work for and with people with disabilities and a migration background that was published by the Federal Association of Non-Statutory Welfare (BAGFW) in 2012 can provide diverse stimuli here: raise awareness among society, improve infor-mation and advice services for those eligible for benefits, develop intercultural skills among service providers, and facilitate networking (ibid, p.3).

References

Cloerkes, Günther (2007): Soziologie der Behinderten. Eine Einführung. Heidelberg.

Dederich, Markus (2009): Behinderung als sozial- und kulturwissenschaftliche Kategorie. In: Dederich, Markus/Jantzen, Wolfgang (Eds.): Behinderung und Anerkennung. Stuttgart, 15-39.

Federal Association of Non-Statutory Welfare (Bundesarbeitsgemeinschaft der Freien Wohl-fahrtspflege, BAGFW) (2012): Joint declaration on intercultural opening culture-sensi-tive work for and with people with disabilities and a migration background. *http://bvkm.de/wp-content/uploads/Gemeinsame-Erklärung-2012-01-23_final.pdf*

Free and Hanseatic City of Hamburg. Hamburg Department of Social Affairs, Family, Health and Consumer Protection (Behörde Soziales, Familie, Gesundheit und Verbrauch-erschutz) (Ed.) (2008): Die Entwicklung der Teilhabe von Menschen mit Behinderung in Hamburg. *www.hamburg.de/contentblob/126200/data/bericht-behinderung.pdf*

Frings, Dorothee (2008): Sozialrecht für Zuwanderer. Baden-Baden.

Gag, Maren/Schroeder, Joachim (2015): Country Report GERMANY – focus: migrants with special needs. In: Schroeder, Joachim (Ed.): Breaking down barriers from education to employment. The journey towards inclusion for vulnerable groups. Sofia, p.167-202.

German Federal Ministry of Labour and Social Affairs (Bundesministerium für Arbeit und Soziales, BMAS) (Ed.) (2013): Federal government report on participation with regard to the living situations of persons with impairments. Participation – Impairment – Dis-ability. Bonn.

German Federal Ministry of Labour and Social Affairs (Bundesministerium für Arbeit und Soziales, BMAS) (Ed.) (2011): Unser Weg in eine inklusive Gesellschaft. National action plan of the federal government for implementation of the UN Convention on the Rights of Persons with Disabilities (CRPD). Bonn.

German Federal Ministry of Justice and Consumer Protection (Bundesministerium für Justiz und Verbraucherschutz, BMJV): Book IX of the German Social Code (*SGB IX*). *www.sozialgesetzbuch-sgb.de/sgbix/1.html*

German Federal Statistical Office: "Bevölkerung mit Migrationshintergrund 2011 um 216,000 Personen gestiegen" (press release dated 19 September 2012). *www.destatis.de/DE/PresseService/Presse/Pressemitteilungen/2012/09/PD12_326_122. html;jsessionid=CA8B4B87EB4166832C4BB370B9CBABEE.cae1*

Hamburg Authority for Employment, Social Affairs, Family and Integration (Behörde für Arbeit, Soziales, Familie und Integration, BASFI) (Ed.) (2012): Hamburg state action plan for implementation of the UN Convention on the Rights of Persons with Disabilities (CRPD). *www.hamburg.de/contentblob/3724988/data/landesaktionsplan-behinderung.pdf*

Hradil, Stefan (2012): Soziale Exklusions- und Desintegrationsrisiken: Soziale Ungleichheit, soziale Abhängigkeit. In: Beck, Iris/Greving, Heinrich (Eds.): Lebenslage und Lebensbewältigung. Stuttgart, 124-133.

Huntemann, Hella/Reichart, Elisabeth (2014): Volkshochschul-Statistik: 52nd Edition, 2013 work year: *www.die-bonn.de/doks/2014-volkshochschule-statistik-01.pdf*

Kauczor, Cornelia (2004): Migration, Flucht und Behinderung – eine transkulturelle Behindertenhilfe als gesellschaftliche und institutionelle Herausforderung für Deutschland. In: Kauczor, Cornelia, Lorenzkowski, Stefan/Munaizel, Musa Al (Eds.): Migration, Flucht und Behinderung. Essen, 83-94.

Klauß, Theo (2003): Bildung im Spannungsverhältnis von Pädagogik und Pflege. In: Kane, John/Klauß, Theo (Eds.): Die Bedeutung des Körpers für Menschen mit einer geistigen Behinderung. Zwischen Pflege und Selbstverletzung. Heidelberg, 39-63.

Lachwitz, Klaus/Schellhorn, Walter/Welti, Felix (2010): Handkommentar zum Sozialgesetzbuch IX. Rehabilitation und Teilhabe behinderter Menschen. Cologne.

Law on the United Nations Convention dated 13 December 2006 on the Rights of Persons with Disabilities and the optional protocol of 13 December 2006 on the Law on the United Nations Convention on the Rights of Persons with Disabilities:

www.bmas.de/SharedDocs/Downloads/DE/PDF-Publikationen/a729-un-konvention.
pdf?__blob =publicationFile

Lindmeier, Christian (2009): Weiterbildung mit benachteiligten Erwachsenen – lebenslang-
es Lernen unter erschwerten Bedingungen. In: Stein, Roland/Orthmann Bless, Dagmar
(Eds.): Lebensgestaltung bei Behinderungen und Benachteiligungen im Erwachsenen-
alter und Alter. Baltmannsweiler, 33-65.

Schroeder, Joachim (2014): Migration. In: Handlexikon "Lernschwierigkeiten und Verhaltensstörungen". Heimlich, Ulrich/ Stein, Roland/Wember, Franz B. (Eds.) Stuttgart, 62-64.

Schroeder, Joachim (2015): Migration. Handlexikon der Behindertenpädagogik. Schlüsselbegriffe aus Theorie und Praxis. Antor, Georg/Beck, Iris/Bleidick, Ulrich/Dederich,
Markus. (Eds.) Stuttgart, 419-421.

Schroeder, Joachim (2016): Die Vielfalt der Behinderungen. Theoretische und empirische
Beiträge der Sonderpädagogik zur beruflichen Bildung unter dem Anspruch von
Inklusion. In: Bylinski, Ursula/Rützel, Josef (Eds.): Inklusion in der beruflichen Bildung:
Vielfalt aufgreifen – Potenziale nutzen. Schriftenreihe des Bundesinstituts für Berufs-
bildung (BIBB) "Berichte zur beruflichen Bildung", Vol. 3. Bonn, 57-68.

Solga, Heike (2005): Ohne Abschluss in die Bildungsgesellschaft. Die Erwerbschancen ger-
ing qualifizierter Personen aus soziologischer und ökologischer Perspektive. Opladen.

Statistics Agency for Hamburg and Schleswig-Holstein: Statistical Yearbook for Hamburg –
2014/2015:
www.statistik-nord.de/fileadmin/Dokumente/Jahrb%C3%BCcher/Hamburg/JB14HH_Ges-
amt_Korr.pdf

Thomann, Klaus-Dieter (2012): Von der Kriegsbeschädigtenfürsorge zum SGB IX – An-
merkungen zur Geschichte des Rechts für Menschen mit schweren Behinderungen:
www.schwbv.de/pdf/Geschichte_des_Behindertenrechts.pdf

United Nations (1948): Universal Declaration of Human Rights.
www.un-documents.net/a3r217a.htm

Weiser, Barbara (2016): Sozialleistungen für Menschen mit einer Behinderung im Kontext
von Migration und Flucht. Eine Übersicht zu den rechtlichen Rahmenbedingungen.
Hamburg.

Last accessed: 14 July 2017.

18 Accessibility in public space and public buildings – an observation protocol for research and teaching at universities
(Sven Degenhardt, Marie Geldmacher, Valentin Keller, Torben Scholz)

Legal framework

The UN Convention on the Rights of Persons with Disabilities (UN CRPD) states in article 3 its common principles. One of these principles is that people with disabilities are to be guaranteed full and active participation in society. This concerns work, education, political and public life, the right of access to the justice system and much more. The execution of these areas is highly complex, but they have one thing in common: They require an accessible infrastructure. People with disabilities cannot participate fully in education if they are unable to get to and into an educational building or move within such buildings like people without disabilities can do. The same applies to the justice system. People with disabilities are only able to participate fully in the justice system if they are able to get to and into a courthouse and are then able to obtain their rights in the context of judicial proceedings.

In article 9 of the UN CRPD the goals for "accessibility" state:

"(1) To enable persons with disabilities to live independently and participate fully in all aspects of life, States Parties shall take appropriate measures to ensure to persons with disabilities access, on an equal basis with others, to the physical environment (…). These measures, which shall include the identification and elimination of obstacles and barriers to accessibility, shall apply to, inter alia: a) Buildings, roads, transportation and other indoor and outdoor facilities, including schools, housing, medical facilities, and workplaces" (UN CRPD 2008, 1428).

An isolated strategy to ensure accessibility for people with disabilities falls too short. Measures to establish building accessibility are no additional, expensive and facultative measures that are granted in a social act to a minority (cf. Degenhardt / Schroeder 2016, 8): "A barrier-free, accessible environment is absolutely necessary for about 10% of the population, necessary for about 30 to 40% and comfortable for 100%" (BMWA 2003, translated by MG).

Nevertheless, it is essential to consider which needs of particular target groups are accorded to which measures during the process of shaping a barrier-free, universally designed infrastructure. Accordingly, the accessibility of the constructional infrastructure has to be split up into the following three levels:

The first level includes the target structure, and the first goal of accessibility is accessibleness. A person has to be able to get to a building – f.e. by public transport from the place of residence.

The second goal is the orientation of a building.

The third goal is the secure usage of the building. People with disabilities have to be able to move and use it in the same manner like all the other people that use the local infrastructure there.

The second level of accessibility within an infrastructural environment is the target group. Depending on the target group, a particular way of implementation is defined. Especially differentiated have to be the following target groups: People with physical disabilities, people with sensory disabilities and people with cognitive disabilities.

The third level is the structure of anchoring. This level views the interaction of laws and standards, institutions, organizations and the, in society acting, knowledge structures and attitudes.

Structure of the legal basis of an accessible civil infrastructure

The question as to how the topic of an accessible civil infrastructure is enshrined occurs a cascade of legal systems. Within the national laws one can find regulations according to accessibility, f.e. the "Musterbauordnung" (model building code) or "Landesbauordnung" (state construction laws) in Germany. In §50 the Musterbauordnung stipulates accessibility in public buildings. This §50 is the groundwork for the particular regional-political implementations in the state construction laws. A key term for barrier-free constructing are the term "Allgemein anerkannte Regeln der Technik" (obligatory generally recognized rules of technology). Those "Allgemein anerkannte Regeln der Technik"/ obligatory generally recognized rules of technology are complicated and imprecise within the law but are of great relevance for the construction law. "Obligatory generally recognized rules of technology are (…) fundamental rules that are acknowledged as theoretically correct within technical science. They are fixed and for their usage decisive with the newest knowledge level, widely known in the circle of professionally trained technicians and, based on continuing practical experiences, are recognized as technical suitable, appropriate and necessary" (Heiermann/Riedl/ Rusam 2013, 862, translated by MG).

Very interesting is the relation between the legal term of the "Allgemein anerkannten Regeln der Technik" and the system of norms and recommendations. Germany has the "Deutsche Institut für Normung" (German Institute for Standardization), called DIN. For more than 100 years the DIN has been publishing the so-called DIN-standards on a wide variety of subjects and have been compiled by the committees for standardization and are regularly reviewed and adjusted, when necessary. These standards are not legal standards and thus not binding. Nevertheless, it is highly recognized that the DIN-standards are influencing the "Allgemein anerkannten Regeln der Technik", but there is also the clear legal statement that the DIN-standards can fall short of the "Allgemein anerkannten Regeln der Technik". This is due to the fast speed in which new knowledge in science and technology is generated. The practical implementation and practical knowledge, which then result in the "Allgemein anerkannten Regeln der Technik", run in continuous processes. On the contrary, the DIN-standards are adapted and customized in cycles. Accordingly, not only the DIN-standards, but also the recommendations of professional associations, expert associations, insurance companies (such as the DGUV), technical specifications (f.e. of the company Deutsche Bahn) as well as EU regulations, have to be consulted for the newest recognition of the "Allgemein anerkannten Regeln der Technik". Assessing the relevant standards and recommendations in the context of accessibility, the following list results:

- ISO 21542 Building construction – Accessibility and usability of the built environment
- DIN 18040-1 Barrierefreies Bauen – Teil 1: Öffentlich zugängliche Gebäude
- DIN 18040-3 Barrierefreies Bauen – Teil 3: Öffentlicher Verkehrs- und Freiraum
- DIN 18041 Hörsamkeit in Räumen
- DIN 32984 Bodenindikatoren
- DIN 12464-1 Beleuchtung von Arbeitsstätten – Teil 1: Arbeitsstätten in Innenräumen
- Planungsleitfäden, z.B. Leitfaden Barrierefreies Bauen des BMUB

- Empfehlungen der Deutschen Gesetzlichen Unfallversicherung (DGUV)
- Technischen Regeln für Arbeitsstätten (ASR): ASR V3a.2, ASR A3.4
- Richtlinie 813.0304 Wegeleit- und Informationssystem Informationselemente für Blinde und Sehbehinderte der DB.

These norms and recommendations have in common that they follow a fundamental principle: The formulation of a protection aim, which has to be achieved. Based on this it is shown how this objective can be reached and, if necessary, it differentiates on the various needs of the various groups of persons. Protection aims can be reached in different ways than stated by the DIN-standards as well, but any deviations in the execution have to prove that the protection aim is still achieved. At this point, the question arises as to what the process looks like from the formulation of a protection aim to a norm with technical measures, lengths, areas, slopes, etc.

On the one hand, the existing public buildings and the public sphere have to be analyzed regarding the protection aim have of accessibility. During this analyzation process, the knowledge of ergonometry and anthropometry have to be included. Ergonometry is the science of human work, and it aims at pushing forward an optimal workplace design by using bio-psychosocial understandings. The basis for the ergonometry is the anthropometry, the teaching of the survey, structuring and usage of the human body dimensions.

Step 1: Determining a protection aim

Step 2: Analyzing the situation

Step 3: Developing measures

(collect data in consideration of the particularities of disabilities)

Step 4: Drafting a standardization

How to get from a protection aim to a standard – doors

In public buildings, the protection aim is to make all entries easy to find, easy to open and close and to make them safe to pass through. It is known from experience that doors are difficult to open for wheelchair users. The door opener is hard to reach out of the wheelchair, and it requires significant strength to move the doors.

In step 3, developing measures, the measurements of a walking and a sitting person are considered at first. Subsequently, the gripping area and the particularities of disabilities have to be included. Following this, in the fourth step, the standard is drafted. In this case, the height of the door handle and the installation dimensions get defined.

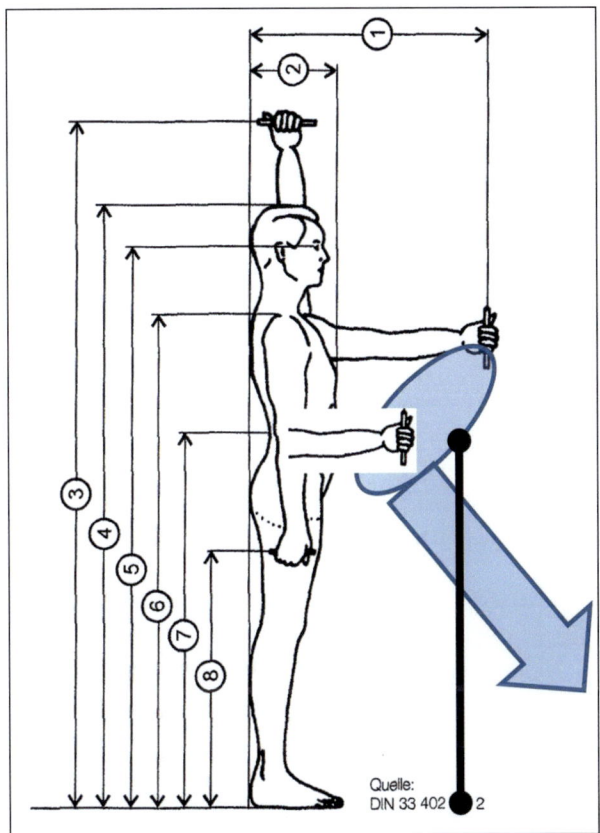

Figure 18.1: Body measurements and frontal gripping areas of an upright standing person (see Lange & Windel 2017, 8; additions by SD)

(For the descriptions, go to "Alternative text for images" page 224)

The data on the measures of in Germany living male adults show the following values (see Lange & Windel 2017):

Five percent of the men have a shoulder height below 134 cm, another five percent have a shoulder height above 155 cm. The median, which means the value in which 50 percent are taller, and 50 percent are shorter, is 145 cm. Regarding the women, the values show that five percent of in Germany living women have a shoulder height below 126 cm and five percent have a shoulder height above 142 cm, the median is 134 cm. Hence the average shoulder height and therefore the height of a stretched arm is between 134 cm to 145 cm. Consequential, from a metrological point of view, 102 cm to 110 cm is comfortably reachable with a right-angled elbow for most of the public. Keeping in mind that the change of angle can cause a play, the optimal range for a door handle is at 105 cm over OFF. Historically this range used to be higher at 120 cm over OFF. Considering the range from the front of the body, the range is at ca. 40 cm (women: 38 cm to 40 cm, men: 43 cm to 45 cm). Thus, it appears that a maximum range of 40 cm presents a comfortable scope from the body front from a person.

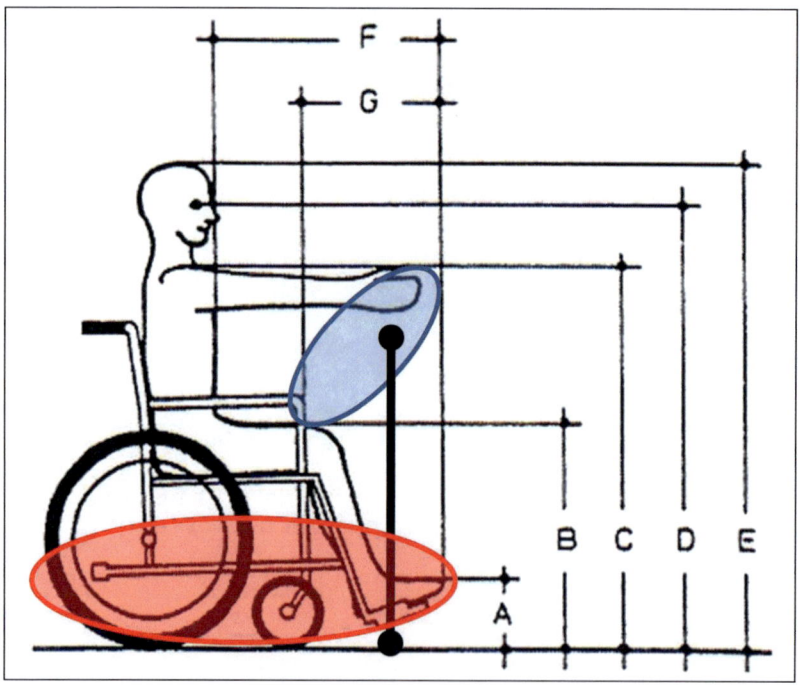

Figure 18.2: Body measurements and frontal gripping areas of a person in a wheel-chair (see Loeschcke et al. 2011, 56; additions by SD)

(For the descriptions, go to "Alternative text for images" page 224)

Sven Degenhardt et al.

The shoulder height of a sitting person ranges between 109 cm (tall man), over 101 cm (human average) to 90 cm (kids between nine to twelve years). Out of these values, the standard for doors states that the door handle can be comfortably used at 85 cm over OFF by wheelchair users. It has to be taken into account though, that upright sitting wheelchair users have different gripping areas than a person that is able to move freely. This means that the measures of a wheelchair have to be considered as well. For instance, if a person cannot freely move his or her upper body, the range from the body front lies at 40 cm in the same area as the tip of his or her feet; a gripping area starting in the front of the wheelchair is nonexistent. So it is not possible to reach the door handle by driving straight at the door.

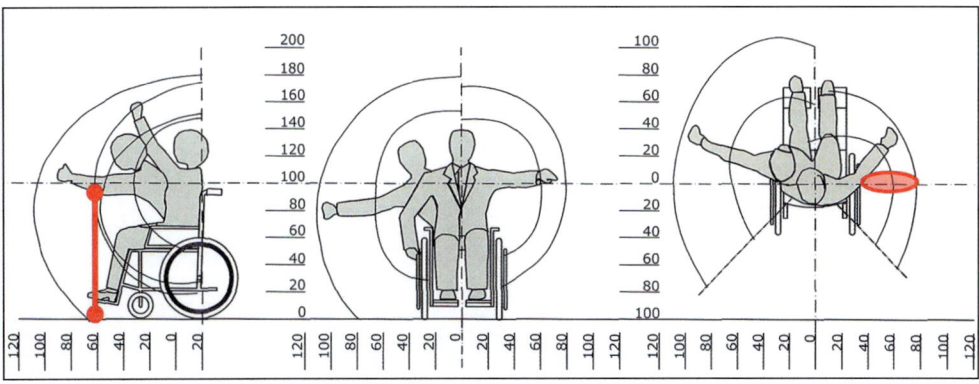

Figure 18.3: Gripping areas of a wheelchair user (see Rau 2011, 243; additions by SD).
(For the descriptions, go to "Alternative text for images" page 225)

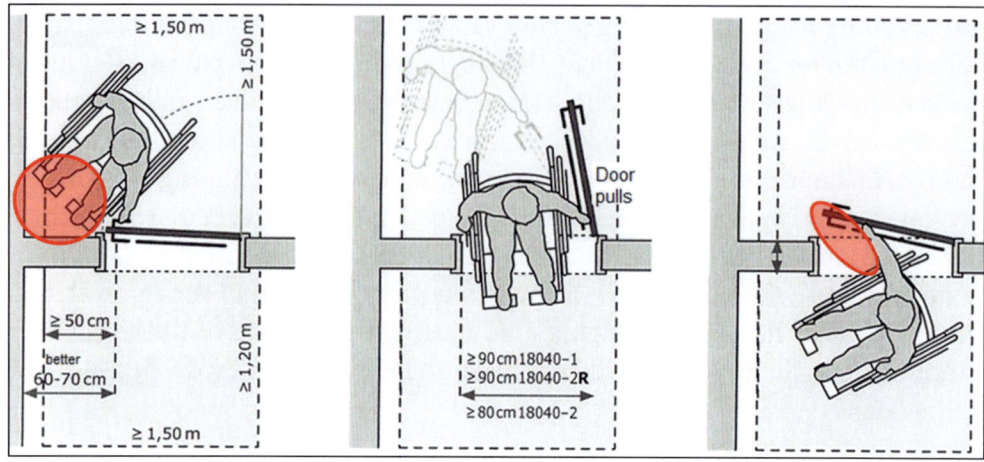

Figure 18.4: Wheelchair positions for opening, passing and closing a door (see Rau 2011, 97; additions by SD)

(For the descriptions, go to "Alternative text for images" page 225)

A person in a wheelchair needs a movement area of 150 cm times 150 cm in front of the door. Since it is impossible to reach the door handle when running-up straight, another movement area of at least 50 cm, better 60 cm to 70 cm, is needed next to the door, so the wheelchair can drive up at an oblique angle. This way the door handle is within reach of the person. Accordingly, a movement area of 50 cm to 60 cm next to the door as well as a maximum reveal depth of 26 cm, by which it is possible for a person to close the door afterwards by his- or herself.

Figure 18.5/18.6: A standardized and not standardized door (photo by SD)

(For the descriptions, go to "Alternative text for images" page 226)

Next to the standard-compliantly door (see fig. 5), the door-buzzer is at standardized height and on the left side is an area of ca. 60 cm, so that wheelchair users can drive up to the door handle. This is not possible in situations like shown in figure 18.6: The door handle is back in a corner and therefore unreachable for wheelchair users.

From a protection aim to a standardization – Movement areas/height and width

The protection aim for movement areas is easy to define: All people have to be able to move safely and without any help in buildings (on floors, in rooms, etc.). Movement areas need to have enough height and width. To determine the necessary space requirements, the measures of a walking person (width, length, height), as well as the specific space requirement of a person using a white cane and of a person using a wheelchair, have to be considered. As a result, the requirements for height as well as the width of movement areas are formulated.

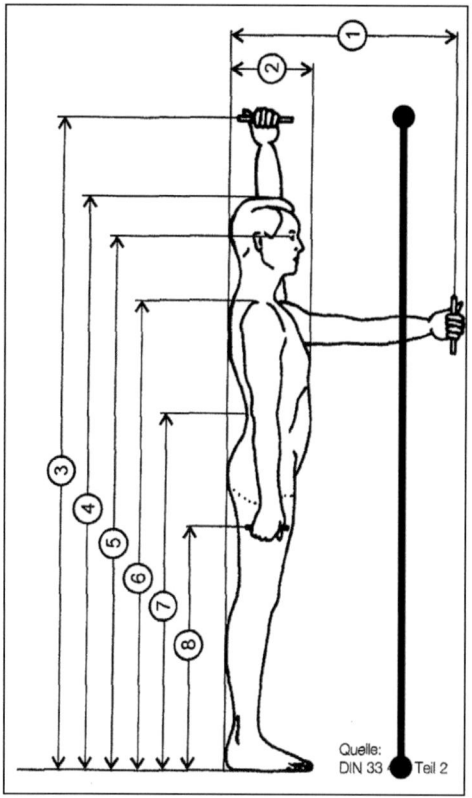

Figure 18.7: Body measurements and maximum
height of a standing person
(see Lange & Windel 2017, 8; additions by SD)
(For the descriptions, go to "Alternative text for images" page 226)

Sven Degenhardt et al.

The body measurements of in Germany living adults between 18 to 65 years show the following results: Five percent of the female populations are taller than 172 cm; five percent of the male population is taller than 186 cm. The value of the height of the movement areas is set, so that there is a safety area above the head. To that, the upraised arm of a standing person is counted as well. By these means, the range over OFF of five percent of the population lies at 202 cm for women and 220 cm for men. Since the highest value is used, the norm has been formulated accordingly: A safe passage height for all people (presumably) without hurting their heads, lies at 220 cm.

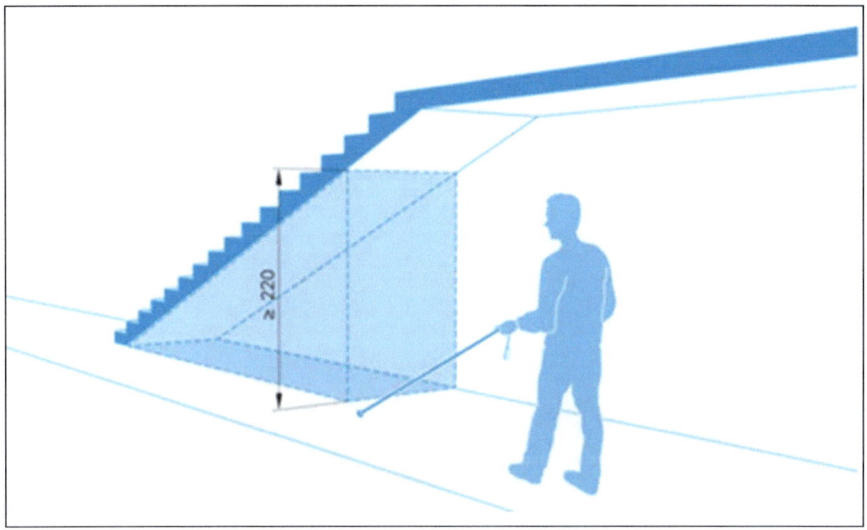

Figure 18.8: Underwalkability of self-supporting stairs (Degenhart et al. 2014, 27)

(For the descriptions, go to "Alternative text for images" page 226)

A free passage height is especially crucial because stairs can be underwalkable. If an obstacle undercuts this passage height, f.e. self-supporting stairs, it is inadmissible within the meaning of structural accessibility.

Figure 18.9: Self-supporting stairs in a room (photo by SD)

(For the descriptions, go to "Alternative text for images" page 227)

The picture (see figure 18.9) shows an example of self-support stairs in a German education institution. No obstacles are preventing the underwalkability, so a person could suffer severe head injuries when possibly bumping against the underside of the stairs.

Sven Degenhardt et al.

Figure 18.10: Self-supporting stairs with standard obstacles (photo by SD)

(For the descriptions, go to "Alternative text for images" page 227)

Figure 18.10 shows what a standardized structural measure may look like, that hinders people from walking into self-supporting stairs.

Looking at the movement areas considering the necessary width, it is essential to include the widths and lengths of a person and particular groups of people. A walking person has a space requirement of ca. 60 cm times 60 cm. If a person is using a one-sided walking aid, he or she needs at least 60 cm times 80 cm, a person with a walking aid on both sides has a space requirement of 60 cm times 100 cm. Walking with a walking frame takes up between 80 cm times 100 cm, roughly the same amount as a person with a stroller. Depending on the type of the wheelchair, a wheelchair user requires 90 cm of width but 120 cm up to 200 cm in lengths.

Transferring these space requirements to the design of floors it becomes evident that an unproblematic crossing of two people on a floor is only possible if the floor is wide enough.

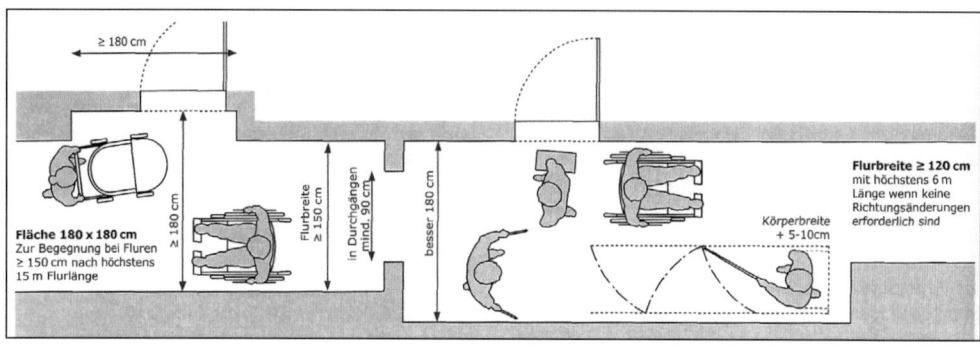

Figure 18.11: Floor widths and encounter areas (Rau 2011, 70)
(For the descriptions, go to "Alternative text for images" page 227)

The minimum passage-width of floors is set at 90 cm in the DIN. If the floors are highly frequented, double the width (180 cm) is statutory. It is possible to reduce the width to 150 cm or even 120 cm if the floor has a low frequency or has only a few changes of direction. After six meters an encounter area of at least 180 cm times 180 cm has to be installed so that two people with f.e. a stroller can pass by in different directions.

To do a proper valuation whether a building or a public space is accessible, many values and measures have to be collected and calibrated with the standards and recommendations.

Therefore, a set of protocol sheets have been developed. These protocol sheets collect data on the following fields in public buildings and the public space:

Sven Degenhardt et al.

1. Toilets
2. Toilets – high in contrast
3. Doors
4. Door plate
5. Glass doors
6. Building entrance
7. Movement space (hallways and floors)
8. Lift measurements
9. Lift tableau
10. Disabled parking
11. Guidance system – sidewalk
12. Guidance system – crossing points
13. Ramps
14. Staircase handrails
15. Staircase recognisability
16. Staircase headroom clearance
17. Staircase design

The concept of these protocol sheets is to use them in various education classes such as teaching, special needs teaching (regardless the chosen focus), in primary education classes or rehabilitation sciences. This is done with the purpose that students may examine various public buildings, such as educational or healthcare buildings, of the political or public life, of arts and culture, justice and administration on the topics of accessibility and barrier liberty. Through the usage of this instrument, students should be enabled to get a sense of infrastructural accessibility of buildings and how the various protection aims are realized. Thereby it is not about "tracking of mangles," but about getting access on how to accomplish protection aims with short-, middle- and long-term measures, so that people with disabilities can use a building independently and have the chance of participation. Furthermore, in this context, the idea of the universal design shall be discussed in depth.

References

BMWA - Bundesministerium für Wirtschaft und Arbeit (Ed.) (2003) Ökonomische Impulse eines barrierefreien Tourismus für alle: Eine Untersuchung im Auftrag des Bundesministeriums für Wirtschaft und Arbeit, Kurzfassung der Untersuchungsergebnisse. (*https://www.pro-retina.de/dateien/ea_barrierefreier_tourismus_oekonomie.pdf*, access at 29.12.2017)

Degenhardt, Sven, Joachim Schroeder (2016) Inclusive Education and Accessibility. Science to Policy Brief. Bonn: Deutsche Gesellschaft für Internationale Zusammenarbeit. (*https://www.giz.de/fachexpertise/downloads/giz2016-inclusive-education-and-accessibility.pdf*, access at 29.01.2018)

Degenhart, Christine, Johann Ebe and Gabriele Famers (2014) Barrierefreies Bauen: Planungsgrundlagen, Leitfaden füpr Architekten, Fachingenieure, Bauherren und Interessierte zur DIN 18040, Teil 1. München: Bayerische Architektenkammer. (*https://www.byak.de/data/pdfs/AuT/Normung/Basiswissen_Links_Hinweise/ByAK-Barriere-freies-Bauen-01.pdf*, access at 29.01.2018)

DIN - Deutsches Institut für Normung e. V. (Ed.) (2010) DIN 18040-1 Barrierefreies Bauen – Planungsgrundlagen – Teil 1: Öffentlich zugängliche Gebäude Ausgabe: 2010-10. Berlin, Wien, Zürich: Beuth.

ISO - International Organization for Standardization (Ed.) (2011) ISO 21542:2011(E) Building construction – Accessibility and usability of the built environment.

Heiermann, Wolfgang, Richard Riedl, Martin Rusam, et al. (2013) Handkommentar zur VOB: Teile A und B, Rechtsschutz im Vergabeverfahren. Wiesbaden: Vieweg & Sohn.

Lange, Wolfgang and Armin Windel (2017) Kleine ergonomische Datensammlung. Köln: TÜV Media.

Loeschcke, Gerhard, Daniela Pourat and Lothar Marx (2011) Barrierefreies Bauen Band 1: Kommentar zu DIN 18040-1. Berlin, Wien, Zürich: Beuth Verlag.

Rau, Ulrike (Ed.) (2011) barrierefrei - bauen für die zukunft Berlin: Bauwerk.

UN - United Nations (2006) Convention on the Rights of Persons with Disabilities. (*http://www.un.org/disabilities/documents/convention/convoptprot-e.pdf*, access at 25.03.2008)

Alternative text for images

Figure 1
Examples of barriers and accessibility

Top left Dining scenario Cutlery and crockery can be made more visually interesting or better visible for people with a visual impairment by placing them on an LED LightBox to enhance the contrast. This place setting can be used in early learning or for people with multiple disabilities.

Bottom left Barrier-free access to a public space (negative example) Here: Isfahan. While there is tactile paving to guide white cane users, access is restricted by concrete blocks that have been positioned to prevent motor vehicles from driving on the pavement. These blocks mean that wheelchair users cannot use the pavement. The narrow gap between the blocks could also present a challenge to white cane users.

Top right Stairwell, exemplary barrier-free access (positive example) with a handrail meeting DIN standards Bottom right Steps in a public space (negative example) Here: Hamburg. The edges of the steps have not been marked and a bench has been integrated into the steps. This might not be discernible to people with impaired vision if they are descending the steps backwards, for example. In a worst-case scenario, the steps may appear to end at the bench plateau. However, they actually continue down after 50 cm – at double step height even! This is entirely unacceptable. People with visual impairments could encounter difficulties if they deviate from the marked route!

(back to text page 8)

Table 10.1
Definition of a person with Disability

Table with 8 rows and 1 spilt.
The content reads: Blindness, deafness or severe hearing impairment, physical disabilites, psychological or emotional condition, chronical illness, other.

(back to text page 103)

Table 10.2
Illnesses, conditions or disabilities (N=400)

Table with 10 rows and two splits. The first split lists the illnesses, conditions or disabilities and the second split the percentage in 2015. Intellectual (e.g. mental handicap – Down Syndrom – 75%), physical disabilitiy 60%, visual difficulties 51,7%, mental health difficulty (mental illness - depression, schizophrenia) 45%, elder disabilites 43,3%, hearing loss 41,7%, long-term illness (e.g. diabetes, dialysis) 26,7%, addiction 25%, HIV/AIDS 18,3%. Total n=400 (2015).

(back to text page 104)

Figure 10.1
Percentage of respondents that knew someone with a disability

Title: Do you know someone with a disability?
The bar graph shows the percentage of different groups of people knowing someone with a disability. On the x-axis the percentage from 0% to 35% is shown. On the y-axis the different groups of people are shown. Member of family 33%, Other relative 17%, Acquintance 15%, Friend 13%, Neighbour 10%, Spouse/ partner 1,7%, Colleague/work contact 0%.

(back to text page 105)

Alternative text for images

Figure 10.2
Level of agreement with the statement 'it is society which disables people by creating barriers'

Title: Society disables people by creating barriers
The bar graph shows the level of agreement with the statement: society disables people by creating barriers. on the x-axis the percentage is shown from 0% to 100%. The bars are divides into 5 percentage groups. Strongly agree 7%, agree 17%, neither agree nor disagree 23%, disagree 30%, strongly disagree 18%.

(back to text page 106)

Figure 10.3
Level of agreement with the statement 'people with disabilities are treated fairly in Isfahan society

Title: People with disabilities are treated fairly in Isfahan
The bar graph shows the level of agreement with the statement: people with disabilities are treated fairly in Isfahan society. On the x-axis the percentage is shown from 0% to 100%. The bar is divided into 5 categories. Strongly agree 12%, agree 33% neither agree nor disagree 18%, disagree 23%, strongly disagree 1%.

(back to text page 106)

Figure 10.4
Do people with disabilities receive equal opportunities in terms of Education?

Title: In general, do you think that people with disabilities receive equal opportunities in terms of education?
The pie chart shows that 59% don't think that people with disabilities receive equal opportunities in terms of education, 40% think they do and 1% doesn't know.

(back to text page 107)

Figure 10.5
Object or not if children with disabilities were in the same class as your child (if you had a child) for different disability types

Title: In general, would you object or not if the children with the following disabilities were in the same class as your children?
The bar graph shows the opinion of people towards the inclusion of children with different disabilities in regular classrooms. Mental health difficulties: Yes 7%, no 7%, don't know 76%. Intellectual and learning disabilities: Yes 8%, no 3%, don't know 79%. Physical disabilities: Yes 57%, no 41%, don't know 2%. Visual or hearing disability: Yes 31%, no 68%, don't know 1%.

(back to text page 108)

Figure 10.6
Reason for objection to children with disabilities in the same class as your child

Title: Why would you object to children with disabilities attending the same class as your child?
The bar graph shows the reasons of people objecting to children with disabilites attending the same class as their own children. The x-axis ranks from 0-30%. On grounds of special needs considerations object 25%, on grounds of the progress of children without disabilities 23%, mobility difficulites 12%, progress of children with disabilites 10%, safety conditions 10%, mental or emotional reasons 7%, other 5%, apperance 1%.

(back to text page 109)

Figure 10.7
Disability and equal opportunities in terms of employment

Title: In general, do you think people with disabilities receive equal opportunities in terms of employment?
The pie chart shows the 76% of the people think that people with disabilities receive equal opportunities in terms of employment, 14% disagree and 10% don't know.

(back to text page 110)

Figure 10.8
Willingness of employers to hire people with disabilities for different disability types

Title: In general, do you think employers are willing or unwilling to hire people with the following disabilities?
The bar graph shows what people think if employers are willing or unwilling to hire people with different kinds of disabilites. 8% think that employers are willing to hire people with mental disabilites, 16% think that they are unwilling to hire people with mental disabilites and 76% don't know if they would hire people with mental disabilites. Intellectual disabilites: 14% willing, 20% unwilling, 65% don't know. Physical disabilities: 10% willing, 25% unwilling, 65% physical disabilites. Hearing disabilites: 20% willing, 31% unwilling, 49% don't know. Visual or hearing disabilites: 10% willing, 30% unwilling, 70% don't know.

(back to text page 111)

Figure 10.9
Level of comfort working with people with disabilities for different disability type

Title: Level of comfort working with people with disabilities for different disability types
The bar graph shows the level of comfort working with people with disabilities for different disability types on a scale between 0 and 10. Mental health difficulties 7,4, intellectual or learning disabilities 6,5, physical disabilities 8,8, hearing disabilities 8,5, visual disabilities 7,5.

(back to text page 112)

Figure 10.10
Accessibility of buildings and public facilities in Isfahan for people with disabilities

Title: In general, do you think that buildings and public facilities in Isfahan are adequately accessible for people with disabilities?
The pie chart shows that 71% don't think that buildings and public facilities in Isfahan are adequatley accessible for people with disabilites . 23% think they are and 6% doesn't know.

(back to text page 113)

Alternative text for images

Figure 10.11
Knowledge of state benefits received by people with disabilities

Title: Do you know if people with disabilities receive state benefits?
The pie chart shows the percentage of agreement towards the question: Do you know if people with disabilities receive state benefits? Yes, they receive beneftis 47%, some people receive benefits 27%, no, they don't receive benefits 23%, don't know 3%.

(back to text page 114)

Figure 11.1
The stress distribution on the femoral head of the subjects with LCPD

This figure represents the stress and strain distributions throughput the whole femoral heads of both subjects. Subject 1 who has suffered from progressed disease has shown less strain level as compared to the subject 2 who is in earlier stages of disease. Similar trend can be observed in the stress distribution of the subject.

(back to text page 119)

Figure 11.2
The curve correction obtained (a) without orthosis (b) with orthosis

In this figure, there are scoliosis subjects shown whether before using the orthosis or after using it. Clearly from the figure, one can distinguish the curvature angels. As the effects of orthosis forces have been applied to the spine, the curvature of the subject has been modified quite significantly.

(back to text page 120)

Figure 14.1
The limbic system of the human brain

A drawn internal view of a human brain is illustrated. The limbic system lies in the center of this, including the Hippocampus and the Amygdala. It is surrounded by the orbitofrontal cortex and the prefrontal cortex.

(back to text page 154)

Figure 18.1
Body measurements and frontal gripping areas of an upright standing person

Illustrated is a drawn figure as an upright standing person. Seven body measures are brought in, from the OFF to a body part: To the fist of a downwards stretched arm, to the elbow of a downwards stretched arm, to the shoulder height, to the eye height, to the head height and to the height of a fist with an upwards extended arm. Additionally, two gripping areas are illustrated: The range between an upwards stretched arm to a frontal stretched arm, and the range between a frontal stretched arm to a right-angled arm.

(back to text page 205)

Figure 18.2
Body measurements and frontal gripping areas of a person in a wheelchair

Illustrated is a drawn person sitting in a wheelchair, stretching the arms out horizontally. Five different body measurements are brought in from the OFF to a body part: To the feet height, knee height, shoulder height, eye height and crown height. The range from the body front and from the knees to the toes is also marked. Also, it is marked that a horizontally stretched arm does not overtop the toes. A blue arrow shows the gripping area of 45 degrees to the floor.

(back to text page 206)

Alternative text for images

Figure 18.3
Gripping areas of a wheelchair user

Three different perspectives of a drawn wheelchair user are illustrated. Each illustration has a measuring scale in cm, starting at the body's core to the surrounding areas. The side perspective illustrates the gripping areas of 180° with a stretched arm when sitting up straight; the area does not overreach the tip of the toes. The tip of the toes is only overreached when the person bends forwards, so the range about 80vcm bending over instead of 60 cm when sitting straight. The front perspective shows the gripping areas when sitting up straight and leaning to the side, the gripping area increases by roughly 20 cm, from ca. 80 cm to 100 cm. The birds-eye view illustrates the gripping areas sitting up straight and when bent over. Because of the back support of the wheelchair, a specific area can only be reached when leaned over.

(back to text page 207)

Figure 18.4
Wheelchair positions for opening, passing and closing a door

Three different stages of a wheelchair user passing through the door are illustrated. First, the wheelchair user drives up diagonally to the door, reaching out with the left arm to the door handle. The position of the feet is diagonal to the door soffit, needing a little bit over 50 cm between the soffit and the wall next to the door. 60 cm to 70 cm is better than 50 cm. Secondly, the person is driving back to open the door, switching the hand to the closing handle with the left hand. The person can then pull itself through the door. The Door needs to be 90 cm wide. Thirdly, the person grabs the closing handle with the right and to close the door, the position of the wheelchair is diagonal again. The reveal depth is 26 cm.

(back to text page 208)

Figure 18.5/18.6
A standardized and not standardized door

The two photos show two doors in the same educational building in Germany. The one shows a standardized door with enough space on the left side of the door handle to drive up diagonally. The reveal depth is also standardized. A green check is drawn into the photo. On the second picture two doors, 90° apart from each other are shown. Both doors have no space next to the handle. A red cross is drawn into the photo.

(back to text page 209)

Figure 18.7
Body measurements and maximum height of a standing person

Illustrated is a drawn, upright standing person from the side. Eight body measurements are marked from the OFF to the body parts: To the fist of a downwards stretched arm, the elbow, the shoulder height, the eye height, the crown, the fist of an upwards extended arm. Also, the body width from the side as well as the distance between the back and the fist of a horizontally stretched arm.

(back to text page 210)

Figure 18.8
Underwalkability of self-supporting stairs

The drawn illustration shows a person with a white cane walking towards the free underside of self-support stairs. It states that an obstacle should be at the height of 220 cm.

(back to text page 211)

Figure 18.9
Self-supporting stairs in a room

The photo shows self-supporting stairs. A red cross is drawn into the photo because there are no obstacles, which means this setting is not permitted.

(back to text page 212)

Figure 18.10
Self-supporting stairs with obstacles

The photo shows self-supporting stairs in the middle of the room with obstacles preventing underwalkability and guidelines along the obstacles.

(back to text page 213)

Figure 18.11
Floor widths and encounter areas

The drawn illustration from the birds-eye view shows a floor with a passage, the widths and necessary encounter areas in two situations: First, the floor is 150 cm wide and has a passage of 90 cm to the next floor. The floor has an encounter area creating a floor width of 180 cm so that a person with a stroller and a person using a wheelchair can pass each other. Secondly, the floor is 180 cm wide after the passage. A person with crutches, another with a suitcase, one using a wheelchair and a person using a white cane are passing each other comfortably.

(back to text page 214)

Authors

...in alphabetic order

Batoul Aminalzarbian, Psychosomatic Research Center, Isfahan University of Medical Sciences, Isfahan, Iran.

Mostafa Arab-Varnousfaderani, PhD Student, Department of Educational Science, Farhangian University of Isfahan, Isfahan, Iran (arabashrafi@gmail.com)

Kowsar Arab-Varnousfaderani, Medical Faculty. Shahrekord University of Medical Sciences, Shahrekord, Iran

Maryam Ashrafi, Islamic Azad University, Khominishahr (Isfahan) Branch, Iran

Hamzeh Baharlouei, PT, PhD Student, Musculoskeletal Research Center, Isfahan University of Medical Sciences, Isfahan, Iran

Dr. Sven Degenhardt, Professor at the Faculty of Education, Department of Disability and Education, education for learners with blindness and low vision, University of Hamburg, Germany (sven.degenhardt@uni-hamburg.de)

Dr. Amrollah Ebrahimi, Associate Professor, psychosomatic Research Center, Isfahan University of Medical Sciences, Isfahan, Iran. Manager of Iranian Section of project: (a_ebrahimi@med.mui.ac.ir)

Mohammad Hossein Ebrahimi; Psychosomatic Research Center, Isfahan University of Medical Sciences, Isfahan, Iran

Marie Geldmacher, M.Ed. student, study subjects: education for learners with blindness and low vision (TVI) education for learners with physical disabilities and education for learners with special behavior, history, University of Hamburg, Germany

Tobias Hensel, Research Associate, PhD student at the Faculty of Education, Department of Disability and Education, University of Hamburg, Germany (Tobias. Hensel@uni-hamburg.de)

Veronika Hilber, Advocacy Officer, International Programmes & Advocacy, CBM Germany

Sayed Mohsen Hosseini, Professor, Department of Biostatistics and Epidemiology, School of Health, Isfahan University and Medical Sciences, Isfahan, Iran

Valentin Keller, M.Ed. student, study subjects: education for learners with blindness and low vision (TVI), education for learners with physical disabilities and education for learners with special behavior, work study/technology, University of Hamburg, Germany

Dr. Frauke Meyer, Research Assistant, Faculty of Education, Department of Disability and Education, University of Hamburg, Germany (frauke.meyer@ uni-hamburg.de)

Ali Mohammadi, Psychosomatic Research Center, Isfahan University of Medical Sciences, Isfahan, Iran

Dr. Farid Mosharaf Dehkordi, Child and Adolescent Psychotherapy, University of Marburg

Javid Mostamand, PT, PhD, Musculoskeletal Research Center, Isfahan University of Medical Sciences, Isfahan, Iran

Hamid Nasiri Dehsorkhi, PhD Student, Clinical Psychologist, Psychosomatic Research Center, Isfahan University of Medical Sciences, Isfahan, Iran (h_nas_ cli_psy@mui.ac.ir)

Saeid Nasiri, M.Sc. student, Psychosomatic Research Center, Isfahan University of Medical Sciences, Isfahan, Iran

Dr. Monika Ortmann, Professor at the Faculty of Education and Social Sciences, Department of Special Needs Education and Rehabilitation, University of Oldenburg, Germany (monika.ortmann@uni-oldenburg.de)

Habibollah Rezaei, Phd, Faculty Member, Medical Education Department, Medical Education Research Center, Isfahan University of Medical Sciences, Isfahan, Iran. (rezaie.habib1@gmail.com)

Sedigheh Sadrameli, M.Sc. student, Psychosomatic Research Center, Isfahan University of Medical Sciences, Isfahan, Iran

Nele Schell, M.Ed. student, study subjects: education for learners with special behavior, Subject: Social science, University of Hamburg, Germany (Nele-Schell@gmx.de)

Torben Scholz, M.Ed. student, study subjects: education for learners with blindness and low vision (TVI) and education for learners with special behavior, biology, University of Hamburg, Germany

Dr. Joachim Schroeder, Professor at the Faculty of Education, Department of Disability and Education, University of Hamburg, Germany (joachim.schroeder@uni-hamburg.de)

Dr. Marie-Luise Schütt, Postdoctoral researcher at the Faculty of Education, Department of Disability and Education, University of Hamburg, Germany (marie-luise.schuett@uni-hamburg.de)

Negin Shah Hosseini, Research Associate, PhD student at the Faculty of Business & Social Sciences, Department of Social Work, Hamburg University of Applied Sciences, Germany (negin.shahhosseini@haw-hamburg.de)

Manfred Steger, Research Assistant, Synergys for Teaching and Learing with OER, University of Hamburg, Germany (manfred.steger@uni-hamburg.de)

Sönke Thies, Research Assistant at the School of Educational and Social Sciences, Department for Special Needs Education and Rehabilitation, Carl von Ossitzky University Oldenburg, Germany (soenke.thies@uni-oldenburg.de)

Uta Wagner, Research Associate, PhD student at the Faculty of Education, Department of Disability and Education, University of Hamburg, Germany (Uta.Wagner@uni-hamburg.de)

Dr. Nikoo Yamani, MS, MD, PhD, Associate professor, Medical Education Department, Medical Education Research Center, Isfahan University of Medical Sciences, Isfahan, Iran (nikooyamani@gmail.com)